LANGUAGE
AND VALUE

CONTRIBUTIONS IN PHILOSOPHY / NUMBER THREE

Proceedings of the Centennial Conference on the Life and Works of

ALEXANDER BRYAN JOHNSON

September 8–9, 1967   Utica, New York

MAX BLACK
L. H. BUTTERFIELD
JOSEPH DORFMAN
STILLMAN DRAKE
DAVID M. ELLIS
K. T. FANN
LARS GUSTAFSSON
DAVID MILLAR
THOMAS F. O'DONNELL
DAVID RYNIN
ROBERT SONKIN
SIDNEY WERTIMER, JR.

Sponsored by Hamilton College and the
Munson-Williams-Proctor Institute

LANGUAGE
AND VALUE

Charles L. Todd / *Russell T. Blackwood*
EDITORS   *Chairmen, respectively, Department of Speech and Theater,*
and Department of Philosophy, Hamilton College

GREENWOOD PUBLISHING CORPORATION
New York and London

Library of Congress catalog card number: 68-58919

SBN: 8371-1494-2

Greenwood Publishing Corporation
211 East 43rd St., New York, N.Y. 10017

Greenwood Publishers Ltd.
42 Hanway Street, London, W1, England

Printed in the United States of America

*Dedicated to Stillman Drake, and
to all others who played a part in the
long-delayed recognition of the genius
of Alexander Bryan Johnson.*

. . . A Treatise on Language, 1828,
has today become an extraordinary bibliophilic rarity.
Whoever reads it feels like one who on a hot, bright July day goes
down into the cellar and sees burning there a forgotten light . . .
or like a person who steps out of such a cellar into the blinding
sunlight.
As in a small, clear crystal ball one can read out of this
book almost the whole development of analytic philosophy from
1900 to our own day, and one finds there, anticipated and
carefully sorted out, in a paternal and pedantic tone,
all our arguments and counterarguments.
Everything is there, the whole development up into the fifties
of our century, and we need only add the names of philosophers
then still unborn.
In the portrait his great intelligent eye shines with penetrating
coldness.

Excerpt from the poem, "Alexander Bryan Johnson," by Lars Gustafsson.
Translated by Robert Marcellus Browning, Hamilton College,
from the German version which appeared in the
West German review Kursbuch *in 1966.*

CONTENTS

I PHILOSOPHER OF LANGUAGE

II ECONOMIST AND BANKER

FOREWORD

♦ ♦ ♦ ♦ ♦ ♦ ♦ ♦ ♦ ♦

IN FEBRUARY 1967 some forty citizens of Utica, New York, and several members of the Faculty of nearby Hamilton College met in Utica's Munson-Williams-Proctor Institute to discuss a proposed conference on the life and works of a former Utican, Alexander Bryan Johnson, a neglected American genius whose philosophical and other writings were largely ignored by his contemporaries and almost totally forgotten for more than a hundred years thereafter. The chairman told his story of an encounter with scholars in San Francisco who had argued that Utica and Hamilton College might fill an important gap in the history of ideas by bringing Johnson's writings together for the first time in one place. They had also urged that the time was ripe for a serious critical appraisal of those writings, and that his hometown might provide an ideal context for such an appraisal. Two of these scholars, Stillman Drake, the twentieth-century discoverer of Johnson's forgotten works on language, and David Rynin, a philosopher at the University of California in Berkeley and editor of the first modern reprint of Johnson's *Treatise on Language,* agreed to come to Utica if such a conference were held. The dates suggested were September 8 and 9, 1967, coinciding with the one-hundredth anniversary of Johnson's death in Utica. A motion to accept the proposal by William C. Murray, President of the Institute, was approved, and an Alexander Bryan Johnson Centennial Conference Committee was named to proceed with arrangements.

An important factor behind the group's adoption of the proposal was a series of events that had taken place prior to the February gathering. A telephone call by William Murray to Bryan Johnson Lynch, of Barneveld, New York, a great-grandson of the author, elicited a typescript of A. B. Johnson's four-volume unpublished autobiography—a document which was familiar to David Rynin, but otherwise generally unknown outside of the Johnson family. Mr. Lynch also appeared with several rare Johnson volumes, pamphlets, and miniature paintings of Johnson and his wife, Abigail, the granddaughter of President John Adams. Another great-grandson, Alexander Bryan Johnson, was found, and through his generosity the Committee gained access to other important Johnson material, including a large collection of manuscript correspondence.

Meanwhile Miss Alice Dodge, Librarian at the Utica Public Library, revealed herself to be a longtime Johnsonite who had amassed the largest library collection of Johnson material in existence. Miss Dodge also told of her past correspondence with a few scholars who had frequently exchanged photocopies of Johnson material with her. More Johnson descendants dropped in at the Institute bearing Johnson writings, letters, and pictures, while similar memorabilia came in from the Savings Bank of Utica, the Oneida Historical Society, and other city archives. In short, within weeks A. B. Johnson had become a familiar spirit to the Utica planners, and few had any doubts that they were on the trail of an American "original."

Locating the Johnson specialists—in addition to Drake and Rynin—who might share their knowledge and appraisals of Johnson's work was surprisingly easy, mainly by virtue of the fact that they were so few, and because a number of them had kept in touch with each other over the years. Drake suggested Joseph Dorfman of Columbia University; Rynin proposed Lars Gustafsson of Sweden and K. T. Fann of Cleveland State University. All agreed that Max Black of Cornell should be a key contributor. A Hamilton College historian recommended L. H. Butterfield, editor in chief of the Adams Papers, of the Massachusetts Historical Society, and Thomas O'Donnell of Utica College. Another Hamiltonian suggested Robert Sonkin of the City University of New York. Finally, the list was rounded out with the addition of David Ellis and David Millar, of the Hamilton History Department, and Sidney Wertimer, a Hamilton economist.[1]

Additional details on the origins of these *Proceedings* will be found in the Introduction. Meanwhile, in behalf of the Conference participants and of future scholars who may find useful these early efforts to provide a composite of A. B. Johnson, the editors wish to express their deep gratitude to all who made the Centennial Conference possible.

William C. Murray, together with Roy C. Van Denbergh, Treasurer of the Institute, Edwin H. Dwight, Director of the Museum of Art, Joseph S. Trovato, his Assistant Director, and the late A. Montgomery Huntington, the Institute's Director of Public Relations, provided the kind of gracious hospitality and delightful setting one finds only rarely at scholarly conclaves. Credit must also be given to the entire staff of the Institute for its careful attention to detail in the arrangements of exhibits and informational materials, as well as its many courtesies to the Conference delegates and visitors.

Richard W. Couper, Acting President of Hamilton College, which cosponsored the Conference, gave encouragement and support from the beginning—even after receiving word that A. B. Johnson in 1832 had haughtily declined an honorary degree from the then twenty-year-old institution. Hamilton's Librarian, Walter Pilkington, confronting a barrage of Johnsoniana for photocopying and filing, gave unsparingly of his time—as did Robert Hevenor, the College's Public Relations Director.

Mention has already been made of the role played by Johnson's two great-grandsons, Alexander Bryan Johnson and Bryan Johnson Lynch, in supplying much of the documentation that made these *Proceedings* possible. In addition, their active participation in the Conference itself added greatly to this belated tribute to A. B. Johnson, as did the presence of so many of his other descendants.

Dr. Louis Jones, director of the New York State Historical Society, and his vice-director, Frederick L. Rath Jr., made helpful contributions during the planning stages and at the Conference itself. Other members of the Advisory Committee were equally generous with their time and ideas, among them Lysle Harrington and William P. White of the Oneida Historical Society; J. Kenneth Donahue, President of Utica College; John S. Gambs, former Chairman of the Hamilton College Economics Department; Albert V. Payne, President of the Mohawk Valley Community College; and Addison White, Vice-President of the Savings Bank of Utica.

Finally, the editors must acknowledge a special debt to S. I. Hayakawa, whose own writings follow in paths pioneered by A. B. Johnson. It was from Hayakawa that they first heard of "that earliest

American investigator into the area of what we now call semantics";
and it was Hayakawa's insistence that "Utica ought to do something
about him" which supplied what Johnson himself would have called
"the kindling appliance" for the Alexander Bryan Johnson Centennial
Conference.

CHARLES L. TODD
RUSSELL T. BLACKWOOD

NOTE

1   When twelve scholars are asked to prepare separate studies of a single
individual, some duplication is inevitable. This was particularly true in
dealing with A. B. Johnson, for each contributor worked from the same
basc and rather limited source material. In preparing their papers for publication, the editors agreed to let a number of the duplications stand, including the repetition of certain biographical data, on the ground that each study
was conceived as an entity within the broad lines of demarcation prescribed
by the author's field of specialization. It should also be noted that the contributors, in their direct citations from Johnson's writings, have preserved,
wherever feasible, Johnson's archaic spelling and sometimes unconventional
punctuation.

INTRODUCTION

♦ ♦ ♦ ♦ ♦ *CHARLES L. TODD*

HOWARD TAUBMAN, writing under a Utica, New York, dateline for the *New York Times* on September 10, 1967, began his article on the Alexander Bryan Johnson Centennial Conference with two questions. "How many Americans," he asked, "have heard of a remarkable American citizen named Alexander Bryan Johnson who died in this city one hundred years ago at the age of 81? How many scholars know his name, writing and ideas?" Mr. Taubman supplied his own answer: "Very few!"

The reply was a relief to many Uticans who, like most upstate New Yorkers, are highly conscious of place, proud of their historic markers, and careful custodians of the reputations of their local heroes. Yet it seemed incredible that they should have forgotten a man who, in addition to his achievements as a philosopher and economic theorist, named seventeen of their city's streets after various members of his family, presided over one of their leading banks for thirty years, and whose funeral on September 10, 1867, was probably the largest in Utica's history. Adding to their bewilderment were the evidences of Johnson's accomplishments brought together in the display cases of the Munson-Williams-Proctor Institute, cosponsor with nearby Hamilton

◊ ◊ ◊ ◊ ◊ *Chairman, Department of Speech and Theater, Hamilton College, and Chairman, Alexander Bryan Johnson Centennial Conference.*

College of the Johnson Centennial Conference. There were the original editions of his twelve books, bearing such portentous titles as *Deep Sea Soundings and Explorations of the Bottom: or, The Ultimate Analysis of Human Knowledge;* dozens of his pamphlets, published by William Williams, Utica's best-known printer; many national magazines of the 1840's and1850's open to pages bearing Johnson's name. There were the paintings and photographs of his stately Greek revival mansion on Genesee Street where Utica's "Bank with the Gold Dome" now stands, together with delicately done miniatures of Johnson and his wife, Abigail, granddaughter of John Adams and niece of John Quincy Adams. Finally, there were the four-volume, unpublished autobiography,[1] the folders of letters to Johnson from his illustrious in-laws in Quincy, from Martin Van Buren, Lafayette, Samuel Houston, DeWitt Clinton, Chief Justice Taney, and other great Americans, and letters written by Albert Einstein, Percy Bridgman, and Aldous Huxley to Johnson's twentieth-century discoverer, Stillman Drake. Even more impressive perhaps was the list of scholars who had come to Utica to pay their respects to Johnson. Utica's state of mind was playfully expressed by Dr. Louis Jones, Director of the New York State Historical Society of Cooperstown, who hinted in introducing one of the visitors that the Conference Chairman and fellow conspirators from Hamilton College had "invented" Alexander Bryan Johnson.

A partial answer to Mr. Taubman's first query can be found in his second, for the number of scholars who "knew Johnson's name, writings and ideas" prior to the Utica Conference can be gauged with some accuracy by counting those listed among the participants in these *Proceedings.* It must be pointed out in all honesty, however, that the local Johnsonites from Hamilton College and Utica College who addressed the Conference achieved their expertise through a crash program begun less than six months before the Conference took place. Their achievements are a tribute not only to their powers of "instant research" but also to the intriguing personality and accomplishments of A. B. Johnson, who persisted throughout his long life in the unrewarding (to him, at least) practice of writing books and thinking thoughts in Utica, New York, mainly for a highly specialized audience in a later century.

It has become a kind of parlor game among modern Johnsonites to speculate on the whys and wherefores of his almost total disappearance from the recorded history of ideas during the past hundred years. Insofar as his philosophical writings are concerned, particularly

A Treatise on Language (1836), *The Meaning of Words* (1854), and *The Physiology of the Senses* (1856), it is obvious that Johnson was far ahead of his time, living in a realm of ideas that few of his contemporaries dared or cared to enter. These are difficult books, even when read in the light of twentieth-century advances in the field of language analysis. Johnson's most sympathetic critic, Timothy Flint of the *Western Monthly Review,* complained that *The Philosophy of Human Knowledge* "required a painful effort of attention," adding, in reference to Johnson's early use of the work in a series of lectures in Utica, "What an audience must that of the Utica Lyceum have been, to have so patiently followed this gentleman through his acute, and fine spun, and sometimes darkly woven disquisitions." [2] Some of his economic theories, as Joseph Dorfman has pointed out, must have proved equally baffling to his nineteenth-century readers, although they would seem fairly tame to a New Dealer or a Great Society planner. On the other hand, many of the political essays which Johnson collected together in his *A Guide to the Right Understanding of Our American Union* were highly topical, dealing with matters which ceased to engage public attention soon after Johnson had written about them. Johnson's fiction, appearing mainly in *The Knickerbocker Magazine* between 1850 and 1852, was, as Professor O'Donnell has made clear, outmoded in style and content even before it was published.

   The very brashness of his philosophical studies, in addition to their abstruse nature, must have put off Johnson's contemporaries. "I am the first philosopher," he announced, "who has gone deeper than language. . . . All speculative philosophies precedent of mine are like tunes, which skillful musicians play on a piano forte." Locke, Hume, and many more of his illustrious predecessors were accused of "playing bo-peep with words," of failing utterly to understand the nature of language. Hume's problem with the table which diminished in size as one walked away from it was rudely dismissed as a failure to understand the multiple meanings of the word "diminution"; the ancient paradox of Zeno involving Achilles and the tortoise, a space-time riddle which had perplexed philosophers for centuries and still does, was treated by Johnson as a mere word game which any child could solve. And all this from a money-grubbing banker in Utica, New York, who apparently had no respect for his betters! Charles Sanders Peirce or William James might have understood, but they came upon the scene a few decades too late. By then, Johnson had vanished into limbo.

   One must also take into account Johnson's publishing methods. Many of his books were published by reputable New York firms such as D. Appleton & Company, Harper & Brothers, etc., but the impatient and well-to-do author could be relied upon to buy up remainders at the first sign of public indifference and distribute them gratis to his friends or to distant heroes like Auguste Comte in France and Sir Charles Haughton in England. *The Meaning of Words* was largely distributed in this fashion. Many copies of *The Encyclopedia of Instruction* were burned in a New York warehouse fire. When it came to his last book, *Deep Sea Soundings,* Johnson limited the edition to one hundred copies, of which he distributed less than half. It is small wonder that the works on which his reputation might have been based are so hard to come by today.

Finally, Johnson was assuredly a victim of the early nineteenth-century prejudice against American authors—a prejudice which he shared. Cooper's works he regarded as "trash," and Irving, he felt, belonged in the nursery with "Jack the Giant Killer." With few exceptions the British reviews ignored his books, and in the eyes of the Yankee intelligentsia American reviews were hardly worth noticing. Had Timothy Flint, for example, published his long and appreciative essay on *A Treatise on Language* in the *Edinburgh Review* instead of in the *Western Monthly Review,* the results might have been quite different. John Quincy Adams, in a sympathetic letter to Johnson, put it succinctly when he said, "It will undoubtedly be many years before an American audience will honor and support such inquiries into abstruse topics."

Stillman Drake has given us in full the story of the rediscovery of Johnson's works some twenty-five years ago in the paper which opens these *Proceedings.* As Drake makes clear, despite the several public and private reprints of his language works in the 1940's, citations from those works in the writings of Irving Lee, and references by Joseph Dorfman to other works, Johnson remained a shadowy figure at best, a kind of literary and philosophical "curiosity" known only to a coterie of specialists and almost totally ignored by the anthologists and historians of nineteenth-century thought in America. Some might argue that this continuing neglect of Johnson by modern scholars indicated that his contributions were indeed minor ones, but this is the easy way out. No present-day student of linguistic analysis, coming suddenly upon the *Treatise* of 1836 or the *Meaning of Words* of 1854 can fail to agree with Lars Gustafsson that a "forgotten light" had been left burning all these years, or that at least as far as the superstructure of our modern approach to language is concerned "everything is there." What was needed, undoubtedly, was more about the man himself, some context in which to place him; for Johnson was a "loner" in time, an anomaly in place. It was this realization which prompted the Alexander Bryan Johnson Centennial Conference on September 8 and 9, 1967. And what better place to hold it than in the hometown of the man whom Drake has termed "the philosophical banker of Utica"?

Johnson's isolation in Utica, a frontier way station on the Erie Canal far from the intellectual ferment of Boston or New York, kept him out of the mainstreams of American thought, particularly in the realms of literature and philosophy. His "inner circles" were the Utica Lyceum, the Temperance Society, and the Young Men's Association. There was no tight little coterie of convivial and gossipy intellectuals gathering at "The Bread and Cheese Club" or "Cockloft Hall," such as Irving, Fitz-Greene Halleck, or Gulian Verplanck found in New York City. (Whether they would have put up with Johnson's solemn sobriety is a matter of some question, but at least they might have recorded their impressions of him.) In short, until the four-volume autobiography, the books, the pamphlets, the letters, and the Johnson family papers finally came together at the Utica Conference, there was no context, and there were very few points of departure toward a composite picture of Johnson. Obviously he was a learned eccentric—but whence came the learning? How far did his eccentricities extend? In some ways he was certainly a man of the world—but of what world? Guests at the Utica Conference wondered at the exhibit of books provided by Stillman Drake—frayed eighteenth- and nineteenth-century volumes by the French *philosophes* Degerando, Condorcet, Condillac, Destutt de Tracy, and others—but these books provide at least a partial answer to "whence came the learning?" A Johnson article entitled "The Immorality of Tight Lacing," from the Utica *Mother's Magazine,* signed "Matilda," hinted at the "eccentricity"; the autobiography provided many more clues. Finally, the efforts of Professors Ellis, O'Donnell, and certain local historians, reinforced by old newspaper clippings, various memorabilia, and (above all) the presence of so many of his descendants, opened a window on Johnson's world and provided some of the context which had been missing for so long.

Nearly all of the studies that appear in these *Proceedings* lean heavily upon a typescript of Johnson's unpublished autobiography. Prior to the emergence of this long document, which was brought to the Conference Committee by Bryan Johnson Lynch, and reproduced for the participants, Johnson scholars had little biographical material to work with beyond a local history called *Pioneers of Utica*, published in 1877 by Moses M. Bagg. Bagg knew Johnson, and filled out his essay on Johnson with information taken from the numerous obituaries which appeared after Johnson's death. He had also seen a manuscript of the autobiography, calling it a "copious and entertaining work." However, since Bagg had other "pioneers" to deal with, many of whom achieved greater contemporary acclaim than Johnson did, his sketch is perfunctory at best. The autobiography itself survived in several hand-written copies, including one owned by Alexander Bryan Johnson of Darien, Connecticut, and New York City. Several typescripts were made in 1930 by Elizabeth Stringham Morton, and these appear to have circulated among members of the large Johnson family. There are now two copies in the Hamilton College Library, and material relating to the Adams family has been reproduced for the Adams Trust at the Massachusetts Historical Society.

The autobiography is a curious work—one which may defy editors for some time to come. It is a repository of letters sent and letters received. It is a ledger in which routine banking transactions and reflections on religion and morality appear side by side, interspersed with detailed accounts of the dying moments of a father, wife, or child, vignettes of life along the Erie Canal, or a trip by stage on a newly constructed turnpike through the forests of central New York. With few exceptions the prose is pedestrian, displaying little of the concise elegance of his public writings. It was begun sometime in 1863 when Johnson was seventy-seven and was completed a few months before his death. The chapter headings which precede each volume give the impression that Johnson saw his life mainly in terms of births, marriages, journeys, and deaths. Only toward the end do these headings record the publication of a book or the termination of a business enterprise; and then, possibly, only because the births and marriages have ceased and most of the living have died. Johnson apparently intended it as a family record to be passed on to his third wife, his children, and his grandchildren; there is no indication of any hope or desire for a wider public. "Such as these memoirs are," he says in the inscription to his wife, "he dedicates this copy to you, to be preserved or destroyed." In his introduction he expresses the humorless hope that because "it lacks the spice of J. J. Rousseau's *Confessions,* it will be more acceptable to my descendents for whom alone I write it, and to whom alone it can probably be interesting." Despite its many shortcomings, however, the autobiography is an essential document for any student of Johnson, for everything is there—the bigness of him and the pettiness, the pride and the despair, the zest and the loneliness of living in an alien time. As has already been indicated, many of the details of Johnson's life taken from the autobiography will appear in the individual studies which make up these *Proceedings.* At the risk of anticipating some of them, however, it seems appropriate to present here a brief chronological account—omitting much that is dwelt upon at length by some of the contributors. Where it seems important, the reader will be referred to the specific papers in which these details are given.

Johnson's story begins in the seaport town of Gosport, England, where his father, Bryan, worked as a paymaster and supplier for the British Navy. Bryan's family was of German-Jewish descent, and the name was changed in England "for purposes of trade," according to family notes. Johnson's mother was the former Leah Simpson, of Amsterdam, Holland, who, Johnson tells us, "never learned to read or write English, but later spoke it with scarcely any accent." Though he tried hard to refresh his memory on the "great events" which took place during his childhood by reading *Dodsley's Annual Register,* one of the few he recalled was the beheading of Louis XVI, which, he said, caused him to shout "Damn the King!"—a sentiment he later blamed on having been "tinctured with republicanism at an early age." His personal recollections do include, however, the mutiny of the Channel Fleet at Spithead in 1797. He also gives us a clinical account of the hanging of a mutineer, with all the gusto he applies to the later hanging of an Oneida Indian in Utica, New York. There are some equally detailed narrations, in a Hogarthian vein, of women wrestlers "naked to the waist and generally large and bloated" performing for British sailors in the city of Deal.

Johnson went to a school in Gosport, but "learnt little in it," playing truant whenever "any review of troops took place." Later he received instruction in "dancing, drawing, and the rudiments of English" at an Anglican school in Kent, but his father removed him after he was "struck on the back with a short horsewhip." This ended his formal education, save for a brief interval at a day school in Finsbury Square, London. "My want of schooling," he wrote, "was compensated for by an insatiable inclination for reading . . . books which assisted in improving my character by infusing into it aspirations to occupy a good social position and especially to dread that I should pass from life without leaving some worthy memorial of my having existed." This obsession with "social position" and leaving a "memorial" was to stay with him throughout his life.

In 1797 Bryan Johnson emigrated to America, leaving his wife and son in London with instructions to join him as soon as he had found a permanent situation. He settled first in New York City, but fled almost immediately to Albany to avoid a yellow fever epidemic which threatened the city. From there Bryan planned to proceed to Canada but was attracted en route by the beauties of Old Fort Schuyler (now Utica) on the banks of the Mohawk, and he never went beyond it.

Meanwhile Alexander and his mother settled down to await the summons, which was four years in coming. The youth wandered around London, did a few odd jobs, went often to the theater, tried his hand at raising rabbits and silkworms, read books in a coffeehouse while waiting for mail and money from his father. Among the books, he relates, were the works of Tom Paine. He also tells us of some "lessons in atheism as well as the flute from a music teacher"—an experience which "fortified my orthodoxy and prevented me from being contaminated by his logick." Finally in 1801 Johnson and his mother embarked from Liverpool for New York, arriving shortly before his fifteenth birthday. Johnson describes himself at that time as "intellectually premature, but physically immature" and suggests that the former quality "fostered a vanity which I fear has attended me all my life."

Bryan Johnson had done well in Utica, having established a Mohawk River trading post in which he managed "to sell goods at lower prices than his village contemporaries and to purchase country produce at higher prices." His son became his father's bookkeeper and financial advisor, urging him constantly to accumulate enough money "that we might live without business . . . for I nourished a notion that country shopkeeping was not an elevated employment." With his son's help, this goal was soon realized, and by 1810 the Johnsons were able to enter into more speculative and respectable ventures. Alexander meanwhile had discovered a circulating library in the law office of Judge Nathan Williams and resumed his heavy diet of reading, concentrating mainly on "philosophy, grammar and etymology," scorning all novels and most poetry. At some period between 1805 and 1810 he submitted several short, anonymous essays to a newspaper in Utica, one of which began with a couplet borrowed from *The Spectator*: "Whatever contradicts my sense I hate to see and never can believe"

—a foreshadowing, perhaps, of the "logical positivism" which was to provide the impetus for his works on the philosophy of language.

Johnson's first and least successful independent business venture began in 1810 when he joined forces with seventeen-year-old Henry Rowe Schoolcraft in establishing glass factories in Vernon, Marcy, and Geneva, New York. Schoolcraft, who later became an eminent authority on the American Indian, had worked with his father in New York State's first glass factory near Albany, and because there was a real possibility that the British would soon cut off their exports of glass upon which most of the United States depended heavily, he persuaded Johnson that the venture would be both profitable and in the national interest. Johnson organized a company in Utica, capitalized at $100,000, and after setting up factories in Vernon and Marcy went off to Geneva with Schoolcraft. The story of their trials and tribulations in Geneva (largely a result of the then current practice of pirating glassblowers) occupies a large portion of Volume II of the autobiography, and differs in certain particulars from that told by Jasena Rappleye Foley in a study of "The Ontario Glass Manufacturing Company." [3] Miss Foley tells of "difficulties among the management" which led to the "removal" of A. B. Johnson, while Johnson lays most of his problems on the shoulders of the unpredictable and often inebriated glassblowers. Whatever the real causes were (and one is tempted to follow Miss Foley's account), Johnson and Schoolcraft withdrew rather hurriedly and without obvious regrets.

"Being relieved from all business engagements, and much desiring to live in New York," Johnson, accompanied by a young Negro slave donated in full livery by his doting father, set off for the city to enlarge his fortune and, at his father's prompting, to engage in some judicious "wife-hunting." He took $16,000 with him, and promptly invested it in New York bank stocks, also "buying up notes at two per cent per month" from various city merchants—including several signed by John Jacob Astor. He became acquainted with Robert Fulton, who did him a favor by exposing a perpetual-motion machine which apparently interested Johnson. Fulton also introduced him into the society of the Congers, the Gracies, the Hunts, and some of the other "better families" in New York; but the young ladies Johnson encountered frightened him with their social graces and city ways, and he soon abandoned that aspect of his quest. His investments went well for a time, but early in 1812 rumors began to spread, particularly in Johnson's boarding house, that the British would soon bombard New York, so the cautious Johnson hastily converted his notes into specie which he stored in the Manhattan Bank ready for a retreat to Utica. The British, much to his embarrassment, never came. However, partially out of concern for his father, Johnson returned to Utica anyway, deciding to reinvest his capital in local enterprises.

The New York sojourn was not without its rewards, for his study of New York banking methods and big city finance paved the way for his first book, *An Inquiry into the Nature of Value and Capital,* published in New York in 1813 and discussed at length in these *Proceedings* by Joseph Dorfman. A chance remark made by one of his New York friends to the effect that the "British were cowards" (retracted when the friend learned that Johnson was an Englishman) inspired his first pamphlet, also published in New York in 1813, *An Inquiry into the Natural Rights of Man, as Regards the Exercise of Expatriation.* The pamphlet is dedicated to "All the Adopted Citizens of the United States," and Johnson signed it with the pseudonym, "A Gentleman of the City of New York." In it he made an eloquent case for the right of any naturalized American to achieve equal status with the native born and excoriated those—particularly British citizens—who felt their loyalties should remain with the King. The book ends with the proposition: "That a man may even feel a dislike to the country of his birth and education, and have good and sufficient reasons for his dislike; and, therefore, neither be depraved in taste or incorrect in principle."

Johnson's return to Utica sans wife, or any prospects of finding one, galvanized his father into immediate action. He and his father were accustomed to taking long walks together up Genesee Street. On one of these occasions they passed a group of young ladies just emerging from class. "Among the female scholars," Johnson wrote later, "I noticed one whose bright appearance, mature but slight form and auburn hair greatly interested me. As we passed my father bowed to her . . . he said she was a granddaughter of President John Adams." His father took him to call at once. Johnson made several visits alone thereafter and "eventually came to address some conversation to her," although it struck him as preposterous that he might assume "the character of a lover to one whom I thought so much my superior." When he did get up courage to propose he discovered that she had gone off to Quincy to visit a "very dear friend" and "felt indisposed to the gaiety of Utica."

A thoroughly crushed Johnson inferred that this "dear

friend was necessarily of the male gender . . . and I hastily concluded to no longer continue my unavailing intercourse, and therefore told the ladies that I intended to return shortly to New York." At this point the autobiography breaks off with the notation "Some Omission"; and the next thing we know Johnson is paying a marriage fee to the minister of the Utica Episcopal Church. A few pages later, as he begins to discuss finances again and is looking back at his courtship, the autobiography gives us another unfinished sentence: "I feel constantly abashed at the . . ."; but once more we are informed that something has been omitted. Johnson's 1814 honeymoon with Abigail and her mother has been recounted by Lyman Butterfield in his essay on "Johnson and the Adams Family," along with his many later encounters and correspondence with John and John Quincy Adams. Mr. Butterfield omits one short item, however, quite possibly out of deference to one of his hosts at the Utica Conference. Johnson told John Adams one day that there was a "college near Utica called Hamilton, after the late Secretary of the Treasury." Adams' reply, as reported by Johnson, will be treasured by all Hamilton men: They had better have called it Bathsheba College!"

Johnson often deplored the fact that he had waited until he was thirty-one to marry. "One should take the step," he wrote later, "when one is in the most marketable condition." He seems to have felt a similar urgency about his other affairs, for once he committed himself to a career in Utica he began to market his talents as fast as possible. Shortly after his marriage he was appointed by the state as a director of the Bank of Utica, which gave him prestige, but no great financial return. Accordingly in 1816 he chartered the Utica Insurance Company with some cleverly worded fine print giving it the power to conduct banking operations—a subterfuge which he hoped would avoid restrictions limiting the number of banks in Utica. The hidden clauses escaped the notice of the State Attorney General, Martin Van Buren, for over a year, but in the end, under pressure from other banks, Johnson was forced to liquidate the company—with some loss of face, but little loss on his investment. Some details of this escapade, which Johnson regretted deeply in later years, are included in Professor Wertimer's essay.

After the insurance company fiasco Johnson decided to study law in the hopes of finding "an honorable and useful employment" for his future. John Adams thought this was a splendid idea, adding his pious hope that such employment would distract his grandson-in-law from writing any more books—"since American books do not sell in America." Shortly after being admitted to the bar, however, Johnson went back to full-time banking and became president of the newly formed Ontario Branch Bank of Utica, a post which he held until ten years before his death. He never practiced law, but his legal training proved useful to him in his later studies of corporations and corporation law appearing in *Hunt's Merchants' Magazine* and elsewhere. In 1819, according to a note appearing in the autobiography, Johnson's total capital amounted to $55,000 and his annual income $4,157. His family expenses in that year are listed as $1,600. He ascribes the low figure mainly to the fact that he "never entertained" unless he had to.

Despite his social reticence, and his frequently expressed desire to withdraw to his study and write, Johnson threw himself with considerable vigor into the various reform movements and social causes which were sweeping the Mohawk Valley region at the time. His crusade for Sunday postal service, resulting in his "excommunication" from the Presbyterian church; his role in the beginnings of the Utica Lyceum and the national lyceum movement; his polemics against the National Bank and the American Colonization Society—these activities are chronicled in detail by Professors Ellis, Wertimer, and Dorfman in the studies that follow. His long and tedious labor on a dictionary of synonyms, which anticipated in many ways Roget's *Thesaurus,* is outlined by Robert Sonkin in this book. Some additional brief notes are needed, however, to fill in the picture of this busy middle period, setting aside for the moment those literary endeavors which are the major source of our interest.

Soon after assuming the presidency of the Ontario Branch Bank, Johnson seriously considered a race for the governorship of New York. In 1821, the state held a constitutional convention in Albany, and Johnson proposed an amendment which was brought before the Convention, calling for the defeat of a proposed restriction against naturalized citizens running for the office of governor. Johnson stated with customary frankness that he felt aggrieved at the new clause "because it excluded me." His amendment was defeated, however, by forces led by Rufus King, and this, as Johnson put it, "repressed all tendency in me to enter into political office . . . since the high prize was precluded from obtainment." Also at about this time Johnson offered his services to DeWitt Clinton to help speed the development of the Erie Canal, an enterprise in which Johnson passionately believed. He promoted this cause with vigor and assisted in securing funds for the hiring of contractors. During General Lafayette's triumphal tour of America in 1825, Johnson, at the urging of John Adams, played host to the great Frenchman in his home on Genesee Street and later, at Lafayette's request, led a drive to collect funds for Poland in its struggle against Russia. Meanwhile he continued to expand his bank investments, putting more than $100,000 into stock shares in new banks which were opening their doors in Oneida and nearby counties.

The portions of the autobiography which cover the period between 1820 and 1840 leap without transition from one episode to another, each in turn producing an extended commentary. The great cholera epidemic of 1832 in Utica, for example, set up a train of thought which bears a startling resemblance to the doctrines of later Christian Scientists, followers of Émile Coué's school of psychotherapy, and modern devotees of psychosomatic medicine. As the disease spread, Johnson "interdicted any discussion of cholera" within his family circle on the grounds that "cholera and terror" were identical and that the best solution would be to stop talking about it. His theory was tested one night when the conversation got out of hand and Johnson suddenly felt ill. He was rushed to a doctor who could find nothing whatever wrong with him; from that point on Johnson "would permit no one to inform me of any cholera statistics." As a result, he stated, "peace and health were promptly restored." He may also have recalled at that point how his father fled from New York City in 1798 in face of the yellow fever peril—after his first encounter with a swarm of fireflies which had convinced him that he was undergoing initial fever symptoms.

Johnson frequently occupied his mind with problems of love and courtship and issued advice on the subject to anyone who would listen, relying again on his faith in what might be called logotherapy. One young friend who sought his advice was instructed, first and foremost, to "make wealth an ingredient in the woman you are to marry." Next he advocated a good "physical constitution—since to marry disease is a miserable neglect of the commonest dictates of ordinary intelligence." The young lady should also possess a "relative strength of intellect as will protect the husband from pain in her social intercourse with his friends." Finally he urged the suitor not to worry about being "in love" from the very beginning. If she has the other attributes, "marry her and love will certainly ensue"—particularly if one uses the vocabulary of love at all times.

Johnson was frequently called upon for advice on religious matters, and here again he often stressed the role of language as a "kindling appliance" in the cultivation of proper attitudes. Though he disapproved of the more extreme forms of revivalism which were sweeping through the Mohawk Valley during the 1830's, his letters to Judge Ezekiel Bacon, one of those who turned to Johnson for help, complimented the evangelists for their "knowledge of the workings of human nature" which led them to "make the audience take an active part by coming to the middle of the church, kneeling, confessing, praying, etc." "Our words," he added, "naturally excite our feelings. We can listen to almost anything while we refrain from words and actions, but you know how prone a man is to become warm in debate, simply from the influence of his words on his feelings." This emphasis on the relationship between words and human behavior, discussed at length in David Rynin's study of *Religion in Its Relation to the Present Life,* and Johnson's preoccupation with audience psychology, may well explain some of his appeal to the "general semanticists" like Irving Lee and S. I. Hayakawa, who began in the late 1930's, under the impact of Adolf Hitler's success with words and symbols, to examine and popularize the role of language in behavior. As David Ellis has suggested, there may also be in Johnson some early glimmerings of the modern preoccupation with "consent engineering" and the "power of positive thinking."

Like Benjamin Franklin (whom he resembles in many ways) Johnson was intrigued by the physical sciences. He produced a short paper for a New York discussion group on "The Nature of Sunbeams," studied new developments in chemistry, physics, and mineralogy, and kept a critical eye on medical practices of the period. When his son Alexander became ill with typhoid fever in 1837 the doctor resorted to "bleeding" his patient, and after the boy's death Johnson denounced it as "murder." Subsequent deaths among his friends and family in Utica seem to have provoked similar skepticism about early nineteenth-century medicine. Johnson also possessed a lively interest in what he called "mechanical contrivances." Dismayed by the condition of his clothes after a trip to Albany on a wood-burning train, he formulated elaborate proposals for putting the engine on the rear of the train, and addressed them to the appropriate authorities. He also entered into correspondence with President Nott of Union College, suggesting certain mechanical improvements in a stove which Nott had patented; he gave up in some embarrassment after receiving a condescending reply from the inventor.

Throughout the 1830's Johnson, a staunch Jacksonian, bombarded the newspapers of Utica, and occasionally of Albany, with biting attacks on the Whigs, lampooning them with homespun fables and allegories under such titles as "The Effects of Whiggery on the English Language," "Whig Mode of Calumny," or "How the Whigs Estimate the People." Fortunately these "casual publications," as he called them, were all carefully identified by Johnson himself and pasted into a set of scrap books which are now preserved in the New York State Library in Albany.[4] Otherwise, the modern scholar might be hopelessly confused by such whimsical pseudonyms as "Old Hunker," "Green Horn," "Oneida," "Anti-Breeches Pocket," "Noah," "Anti-Gouger," "Anti-Humbug" and "Philo-Equality." On the other hand, many of his contemporaries must have recognized the Johnson touch, for he came under sharp attack in Utica and was frequently denounced in posters and handbills distributed throughout the city. His Jacksonian supporters, however, were equally fervent and, after reading one of his speeches or letters to the press, urged him several times to run for Congress or the Senate—suggestions which he firmly ignored. In 1835 the Oneida County Democrats sent him as their delegate to the national convention in Baltimore where he voted for Martin Van Buren to succeed Jackson—though he later broke with Van Buren and chided him in his satire, *The Philosophical Emperor*. The year 1840 found him in attendance as a spectator at the Richmond, Virginia, convention which nominated Harrison and Tyler. Though Daniel Webster left him unmoved, he seems to have been impressed by the trappings of the convention, particularly the slogan, "Harrison and Tyler will burst Van Buren's Boiler."

In addition to his many forays into national political issues, including his attacks on the Maine Liquor Laws and his arguments in behalf of the annexation of Texas (which won him a letter of thanks from Sam Houston), Johnson also found time to lecture on literary and cultural topics. In 1834 he was honored by an invitation from the American Lyceum to speak at its fourth annual convention in New York City on his plans for a new dictionary; but when he arrived at the meeting the audience was so sparse that he walked out, leaving his paper in the hands of a secretary—an act he later regretted. The 1830's were also for Johnson a period of active investment in Utica real estate. One of his few mistakes involved a number of similar investments in Little Falls, New York, which, he felt, would shortly become the commercial hub of the Empire State.

Abigail Johnson, who brought her husband into the magic

circle of the Adams family and bore him nine children, died in 1835 —presumably of cancer. Her last moments, along with the details of her autopsy, are related with gruesome thoroughness in the autobiography, as were most deaths in the Johnson family. His grief as he describes it was certainly genuine, but his loneliness was also intense, and within eighteen months Johnson was "wife-hunting" once more. Quite obviously, Johnson fancied his hardheaded approach to matrimony and wanted his descendants to profit by his example, for the pursuit receives more than its necessary share of attention in his memoirs. It begins with a series of remarkable letters to an unnamed young lady whom he had met briefly in Utica a few months before. With "utmost candour" he listed his assets and inquired into hers. After what was apparently a one-sided correspondence which proved too much for his self-esteem, he informed her through her family that he had reconsidered the whole thing, and confided to his autobiography: "the lady was too rich to be influenced by my property, and I was too rich to be influenced by hers—though it was considerable." Finally after numerous family conferences and another bout of correspondence he won the hand of Eliza Masters of Madison County and married her in November 1838. Once again he could not resist pointing out that love is an unnecessary ingredient during the preliminary stages of courtship. "I felt confident," he wrote, "that her youth and beauty would enlist my feelings for her"—and apparently they did. This marriage, which produced four children, ended tragically in 1852 with his wife's death from burns received in a fire at his home on Genesee Street. This time Johnson's grief and loneliness brought him close to the edge of complete breakdown ("I feared my intellect would give way"), and his children arranged almost immediately for him to take an extended European trip, accompanied by one of his sons. Johnson had to be forcibly restrained from leaving the ship and returning to New York on the pilot boat, but after getting under way, he found some solace in the presence on board of the Anglican Bishop of Western New York and Jenny Lind, the "Swedish Nightingale." Johnson's long account of his travels is utterly undistinguished, and there is no indication that he made any effort to follow up old contacts with foreign intellectuals or to gain entrée into the circles which might have been open to an American of some literary accomplishment. The travelogue brightens only when he runs across a friend of a friend back home.

Johnson's third marriage—to Mary Livingston of Columbia County—goes virtually unrecorded in the autobiography, but some of his descendants recall family legends indicating that his children took a firm hand in the arrangements. After his marriage, he tried hard to settle down and write his books in whatever peace and quiet could be salvaged for him, but there were many difficulties still ahead. The Ontario Branch Bank, whose parent company was in Canandaigua, New York, was reorganized in 1855 as an independent institution known as "The Ontario Bank." Shortly after the reorganization, while Johnson was spending as little time at his office as possible, appalling shortages were discovered which were eventually traced to one of the cashiers, a relative of Johnson's. Sidney Wertimer's paper on Johnson's *Treatise on Banking* discusses this affair, which made national headlines. The effect on Johnson is related in the melancholy prose of M. M. Bagg's *Pioneers of Utica:*

> Sad indeed it was that now, when he had gained a reputation as a banker as high as any man's, the great misfortune of his life should befall him, and that this misfortune should consist in a blow struck at his very reputation itself. Without any fault of his the bank . . . was insolvent. The event, in all its painful aspects, the ruin produced, the brief period of its accomplishment, constitute a case almost without parallel in banking. . . . Though overwhelmed by this great and unexpected calamity, Mr. Johnson devoted himself with the energy, industry and sagacity of his best years to save all that could be saved from the wreck.[5]

From this point on Johnson's autobiography turns away from the world of finance, politics, births, and deaths; and, as though he were impatient with the entire narrative, rushes to its conclusion with a series of reflections on his futile search for fame as a philosopher. "My studies," he writes on one of his final pages, "have been intellectually beneficial to myself and to that extent they solace me for the time I have devoted to them. . . . I shall leave much unprinted manuscript [it is doubtful that there is a great deal—save in the form of letters] but whether any of it deserves publicity I cannot conjecture. Judging from the past, the dead may well be left to bury the dead." He wrote these words in February 1867. Seven months later Johnson was dead at the age of eighty-one. One of his last known statements was a letter written a week before his death to the Rector of Trinity Church in Utica. Hardheaded to the last, he admonished his minister that "each sect holds its members to the same doctrine by only an enforced agreement; for naturally two men never thought alike without an artificial concert." He also announced firmly: "If I were to go through life again, I would never give employment to any young man who did not habitually attend church."

Johnson's major works on language theory were produced over a span of thirty-six years, beginning with the publication in pamphlet form of his 1825 Lyceum lecture, which became the first chapter of *The Philosophy of Human Knowledge, or A Treatise on Language.* This work was revised and enlarged as *A Treatise on Language* in 1836, and was the first Johnson book discovered by Stillman Drake. He reprinted it in an edition of forty-two copies on a hand press in San Francisco over a hundred years after its writing. In 1841 Johnson brought out his *Religion in Its Relation to the Present Life,* first presented as a series of lectures delivered before the Young Men's Association of Utica, a successor to the old Lyceum. The work, which Johnson described as "designed to present a summary of morality in small compass," restated earlier theories on the meaning of words and limits of significance, with emphasis on the behavioral aspects of language in respect to religious feeling. David Rynin's essay on this work quotes liberally from the Johnson text. The next major book on language, published twenty-six years after *The Philosophy of Human Knowledge,* bears the full title, *The Meaning of Words: Analysed into Words and Unverbal Things, and Unverbal Things Classified into Intellections, Sensations and Emotions.* Republished in 1862, it is a restatement of many of his earlier concepts, but in it Johnson attempted to resolve the dilemma posed by those words whose meanings cannot be verified or tested by the physical senses. As Johnson explained it in his autobiography: previously he "had analysed unverbal things into only sights, sounds, tastes, feels and smells—omitting emotions and intellections." This type of division, he added, "is a defect of analysis which I corrected in subsequent publications when further reflections had more fully developed my system." Whether or not Johnson would have been wise to leave well enough alone, and thus avoid a number of thorny philosophical problems, is a matter which receives some attention in the Symposium included in these *Proceedings.* Johnson himself seems to have regarded *The Meaning of Words* as the best of his language studies.

The Physiology of the Senses: or How and What We See, Hear, Taste, Feel and Smell (1856) and *Deep Sea Soundings and Explorations of the Bottom: or, The Ultimate Analysis of Human Knowledge* (1861) are again investigations into the problem of meaning growing out of his earlier works. The former deals in a methodical fashion with such propositions as "the degree in which any given sensible knowledge is common to different men . . . our progress in the acquisition of sensible knowledge . . . the limits and latitude of sensible knowledge." The latter book, which Rynin calls "Johnson's most metaphysical work," [6] is a terse summation of what had gone before, embellished with drawings of "the tree of knowledge" with its various branches, "sound," "sight," "envy," "love," "intellect," etc. Johnson regarded it as "little more than a brief epitome of several books previously published by me."

Finally, despite their painful oversimplification and moralistic, pompous prose, one cannot ignore Johnson's efforts in *The Encyclopedia of Instruction: or Apologues and Breviats on Man and Manners* (1857) to elucidate some of his language theories in uncomplicated terms for the benefit of his sons in college and the general reading public. Such essays as "The Effects of Language on the Speaker and Hearer," "How to Obtain any Virtue You Desire," and "The Education of the Feelings" draw heavily upon his more abstruse early writings; but the style is homiletic, and the examples are taken not from science or philosophy but from everyday life. In its own simplistic way the concluding essay on "Death" is one of the most affecting. Even age itself is reduced to a "verbal thing," for "Every man's own duration (be he young or old) stretches back further than his memory. He practically knows no longer duration except in words." [7]

It is not within the compass of these introductory comments to summarize further the body of Johnson's studies in philosophy and linguistic analysis, for the entire framework of his beliefs will be examined in the essays that follow. We owe it to Johnson, however, to let him tell us in his own words, as best he can in his final years, what he was driving at in those curious, pioneering forays of his. There is a certain touch of irascibility in his précis—as though he were going to "give it one more try," at least for the sake of his children, and his children's children.

> The purport of the book [referring to the *Treatise*] is to teach men to interpret words by the unverbal things that words refer to; and not to interpret words by other words. I assumed that every proposition has an unverbal meaning, and when that unverbal meaning is found, language is properly at the end of its office. To persevere in interpreting any given word or set of words by other words is to pursue a round without end. I assumed that words are in themselves unmeaning sounds— French sounds, German sounds, English sounds; while the

meaning that is unverbal is neither French, English, nor German, but some unverbal subjective something in man's consciousness; or some objective unverbal thing that our senses reveal. Nearly all preceding philosophies went no further than phraseology. You were required to interpret the word idea, mind, matter, etc. into some other words; and every philosopher would inculcate a different unverbal meaning, and hence all such discussions are related to the verbal meanings of words. I discarded all such process—my philosophy relating only to unverbal existences, or things. I know not to this day that any person understands the above explanation in the manner I intend it to be understood; though nothing seems to me more plain, simple, and self-evident; and it must eventually come to be admitted. I assumed further that unverbal things are analysable into seven different classes: sights, sounds, tastes, feels, smells, emotions, and intellections. Each of the said classes is generically different from any and all others. By this classification scarlet is a sight, heat is a feel, thunder a sound, odour a smell, sweet a taste, anger an emotion, and thought an intellection. To know the particular one or more of these unverbal things that any words or proposition signifies, you must be taught by your own consciousness; each unverbal thing being alone its only proper expositor. It is certainly not the word or words that you employ about it. . . . To manifest the distinction between words and unverbal things is the first substantial advance made in metaphysical knowledge.

In his appraisals of his own work, Johnson's protestations of inadequacy often become a little tiresome. Much of it seems genuine enough, but it is often difficult to avoid the impression that his modesty is a kind of rhetorical convention aimed defensively at bolstering his public ethos. More believable, perhaps, are those moments of imperturbable satisfaction when Johnson looks down upon his creations and finds them good. The remorseless objectivity which pervaded his entire outlook on life carries over into his attempts to self-appraisal; and, oddly enough, even when he verges on arrogance the reader is not apt to be disturbed by it.

His first book, *An Inquiry into the Nature of Value and Capital,* published in 1813, elicited the later comment from Johnson: "Its success was less than I expected or as the book deserved," and Joseph Dorfman's essay on this work would seem to bear out the latter portion of this statement. A familiar note enters into Johnson's evaluation when he adds that he would alter nothing in it except some of the "composition which my defective education made very faulty." On this point Johnson is more often than not rather proud of his "defective education," for, as he is at pains to point out,

> An education self-acquired conduces probably to originality of conceptions; while regularly educated persons repeat current ideas, rather than originate them. A self-educated man is like a seedling tree; the grafted tree produces like fruit with the graft, but a seedling is an original and may produce fruit better than the graft—or worse.

During the same year that *The Nature of Value and Capital* appeared, Johnson also produced a poem called "The Court of Hymen." He referred to it as belonging among his "abortive writings," but in talking to John Quincy Adams about it, he announced blandly, "I judge poetry by translating it into prose, and if I find the composition sensible prose, I deem the poetry good—otherwise not. Judged by this rule, I think my poem was not bad." This, incidentally, pretty well sums up Johnson's attitude toward poetry in general.

Johnson seems to have regarded many of his earlier pieces as mere efforts at self-improvement. In sending a short essay on population to John Adams, for example, he remarked: "I do not send it as a specimen of my philosophy, for I view it as a species of chamber exercise . . . a species of Mnemonics." His chief mnemonic exercises consisted of poring through dictionaries, listing synonyms, and struggling against the evils of tautology and "pleonasmus"—in the interest of "compressibility."

Johnson locked horns with his own vanity in the very first of his lectures at the Utica Lyceum on the "Philosophy of Human Knowledge," which later became the first chapter of the *Treatise*. He began with the charming apologia,

> It is my misfortune to possess a strong inclination for abstruse studies. Its indulgence has diminished my convivial enjoyments, and employed the ardour which, at my age, is usually expended in political discussions—vociferous in the defence of rights not invaded, and vindictive in the redress of wrongs not inflicted.[8]

The lecture ended, however, with Johnson invoking an "insidious" enemy, a demon "that lures me from the substantial pursuits of life":

> His language was harmonious;—his actions were profoundly respectful. Delight hung upon his lips, and irresistible conviction accompanied his communication. An unusual complacency expanded my breast. . . . When suddenly approaching the fiend, his eyes were averted, and his face was distorted with laughter.

He dissolved into air, and, as he vanished, I discovered that his name was Vanity.[9]

Vanity is always present with Johnson, even as it masquerades as modesty, but the author invariably recognized his enemy and rarely failed to announce his presence. After another of his Lyceum speeches, one which he labeled "original in the manner I treated the subject," a letter of praise from an old friend elicited the reply: "praise is a necessary ailment in a literary man . . . in proportion to the quantity he receives, an author will either produce a few sterile pamphlets, or luxuriate into quartos and folios." A laudatory letter from Timothy Flint provoked an unusual exposure of Johnson's feelings: "I literally starve for excitement . . . a mouthful of praise is a luxury to me." And still another compliment brought forth: "Praise is . . . salutary only where the receiver is too strong to be subdued by inebriation."

Such revelations as these are usually reserved for private correspondence with those whom Johnson trusted. Like John Quincy Adams, with whom Johnson had many qualities in common, he would rarely lift a finger to advance his own cause or solicit public approbation. Adams, despite his yearning for the office of the Presidency, sat stiffly at home waiting to be crowned, and stood by what he called his "Macbeth policy"—"If chance will have me king, why, chance may crown me without my stir." Johnson, no doubt, would have accepted public office had it been handed to him; but he too had his "Macbeth policy," and invoked it frequently—particularly in relation to his language works. "I have never made any effort," he wrote, "to give any work of mine a notoriety with the public, and to this may probably belong the little notoriety that any of them ever acquired. I thought if they merited public notice, they would eventually attain it and I left them to float or sink by their own buoyancy." The feminist Fanny Wright tried to help him promote his books, and so did others, but Johnson was rarely cooperative. Even John Quincy Adams, not averse to advising others on how to gain attention, was rebuffed. In one of Adams' more avuncular letters to Johnson he suggested that Johnson might improve the *Treatise* with more biblical allusions. Johnson transcribed the letter into the autobiography with the terse comment, "I copy this letter from Mr. Adams in deference to his social position."

During the last ten years of his life, a period in which Johnson produced four of his twelve books, he grew more and more casual about their fate—or at least he tried to give that impression. When *The Physiology of the Senses* appeared in 1856, he "as usual distributed copies to several of my friends from whom I received pleasant responses." He copied only two, however, one of which complains that the book came to him in "modest silence." In 1857, he published *The Encyclopedia of Instruction,* dedicated to his old friend Henry Rowe Schoolcraft. The destruction of many copies of this book by fire was shrugged off with: "It made the work less diffused among the community than any of my other works." He said nothing of its reception save that a reviewer had found it "puerile"—to which Johnson replied that "it was meant for children [which is wasn't]." Also in 1857, he published a collection of newspaper and magazine articles on many subjects, mainly political, under the title *A Guide to the Right Understanding of Our American Union.* "Soon after its publication," Johnson says, "my bank troubles recalled me from the pleasant recreation of literature, and I know less of the fate of this volume than any I have published." He enlarged upon this "pleasant recreation" theme frequently as he grew more hopeless about his audience, and ended his last book, *Deep Sea Soundings,* with the statement: "I have attained my purpose, for 'while some in war and some in trade delight/my pleasure is to sit alone and write'." A few lines earlier, however, Johnson stated flatly that his works on language "will be improved upon, certainly, and succeeding investigators will, I hope, accomplish more . . . but, they constitute a better intellectual philosophy than can be found anywhere, and more intelligible."[10] And on one of the final pages of his autobiography, Johnson summed up as follows:

> And now in taking leave of my various writings . . . I feel that I have laboured in vain so far as my teachings have been accepted by the world, or influenced the thoughts of reflective men. Teachings, which like mine, require an eradication of existing notions labour under disadvantages which may well be deemed insurmountable, while teachings which harmonize with prevailing opinions are readily accepted. . . . In artistic conception I believe they are unsurpassed for brevity of expression and perspicuity of meaning.

Johnson, in his last days, made peace—or at least a kind of truce—with his old enemy Vanity. He had no doubts whatever as to the uniqueness and ultimate challenge of his writings in the shadowy realm of language analysis. He knew what he had done, and despite the many protestations of inadequacy one suspects that a hundred years of waiting would not have seemed too long a time.

Many of the delegates of the Utica Conference found themselves speculating on how Johnson might have reacted had some friendly medium arranged for him to be present. Among other things, one suspects he would have wanted his children there, and some of his close friends—especially John Quincy Adams. He would certainly have appraised his many descendants in the audience with a critical eye—to see if they had chosen well in their marriages, imbued their children with high moral principles (avoiding spiritous liquors and tight lacing), accumulated sufficient capital through means other than shopkeeping, and gone to church regularly. He would have welcomed the presence of the writer from the *New York Times,* but he would not have sought him out. The frequent comparisons with such moderns as Wittgenstein, Russell, Bridgman, Richards, et al. would have sent him scurrying across the street to the Utica Public Library; and he might have found it hard to believe that not one of them had read his *Treatise.* Stillman Drake's praises would have strongly tested his resistance to "inebriation." As for Max Black's surgical approach to his language theories and the careful reservations expressed by David Rynin, we can be sure that he would have recalled his own application of the scalpel to earlier philosophers. One thing is certain—Johnson's twentieth-century critics would not have escaped without a philosophical argument, for his gravestone in Utica's Forest Hills cemetery states the priorities quite clearly:

THE AUTHOR OF MANY BOOKS:
A LAWYER BY EDUCATION:
A BANKER DURING ACTIVE LIFE:
A STUDENT OF PHILOSOPHY ALWAYS

NOTES

1 All quotations from A. B. Johnson cited in the Introduction, along with excerpts from letters written by and to Johnson, are taken from his unpublished autobiography unless otherwise noted. The editors and a number of the contributors to these *Proceedings* worked from a typescript produced in 1930 by Eliza Stringham Morton from a manuscript copy owned by members of the Johnson family. The typescript was made available by Bryan

Johnson Lynch, a great-grandson of A. B. Johnson, and two photocopies are on file at the Hamilton College Library.

2 *Western Monthly Review,* Vol. II (March 1829), p. 577.

3 Jasena Rappleye Foley, "The Ontario Glass Manufacturing Company," *Journal of Glass Studies,* Vol. VI (1964), p. 138.

4 A microfilm copy of the two-volume scrapbook is in the Hamilton College Library.

5 Moses M. Bagg, *Pioneers of Utica* (Utica: Curtiss & Childs, 1877), p. 327.

6 David Rynin, Introduction to Johnson's *A Treatise on Language* (Berkeley: University of California Press, 1947), p. 10.

7 *The Encyclopedia of Instruction* (1857), p. 407.

8 Address to the Utica Lyceum, February 17, 1825, p. 3.

9 *Ibid.,* p. 16.

10 A. B. Johnson, *Deep Sea Soundings and Explorations of the Bottom* (Boston, 1861), p. 78.

BIBLIOGRAPHY

PUBLISHED WORKS BY ALEXANDER BRYAN JOHNSON

This bibliography is based largely on notes prepared by David Rynin for his 1947 edition of Johnson's A TREATISE ON LANGUAGE (University of California Press). Several additional items, brought to the attention of the editors during the Utica Conference, have been added. The Editorial Board of the Alexander Bryan Johnson Papers at Hamilton College will be grateful for any information concerning other Johnson material.

A number of Johnson's communications to the press, many of them anonymous, as well as a selection of reviews of his books, are contained in two scrapbooks kept by Johnson which are now deposited in the New York State Library, Albany. Three bound volumes of manuscript letters are on temporary loan at the Hamilton College Library, courtesy of Alexander Bryan Johnson of New York and Darien. A facsimile typescript copy of the unpublished autobiography, made available by Bryan Johnson Lynch, of Barneveld, N.Y., is on permanent deposit, along with other documents.

BOOKS

1. (1813) *An Inquiry into the Nature of Value and of Capital, and into the Operation of Government Loans, Banking Institutions and Private Credit, with an Appendix Containing an Inquiry into the Causes which Regulate the Rate of Interest, and the Price of Stocks.* Published for the author by John Forbes, Printer, New York. 8vo., vi+117 pp.

2. (1828) *The Philosophy of Human Knowledge, or A Treatise on Language* (New York: G. & C. Carvill). 4to, vi+200 pp.

3. (1836) *A Treatise on Language: or The Relation Which Words Bear to Things* (New York: Harper & Brothers). 8vo., xxvi+274 pp.

4. (1841; 2d ed. 1862) *Religion in Its Relation to the Present Life. In a Series of Lectures, Delivered before the Young Men's Association of Utica* (New York: Harper & Brothers). 12mo., 180 pp. (The book also appeared under the title *Morality and Manners.*)

5. (1841) *The Philosophical Emperor: A Political Experiment; or the Progress of a False Position, dedicated to the Whigs, Conservatives, Democrats and Loco Focos individually and collectively, of the United States* (New York: Harper & Brothers). 18mo., 112 pp.

6. (1854, 2d ed. 1862) *The Meaning of Words: Analysed into Words and Unverbal Things, and Unverbal Things Classified into Intellections, Sensations, and Emotions* (New York: D. Appleton & Co.). 8vo., 256 pp.

7. (1856) *The Physiology of the Senses: or How and What We See, Hear, Taste, Feel and Smell* (New York and Cincinnati: Derby and Jackson). 12mo., 214 pp.

8. (1857) *An Encyclopedia of Instruction; or, Apologues and Breviats on Man and Manners* (New York: Derby and Jackson). 12mo., 409 pp. (This work also appeared under the title *Guide to Knowledge and Wealth.*)

9. (1857) *A Guide to the Right Understanding of Our American Union, or Political, Economical and Literary Miscellanies* (New York: Derby and Jackson). 18mo., 407 pp.

10. (1861) *Deep Sea Soundings and Explorations of the Bottom; or The Ultimate Analysis of Human Knowledge* (Boston: privately printed). Small 8vo., 78 pp.

PAMPHLETS

(1813) *An Inquiry into the Natural Rights of Man, as Regards the Exercise of Expatriation; dedicated to all the adopted citizens of the United States; by a gentleman of the city of New York* (New York: Pelsue and Gould).

(1824) *Address before the Utica Lyceum, Delivered February 5, 1824* (Utica: H. Gray). 8vo., 13 pp.

Oration Commemorative of American Independence, Delivered at Utica: July 5, 1824 (Utica: William Williams). 8vo., 16 pp.

An Address to the Utica Forum, Delivered December 9, 1824 (Utica: William Williams). 8vo., 16 pp.

(1825) *Address to the Utica Lyceum, February 17, 1825,* Prefatory to His Course of Lectures, "The Philosophy of Human Knowledge" (Utica: Merrell & Hastings). 8vo., 16 pp.

(1829) *Address to the Utica Temperance Society, Delivered July 29, 1829* (Utica: William Williams). 8vo., 16 pp.

(1831) *Method of Acquiring a Full Knowledge of the English Language, Propounded at Their Invitation by A. B. Johnson, Utica, August 10, 1831, before the New York State Lyceum* Utica: Northway & Porter). 15 pp.

(1832) *A Discourse on Language* (Utica: William Williams). 28 pp.

(1834) *Speech before an Auxiliary of the American Colonization Society, Utica, January 13, 1834* (Utica, William Williams). 16 pp.

Speech before a Meeting of the Democratic Citizens of Utica, on the Subject of the United States Bank, March 25, 1834 (Utica: E. A. Maynard).

Letter to Nathan Williams, Containing His Views on the Coming Election (Albany: Albany *Argus*). 4 pp. An "extra" issued by the *Argus*.

On the Political Contest (Utica).

(1846) *Thoughts on the Necessity for, and Action of, the Approaching State Convention* (Utica: I. S. Clark). 51 pp. Reprinted from articles in the *Democrat*.

(1850) *A Treatise on Banking* (Utica: Seward and Thurber). 8vo., 44 pp. Reprinted from *The Bankers' Magazine*, vol, III, pp. 733*ff.*

(1862) *The Advanced Value of Gold, Suspended Specie Payment, Legal-Tender Notes, Taxation and National Debt, Investigated Impartially* (Utica: Curtiss & White). 8vo., 32 pp.

The Union as It Was, and the Constitution as It Is. N.p., author not named.

(1863) *Where We Stood and Where We Stand.* By the Author of *The Union as It was.* N.p., 13 pp.

(1864) *Our Monetary Condition.* N.p., 8vo., 21 pp.

The Approaching Presidential Election. N.p., 8vo., pp.

PERIODICAL AND NEWSPAPER ARTICLES

(1833) "Immorality of Tight Lacing" (signed "Matilda"). *The Mother's Magazine*, Vol. 1.

(1847) "The Wilmot Proviso." Utica *Observer,* August 24, 1847.

(1849) "How to Live Where You Like, a Legend of Utica." *Knickerbocker Magazine,* November 1849.

"The Argumentative Husband and the Husband Who Denied His Wife Nothing; or A Secret Worth Knowing." *Knickerbocker Magazine,* December 1849.

(1850) "Feminine Perfections, or the Unreasonable Bachelor." *Knickerbocker Magazine,* January 1850.

"How to Prosper: or the Fatal Mistake." *Knickerbocker Magazine,* February 1850.

"The Hermit of Utica." *Knickerbocker Magazine,* March 1850.

"How to Be Happy." *Knickerbocker Magazine,* April 1850.

"The Philosophical Emperor: or an Experiment in Morals." *Knickerbocker Magazine,* May–June 1850.

"Story of the Man Whom Nobody Can Benefit, and the Man Whom Nobody Can Injure." *Knickerbocker Magazine,* July 1850.

"The Three Views of Life." *Knickerbocker Magazine,* August 1850.

"A Day at Utica: or the First House-warming." *Knickerbocker Magazine,* September 1850.

"The Obstacles to Success." *Knickerbocker Magazine,* October 1850.

"Advantages and Disadvantages of Private Corporations." *Hunt's Merchants' Magazine,* December 1850.

"Legislative History of Corporations in New York; or The Progress of Liberal Principles." *Hunt's Merchants' Magazine,* December 1850.

(1851) "The Philosophy of the Union; or The Principles of Its Cohesiveness." *United States Magazine and Democratic Review,* January 1851.

"The Constitutional Power of Congress over Public Improvements." *United States Magazine and Democratic Review,* February 1851.

"The Internal Management of a Country Bank" (an unsigned review of Thomas Bullion's book of this title). *Hunt's Merchants' Magazine,* February 1851.

"The Present and Prospective Value of Gold." *Hunt's Merchants' Magazine,* March 1851.

"The Veto Power of the President." *United States Magazine and Democratic Review,* March 1851.

"Duties, Omissions, and Misdoings of Bank Directors." *Hunt's Merchants' Magazine,* April 1851.

"The Philosophy of Joint-Stock Banking" (a review of G. M. Bell's book). *Hunt's Merchants' Magazine,* August 1851.

"The Threefold Nature of Man: A Legend of the Oneida Indians." *Knickerbocker Magazine,* August 1851.

"The Philosophical Sparrow." *Knickerbocker Magazine,* September 1851.

"Relative Merits of Life Insurance and Savings Banks." *Hunt's Merchants' Magazine,* December 1851.

(1852) "The Lunatic Asylum of Boresko." *Knickerbocker Magazine,* March 1852.

(1854) "The Maine Liquor Law." Rome (N.Y.) *Daily Sentinel,* October 25, 1854.

(1856) "Our Political Disorders and Their Remedy." Utica *Observer,* July 30, 1856. (Reprinted from the Albany *Atlas & Argus.*)

"The Principles of American Liberty." Albany *Atlas & Argus,* 4 September 1856.

"The Political and Economical Influence of Usury Laws." Albany *Evening Journal.*

(1857) "The Almighty Dollar; or, Money as a Motive for Action." *Hunt's Merchants' Magazine,* January 1857.

OTHER PUBLICATIONS, FORM UNCERTAIN

(1818) Prospectus for a book entitled *The Philosophy of Human Knowledge.*

(1830) Prospectus: *A Collated Dictionary; or A Complete Index to the English Language.*

(1834) The Alternative of Continuing Our State Debt, or Liquidating It by Taxation. (Exact title not known.)

"The Bank Panic and Pressure." (Published October 6, 1834.)

(1835) "The Mode of Selecting a New President." (Published June 9, 1835, and addressed to the Democratic Electors of the 17th Congressional District of New York.)

"An Obituary Notice of the Life of Judge Nathan Williams."

(1837) "The Suspension of Specie Payments." (Address to a convention of bank representatives at New York, 1837.)

(1842) "The Alternative of Borrowing Disadvantageously, or Suspending the Public Works."

"The Alternative of Debt or Taxation." (See also first title under 1834.)

(1844) "The Annexation of Texas."

(1845) "Texas Annexed."

(1846) "The Excise License Question."

(1848) "The Anatomy of Politics." (Published March 21, 1848.)

"The Slavery Question." (Published August 30, 1848.)

"Merits and Demerits of Existing Parties." (Published September 2, 1848.)

"The Vices of Political Minorities."

(1849) "The Southern Disunionists." (Published December 17, 1849.)

(1851) "The President's Constitutional Advisers."

(1854) "Reserved Rights of American Citizens."

"The Kansas-Nebraska Question." (Two articles, the second published March 20, 1854.)

(1855) "Eulogy on a Body Corporate."

(1856) "The Clayton-Bulwer Treaty."

(1857) "Political and Economic Influence of Usury Laws."

I

PHILOSOPHER OF LANGUAGE

Succeeding investigators will, I hope,
accomplish more. . . .
A. B. Johnson's autobiography

BACK FROM LIMBO:
THE REDISCOVERY OF
ALEXANDER BRYAN JOHNSON

♦ ♦ ♦ ♦ ♦ *STILLMAN DRAKE*

FOR NEARLY thirty years I have looked forward to this occasion. We are here to honor the memory of Alexander Bryan Johnson, one of Utica's first citizens in every sense of the word. I am happy to take part and proud to do so in the company of distinguished scholars drawn from many fields, whose very presence shows the permanent place that Johnson has earned in the history of ideas. For this I must thank Hamilton College, the Munson-Williams-Proctor Institute, and all the persons and organizations that have cooperated to make the occasion possible.

Many aspects of Johnson's life and works are about to be discussed by experts in various phases of his activity and by specialists in the history of Utica. It is fitting that the professional appraisal of his life and work should fall to them. But first in order of time, if not of importance, is the story of events which brought Johnson's work, after a century of neglect, to its proper place on the American intellectual scene.

It was in 1938 that, as Professor David Rynin said in the

◊ ◊ ◊ ◊ ◊ *Professor of History, Institute for the History and Philosophy of Science and Technology, University of Toronto. Among his published books are* Galileo: Dialogue Concerning the Two Chief World Systems *and* Discoveries and Opinions of Galileo.

Introduction to a modern edition of Johnson's *Treatise on Language,* I "by chance found a copy" of that book, which I "luckily recognized for what it is, a philosophical classic." [1] Apart from the fact that in what Professor Rynin acclaimed as a philosophical classic, I recognized only an antimetaphysical bombshell, that account is correct. In a sense it gives the whole story and gives it very succinctly. The discovery was certainly a lucky chance. But it is now generally agreed that every event has causes, and that when we speak of "chance" and "luck," we do not mean to deny that causes exist; we mean only that they are obscure, or unknown to us. It is not always possible to trace such causes accurately and completely, and they may not all be of equal significance. But to the historian of ideas they are all of possible interest. In the present instance the long neglect of Johnson's thought is no less surprising than the resemblance between it and that of other men who came after him but knew nothing of his work. This story of its rediscovery may throw light on both those puzzles.

The history of ideas presents many examples in which an important concept has been announced before its time, so to speak, and has been recognized as valuable only later. Sometimes the later writer has found the idea in the writings of an earlier man, and then he may have hailed the genius of his predecessor, or he may have tried to conceal his ancient source. The latter possibility is ever present, and gives special trouble to historians of science. Again, the later writer may have developed the idea quite independently, and its discovery in the works of an earlier writer may occur only much later. To trace the actual facts in all cases is not always possible; the historian may be obliged to make conjectures. It therefore seems to me that where an actual detailed account of events can be given in one instance—as in that of A. B. Johnson's critique of language—it should be given in full, as a possible guide to the reconstruction of other instances far in the past.

No one has yet demonstrated an indebtedness of Johnson to earlier writers for his fundamental method of attack on philosophical problems. It also appears that writers in the present century who developed a similar method of attack owe no debt to Johnson, directly or through any philosophical tradition.

Such a situation is rare in the history of ideas; perhaps it is unique. Most instances of the anticipation of later ideas have been found through the discovery of manuscript or other unpublished material, or occasionally where a publication was obscured by reason of its place or language. But Johnson's important work was published in

4   LANGUAGE AND VALUE

English in New York, and not once but twice, eight years apart. It was also published in diluted form in some of his numerous other pamphlets and books. I can think of no truly parallel case of neglect and belated recognition since the invention of printing, five centuries ago.

An isolated idea may indeed be put forth in a lengthy book and escape notice as original and valuable. But Johnson's contribution is not an isolated idea; it is a truly new line of thought concerning a very much agitated question—the nature of philosophical problems. Johnson's line of thought is not merely suggested, but is worked out consistently and in considerable detail. No one before him seems to have hit on it, let alone to have worked it out. Yet for centuries men of high intellect had concerned themselves with the same problems. Among themselves, they had expressed differences of philosophical opinion—or that is how I should describe the differences between John Locke, George Berkeley, and David Hume. Johnson was able to show that each of those three philosophers had on occasion slipped into a linguistic trap, in the belief that some truth about nature was being shown. Johnson's contribution was thus no mere difference of opinion, but a promising and novel method of semantic analysis. It was published repeatedly. But it attracted no attention from recognized philosophers.

The normal explanation would be that Johnson's proposed analysis was worthless. But the modern, independent development of linguistic analysis in philosophy obviates that explanation. Johnson's method of investigation, if not all of his conclusions, has been entirely vindicated.

Another possible explanation would be that Johnson's method was not clearly set forth and illustrated. But no one has taken or is likely to take that position. Indeed, the opening lecture of the *Treatise* makes it unmistakably clear that Johnson realized the novelty of what he wished to say, as well as the difficulty of preventing his listeners or readers from confusing it with quite ordinary critiques of language. "I allude to no defects of language that you ever heard of or conceived," he said. "I also allude to none that can be obviated. The most that I hope to perform is to make them known, as we erect a beacon to denote the presence of a shoal which we cannot remove." He spared no effort to clarify his view of the manner in which words get their meanings and to show its relevance to the problems of philosophy.

I hope I have sufficiently convinced you that the problems presented to the historian of ideas by the neglect of Johnson's *Treatise on Language* are both interesting and unusual. Their solutions must be sought in a variety of circumstances that must have combined to push the book into limbo. It is easy to suggest a few of these: Johnson was an American venturing on abstruse matters at a time when America was considered (and considered itself) a rude and uncultured land; Johnson's views, if understood, might threaten religion in an intensely religious age; Johnson lived far to the west of the American universities, and had no connection with them; Johnson was a banker, and therefore a mere amateur in the eyes of philosophers. There is always a great surplus of amateur productions in philosophy to which philosophers can scarcely afford to pay attention. The effect that each of these factors had on the neglect of Johnson's *Treatise* by philosophers is an interesting question for historians.

But the rediscovery of Johnson's *Treatise* presents a further challenge to historians of ideas. The phenomenon of simultaneous discovery is one of the most illuminating reflections of a cultural epoch. Now the *Treatise* was rediscovered independently within a year or so by two men, unknown to one another, in widely separated places, under totally different circumstances. That fact needs explanation in terms of cause and effect. Chance and luck might pass as explanations for one incident, but not for two so closely related and yet so different. What was the intellectual climate that suddenly made the *Treatise* of interest to a businessman in one city and a scholar in another?

A young German philosopher, inspired by the creation of symbolic logic, had turned his attention to language, with devastating effects for conventional philosophy. The English translator of his work had ventured a work of his own, a semipopular book called *The Meaning of Meaning*. A Polish engineer had found in linguistics the basis for a visionary reform of the human race, set forth in two books, *The Manhood of Humanity* and *Science and Sanity*. A great depression and the threat of an unscrupulous dictator had inspired an American popularizer to apply the ideas to politics in a book called *The Tyranny of Words*.[2] All these are demonstrably factors in the double rediscovery of Johnson's *Treatise,* and goodness knows how many other things may have been involved.

But was Johnson really important? Was the rediscovery of his *Treatise* important? My opinion is affirmative on both questions, but my opinion is obviously biased. It is up to historians of ideas to explore the mines and determine whether they will repay further working. From what I have learned of Utica, it is no mere accident that the first

6

and perhaps the greatest original American contribution to philosophy —or rather to the theory of knowledge—originated here. I should not wonder if many other cultural aspects of this early western outpost now begin to receive the attention they deserve from American historians of ideas as a result of this conference on A. B. Johnson. For in my opinion his pioneer examination of our most fundamental means of communication, language, is destined to take a place in the history of Western culture far above that which anyone else imagines at present. It is only when all the questions I have mentioned above have been explored, and their ramifications begin to be perceived, that Johnson, in his restless and versatile contemplations and activities, will be recognized as a prophet of our own time; a lonely, self-taught thinker whose voice cried out in the wilderness, and who—had he been heard—might have changed the intellectual history of mankind.

Because I believe that, I shall try to present in as much detail and as accurately as I can the story of Johnson's return from limbo. If my view is correct, no scrap of data should be left out. I do not know which of the anecdotes I shall relate may turn out to be enlightening to the historian, which ones merely amusing, and which ones wrong despite my best efforts.

Of the many people who deserve credit for their contributions to the rediscovery of A. B. Johnson and to the awakening of interest in his life and works, I should like first to mention three of my closest friends at the University of California in 1930: Daniel Belmont, Mark Eudey, and Henry Ralston. Belmont and I were then fellow students in the department of philosophy. After my graduation in 1932 he won a fellowship which enabled him to study at Cambridge under Professor Ludwig Wittgenstein. That good fortune of his turned out to be still luckier for me, and ultimately for A. B. Johnson. For it was from Belmont, after his return from England, that I was able to learn much about the nature of philosophical problems and about their frequent, if not invariable, origin in misapprehensions of the nature of language. But by that time we had both left Berkeley and were at work outside the university.

About the beginning of 1938 I organized a sort of cooperative seminar with my friends in order that I might take advantage of their special knowledge in divergent fields. The idea was that each of us would serve as instructor at two or three meetings of the group, as the price of receiving instruction at the others. Meeting weekly in the evening at one another's house, we thus heard from Belmont about modern trends in philosophy, from Mark Eudey about astrophysics and cosmogony, and from Henry Ralston about evolution and genetics. Other friends dealt with such a variety of topics as electronics, history, and naval strategy, while I undertook to talk on comparative philology.

In order to brush up on that subject, I went one Saturday afternoon to a San Francisco bookstore in which I had lately noticed a number of works on linguistics. Among them I saw a book labeled *Johnson's Treatise on Language.* The book was obviously too old to contain any scientific philology, but I took it off the shelf anyway, wondering if it might be some rare work by Dr. Samuel Johnson of dictionary fame. The title page quickly showed that idea to be mistaken; the book was by one A. B. Johnson, whose name was new to me. But I did not put it back on the shelf, because my attention was arrested by its subtitle: "The Relation Which Words Bear to Things." Now, that had nothing to do with my principal interest at the moment, but it chanced to bear directly on the matters that Belmont had studied under Wittgenstein at Cambridge and that he had just been discussing in our seminar. I therefore looked further into the book, and found it to be composed in numbered paragraphs, beginning with the sentence, "Man exists in a world of his own creation." Curiously enough, Wittgenstein's one published book at that time was known as the *Tractatus,* or treatise; it was composed in numbered sentences, and began with the sentence, "The world is everything that is the case." [3] Struck by those coincidences, I read Johnson's preface and glanced through his table of contents, noting at once other similarities in style and intention on the part of the two writers. Reading then at random a few paragraphs of the *Treatise,* I became the first modern Johnsonian in a matter of minutes. Clearly, whoever the man might have been, he knew what he was talking about, was aware of the special difficulties that would attend its communication to others, and had a peculiar gift of expression.

The book was priced at two dollars, which in those times of economic recession was exorbitant for an old book by an unknown author. But the dealer, Mr. Malcolm McNeill, was not inclined to bargain with me. He contended that any book more than a century old, particularly an American book so venerable, was worth two dollars or it was worth nothing. As a bookseller, he would not consider the latter alternative. I urged it on the grounds that if the book had any real merit, I should have heard of it at the university. I lost the argument, but I did happen to have two dollars with me, and luckily I decided to let comparative philology go for that day and to buy the *Treatise* in-

8

stead. I started to read it on the streetcar home, and with only an interruption for dinner I continued reading it far into the night, finishing it on Sunday morning. Since that memorable weekend nearly three decades ago I have read the *Treatise* through many times, never without renewed admiration for its neglected author.

I soon showed my new find to Mark Eudey, who of course had also been recently awakened to the importance of the topic at our seminars. He read it, and we then concocted a practical joke on Daniel Belmont. Each of us prepared a paper arranged in the style of Wittgenstein's *Tractatus,* but composed simply by taking a selection of sentences from the list of paragraph headings that served as table of contents of Johnson's original book (and which has unfortunately been omitted from all modern editions). These papers we showed to Belmont at lunch one day, saying that each of us had tried to set down the most essential points we had learned from his seminar discourses, amplified by some thoughts of our own, and since we were not in complete agreement, we wanted him to referee the matter. This he obligingly did, writing out his comments on our two papers and giving them to us a week later, without ever suspecting that they were a hoax, cribbed word for word from an author who had written more than a century before. When we revealed that fact, he was amazed to the point of incredulity, so close were Johnson's insights to the best contemporary thought. I then lent him the book and began to check the principal bibliographies of philosophy, as well as a very long bibliography of semantics which had recently been published, but I could find no mention of Johnson anywhere.

It may seem odd, in retrospect, that Johnson's *Treatise* has gone entirely unnoticed by historians of philosophy. But there are reasons for their silence, of which I shall mention only one. On the last page of the *Treatise,* summing up his work, Johnson said:

> Our misapprehension of the nature of language has occasioned a greater waste of time, and effort, and genius, than all the other mistakes and delusions with which humanity has been afflicted . . . and though metaphysics, a rank branch of the error, is fallen into disrepute, it is abandoned like a mine which will not repay the expense of working, rather than like a process of mining which we have discovered to be constitutionally incapable of producing gold.

Professional philosophers could scarcely be expected to admit to their ranks the writer of those words, especially in Johnson's day. Thus I believe that the amateur status of the committee that welcomed Johnson back from limbo was not entirely a matter of chance. Though I am getting ahead of my story, I shall say now that the lukewarm reception of the *Treatise* by philosophers who reviewed its republication in 1947 lent support to that view. So did the fact that an independent rediscovery of the *Treatise,* not long after I had found my copy, was made by another man whose interests were far from those of recognized philosophers.[4] Nor does it seem irrelevant to the same point that Henry Ralston, who was next to borrow my copy, promptly became the most enthusiastic Johnsonian of us all. Ralston, a biologist, was even less familiar with formal philosophy than the rest of us, and perhaps for that reason he endorsed the entire *Treatise* without any reservation.

By this time quite a number of my acquaintances wanted to read the *Treatise,* while I quite naturally became reluctant to lend my copy further and risk its loss, for none was to be found in any library on the Pacific Coast. I made the most determined effort to find another copy through book dealers, but without success. Finally I agreed to print some copies for my friends if enough money could be raised to buy paper and a press. Thus it was that in May 1939 I embarked on a totally unfamiliar project, which I had ample opportunity to regret before it was done. Working evenings and weekends, I needed more than a year to complete it. When the printing was finished in August 1940, Belmont undertook the job of binding the forty-two numbered copies, which were distributed to the subscribers at the end of that year.

I sent copies to Aldous Huxley and to Professor Eric Temple Bell, from whom I received thanks and comments. Huxley saw in it, as I did, some remarkable anticipations of the operationalist philosophy of the late Professor Percy Bridgman. Later on I sent a copy to Bridgman, who confirmed our opinion, though he remarked that Johnson was clearly unacquainted with the actual procedures of the physical scientist, procedures that lay at the heart of his operationalism. I sent a copy also to Albert Einstein, who recognized in Johnson a truly original thinker capable of working out his ideas in a clear and uncompromising way. In my opinion, that tribute alone justifies all Johnson's lonely labors and our gathering here today to do him honor.

By systematic searching and correspondence I was able to find out a little about Johnson, to compile a reasonably complete bibliography of his writings, and to identify many of his sources. In all these efforts Miss Alice Dodge of the Utica Public Library was im-

10

mensely helpful. We used to supply one another with typewritten copies of rare Johnson items in our respective collections. And over a period of years I was able to acquire, with the help of book dealers scattered from California to Vermont, copies of all of Johnson's printed books and many of his pamphlets. In that way I became aware of the broad scope of his genius, which is no less astonishing than the highly original quality of his mind as shown in his analysis of the nature of philosophical problems.

Early in 1943 my friend Robert P. Willson called to my attention a book in which several quotations from Johnson's *Treatise* were given. Called *Language Habits in Human Affairs,* it had been published in 1941 by Professor Irving J. Lee of Northwestern University. Lee's book marked an epoch in the revival of interest in Johnson's work, constituting as it did the first publication of citations from the *Treatise* in the present century.[5] Early in 1944 I wrote to Lee, being curious to know whether a copy of my privately printed edition had come to his attention. His reply is interesting, for it shows that Johnson's return from limbo would not have been delayed much longer even if chance had not put a copy of the *Treatise* in my hands at a time when other circumstances had made me capable of appreciating it. Lee, then a captain in the army, wrote in reply:

> I am happy to discover some one else who found A. B. Johnson a remarkable, even though unknown figure. I came upon the *Treatise on Language* while doing some early work in semantics. In the usual routine of going through the Union Catalogue, etc., I found a copy in the John Crerar Library in Chicago. There was nothing exciting about the physical discovery, but on several occasions during the writing of my book I was disposed to stop everything and do an edition of Johnson.

Lee suggested that I write a paper on Johnson for a new journal called *ETC., A Review of General Semantics,* edited by Professor S. I. Hayakawa. In the same letter, he urged me to prepare a modern edition of the *Treatise* such as he himself had projected. I replied that such a task would require extensive historical and bibliographical information that I lacked, and that I had already tried to induce Daniel Belmont to undertake such an edition, but that he had declined for the same reason. For us to study all the books concerning similar problems that had been written around Johnson's time (with some of which he was familiar) was out of the question; we had neither the time nor the facilities to do so.

I did, however, submit a paper to *ETC.*, outlining Johnson's life and his linguistic analysis. That paper appeared in the summer issue of the journal in 1944. I distributed a number of reprints of it, of which one was sent to Professor Wittgenstein, who sent me a courteous acknowledgment.

As I have said, Lee's independent rediscovery of the *Treatise* shows that the time was at last ripe for the emergence of A. B. Johnson in the modern world. Lee's deep interest in the *General Semantics* of Alfred Korzybski (an enthusiasm which I have never shared) led him to the *Treatise* in Chicago not long after my acquaintance with Wittgenstein's writings enabled me to recognize its merit when I ran across it in San Francisco. It would be hard to imagine two more divergent philosophical backgrounds leading to the same discovery. But the history of ideas, like the history of science, provides other instances of simultaneous discovery when a particular problem is "in the air." Very often such discoveries are made by people well outside the mainstream of conventional thought, as in the present case.

It is much to be regretted that Professor Lee is no longer with us, for I should have liked to meet him. Before his untimely death, however, he contributed further to the spread of Johnson's ideas. In 1948 he persuaded Mr. John Chamberlin of Milwaukee to publish Johnson's *Meaning of Words* in an edition of five hundred copies, and in 1949 he cited Johnson at some length in another book of his own.[6]

About the time I first wrote to Lee in the spring of 1944, Daniel Belmont was invited to speak before the Philosophy Club on the Berkeley campus and he chose as his topic Johnson's *Treatise*. Professor Rynin was present and became deeply interested. Having bought a copy of my privately printed edition, he asked whether my copy of the original would be available if he could persuade the University of California Press to publish a modern edition. I readily agreed to assist in any way to make Johnson's work more generally accessible, and offered not only the book but my bibliography of Johnson and my notes identifying his probable sources. Professor Rynin was privileged to consult Johnson's manuscript autobiography through the courtesy of Mr. Alexander Bryan Johnson III, and wrote a biographical introduction, as well as a critical essay which discussed Johnson's work in modern philosophical perspective. To the text of the *Treatise* he added the variant readings and additional passages found in the edition of 1828, Johnson's *Philosophy of Human Knowledge,* and some material from

The Meaning of Words. All this took time, and it was not until February 1947 that Professor Rynin's scholarly modern edition of the *Treatise* issued from the press. Though it was reviewed in many places both in America and in England, Johnson's name still continued to be omitted from histories of philosophy, and even from a later book specifically concerned with the history of philosophy in America.

In 1945, while the new edition of the *Treatise* was in preparation, my friend Henry Ralston had become associate professor of physiology at the University of Texas in Galveston. There he contributed to the spread of Johnson's views by issuing in mimeographed form for the use of his students and friends another scarce book of Johnson's, *The Physiology of the Senses*. Professor Ralston remarked to me that he found the book particularly interesting with regard to the problem of referred pain, which appears not to have received special attention among physiologists until a later time.

Quite independently of all the activities I have mentioned thus far, Johnson was called to public attention in 1946 by Professor Joseph Dorfman in the first volume of his *The Economic Mind in American Civilization, 1606–1865*.[7] I wrote to Professor Dorfman, questioning the basis for a statement of his concerning Johnson's political position during the Civil War. His courteous reply showed that he knew a great deal more about many phases of Johnson's thought than I did, though by that time I had made a fairly extensive study of Johnson's writings in every field. It seems to me sufficiently curious to deserve mention that although I have spent most of my life in the field of investment banking, I have found Johnson's critique of language much more interesting than his successful banking career—as perhaps Johnson himself did. It would be interesting to know whether his attention was turned upon language by problems of law and finance rather than by philosophy. That would be by no means impossible, and well deserving of investigation in the context of surviving letters and unpublished manuscripts.[8]

In 1948 the distinguished antiquarian bookseller Jacob Zeitlin of Los Angeles, who had become interested in Johnson through personal conversations with me in 1942, instigated the printing, in a fine limited edition of two hundred copies, of a letter of A. B. Johnson to the Honorable Nathan Williams (dated October 6, 1834, and printed in the *Albany Argus Extra* of October 17, 1834) to which Mr. Zeitlin added a brief preface.

Professor Rynin's edition of the *Treatise* was sold out long before 1959, when it was reprinted in paperback form. That new issue received an enthusiastic review in England by Lancelot Law Whyte, the author of several important critiques of science and of society. Mr. Whyte had visited me when he was in California around 1955, to discuss Johnson's work and to see my collection of his books. The new edition of the *Treatise* also received an extensive and favorable review in Italy, where the operationalist philosophy is more highly esteemed than here in the land of its birth. An Italian translation of the *Treatise* was even projected at one time, though it did not materialize. More recently, Johnson has been honored in Sweden and in Germany through the labors of Dr. Lars Gustafsson. Thus there can be no doubt that A. B. Johnson is at last safely back from obscurity, to which he will never again be relegated. For he is no longer merely a local, nor even a national, but an international figure.

Early in 1966 Professor Charles L. Todd was in San Francisco, where Professor S. I. Hayakawa spoke to him enthusiastically of Johnson's pioneer place in semantics. He put Professor Todd in touch with me, and on a later occasion we all dined together. It was at that dinner in San Francisco that the idea of the present centennial celebration was first discussed. Today, thanks to Professor Todd's tireless energy, it is a reality. To me it is a dream come true, and my only regret is that not all the people I have mentioned could be here to share in it.

Nothing I have ever done gives me more satisfaction than my rediscovery of A. B. Johnson. Your presence here to honor him makes me feel that I have partly repaid my enormous debt to him for having freed me from many errors and prejudices, and having shown me how to avoid many delusions into which one may fall through a misunderstanding of language. But scarcely less is my debt to those friends who put me in a position to benefit from the happy chance that first placed the *Treatise* in my hands, and to others whose support made possible its reprinting. Only a few of those friends have been mentioned by name today, but all took part in welcoming back one of America's most profound and original thinkers, the Philosophical Banker of Utica.

14

NOTES

1 A. B. Johnson, *A Treatise on Language* . . ., edited by David Rynin (Berkeley: University of California Press, 1959), p. 3.

2 Ludwig Wittgenstein, C. K. Odgen, Alfred Korzybski, and Stuart Chase. Any discussion of these matters here would go far beyond the scope of this paper.

3 Ludwig Wittgenstein, *Tractatus Logico-Philosophicus* (London, 1922). Through Belmont's kindness, I also knew Wittgenstein's then unpublished "Blue Book," which was still more helpful in the recognition of Johnson's genius.

4 Professor Irving J. Lee, who wrote in 1947: "For almost a year before the winter of 1940, I had been systematically going through everything in the catalogue listings under 'Language' in the John Crerar Library in Chicago. The going had been slow and dusty. And then a subtitle stood out clear and clean: The Relation which Words Bear to Things. The book was entitled *A Treatise on Language* by A. B. Johnson, published in 1836 by Harper & Brothers. . . ."

5 My privately printed edition did not constitute publication, as did Lee's book. Earlier in the century, I am informed by Professor Joseph Dorfman, Johnson's economic theories had received attention in publications by Professor Wesley C. Mitchell, but his studies in language and meaning remained unnoticed.

6 *The Language of Wisdom and Folly,* edited and with an Introduction by Irving J. Lee (New York, 1949), pp. 113–123, 188–198.

7 New York, 1946; reprinted, 1966.

8 Both Daniel Belmont and Mark Eudey, who shared my early interest in Johnson's work, are presently engaged in San Francisco in work related to investment banking, as I was until the present year. In the same field is Johnson's direct descendant and namesake, Mr. Alexander Bryan Johnson, who is partner in the firm of Cyrus J. Lawrence and Sons, New York.

NINETEENTH-CENTURY APPRAISALS OF ALEXANDER BRYAN JOHNSON

◆ ◆ ◆ ◆ ◆ *RUSSELL T. BLACKWOOD*

> We cannot pretend to give an opinion on
> the work. The fact of its being an emanation
> from Mr. Johnson's brain is a sufficient
> guarantee of something above mediocrity.
> Evening Telegraph, *Utica, September 8, 1854*

IT IS SURELY fair to say that the philosophic work of Alexander Bryan Johnson confused most of those few who attended to it. It is easy enough to say that he was a man ahead of his time, which is true enough. But it is not correct to picture the man as an anchorite lost in a private reverie, out of touch with his contemporaries. He was a public figure of some consequence in New York State; if not an institutional scholar, he was reasonably well read. He spoke and acted with authority in a wide range of endeavors and even when wrong was respected. The success of his public life was conventional and was conventionally admired; the results of his private meditations were not at all conventional and therefore tended to bewilder. No doubt a few of Johnson's contemporaries understood his philosophy of language, but in the main they were confused, a fact which deprived him of the useful criticisms of an understanding audience.

It was Johnson's practice to present copies of his philosophic works to those friends and relatives who, in his view, might be able to understand them. (His publishers seem to have done little, if anything, to promote their sale.) The local newspapers were generally

◇ ◇ ◇ ◇ ◇ *Chairman, Department of Philosophy, Hamilton College, and author of various articles on the logic of religious knowledge.*

16

courteous in reviewing the work of the prominent citizen; the friends and relatives usually amiable.

Among the friends, S. DeWitt Bloodgood of New York wrote of *The Physiology of the Senses* that it was "the most subtle analysis I ever met with . . . very original, very acute, and very conclusive." [1] Samuel Dakin, who later became the publisher of *Knickerbocker Magazine,* predicted that Johnson's work was "destined to produce many salutary reforms in philosophy." Fanny Wright, the colorful feminist, took a longer view in her prediction that "it would be a hundred years or more" before anyone recognized Johnson's true genius. Senator Charles Stebbins found that Johnson's books had to be "studied rather than read" and hoped that their author "would live to see and enjoy the public acknowledgment."

Other friends were equally well meaning, but less studious. Gerrit Smith, the abolitionist, hoped that the contents of one of the books "would please me as much as the dedication did." P. A. Proal, rector of Trinity Church, Utica, was so overcome by the author's inscription to him that he failed to mention the contents of the book. Benjamin Silliman, Yale's Professor of Science, wrote that "because of the number and pressure of my avocations, it may be some time before I can read your work." To the historian of ideas, surely the most discouraging reply is a letter from Auguste Comte. Writing from Paris in 1854, the philosopher-sociologist declined further correspondence with a philosopher he might have found quite congenial:

> I pray you to accept my entire thanks for the small volume which I received yesterday, with your honored letter of the thirteenth of September. But although the question which you have broached may be one of the most fundamental which we can agitate, I cannot promise you to read such an essay. For my part, I read nothing except the great poets ancient and modern. The cerebral hygiene is exceedingly salutary to me, particularly in order to maintain the originality of my peculiar meditations. Nevertheless, without reading your book, I will confide its scrupulous examination to one of my best disciples. The question which occupies you has not been directly treated in my positive philosophy, but I have fully demonstrated my positive theory of Human Language in the fourth chapter of the second volume of the great work, or system of positive politics of which I have just published the fourth and last volume and according to the general plan of my labours, I can never return to the subject.

There is no record of the result of the disciple's examination.

Most of the newspaper reviews of Johnson's books were polite, but perfunctory. The *Utica Morning Herald* found that *The Physiology of the Senses* "possesses the same excellences of style as have marked the previous productions of its author." The *Utica Daily Gazette* felt that it would "hazard little in saying that it is a contribution to the science of mental philosophy, of striking original power, presenting, in some 200 of 12mo pages, more thought bearing directly upon his subject and entrenching his positions, than is often found in the most unwieldy quartos." The *London Athaneum* was somewhat more perceptive in its observation that "Mr. Johnson is rather a metaphysician than a physiologist, and has in a very original way endeavoured to work out the problems involved in seeing, hearing, feeling, touching, and tasting." Somewhat inconsistently, the review concluded: "Although we do not think Mr. Johnson has made any discovery in *The Physiology of the Senses,* we can recommend his book to those interested in the special department of inquiry of which it treats." One reviewer contended that "it is well adapted to schools, as a book for occasional class reading, and for private study at home." In fact, the Secretary of the State of New York, Samuel Young, promised to have another of Johnson's books, *Religion in Its Relation to the Present Life,* certified as "acceptable in the common schools." The record does not indicate that anything came of the promise. But if school adoption was Johnson's plan, one can only be puzzled by his contention that the book's failure partly derived from the publisher's decision to abridge the subtitle from "Lectures to the Young Men's Association" to "Lectures to the Young." In the author's mind, this "implied the book was designed for children and thus belittled its contents to those who judge books by their title." With some vigor, Johnson claimed the work "was designed for men."

The *Westminster Review* for October 1856 admired *The Physiology of the Senses* in a brief review that deserves full citation:

> We have received from the United States an unpretending little book, the product (apparently) of an amateur in science, which is much more worthy of attention than such productions usually are. Its author is evidently a thinking as well as an observant man, who has set down a number of points relating to the physiology of the senses, which have from time to time suggested themselves to him; and although many of these are familiar to such as have studied the subject more systematically, yet others are either new in themselves, or derive a novel aspect from the guise under which they are presented. The book, moreover, has the charm of being eminently suggestive, and is

distinguished by an agreeable raciness of style; so that the perusal of it will serve as a pleasant and not unprofitable recreation to the man of science, whilst it will convey much valuable information to the general reader,—its great charm being that it develops a significance in the things of familiar experience which the million passes unnoticed; but is always pleased to recognise when pointed out.

But not all of Johnson's contemporary critics were unreserved in their praise. John Quincy Adams, Johnson's wife's uncle, argued that his philosophy of language contained a basic flaw. In a letter commenting on the *Discourse on Language,* Adams wrote:

> Your subject, if I understand you, is the inherent imperfection of language by its undertaking to generalize that which nature produces individually. The position is perhaps incontrovertible, but is this imperfection remediable? Is not the classification of objects produced individually by nature an enlargement of the powers of language? The producing power of nature is infinite, but the mind of man is finite to conceive and still more finite to impart.

Johnson complained that the former President, now Congressman, had entirely missed his drift: "Language is doubtless all that Mr. Adams maintains; but the more we understand its nature, the less we shall be deceived by its inevitable generalities and other defects."

A few years later Johnson showed warmer appreciation for his distinguished relative's comments. In 1836 Adams wrote what Johnson took to be "the best criticism that my book ever received." In a remarkably perceptive letter regarding the *Treatise on Language,* Adams noted an issue which was to be enlarged on more than a century later. He also made a reflexive point which Johnson did not ignore. John Quincy Adams wrote:

> Without being able to assent to many of its opinions, and particularly to that which if I understand the work looms the foundation of your theory—namely that sensation is the only source of human knowledge, and that every word not expressive of some sensuous impression is insignificant.[2] I must admit that the view you have taken of the whole subject is new and sustained with great meditative power, a power which I can trace to neither sight, sound, taste, feel or smell. . . . The word "mind," itself, in your system is insignificant, it means nothing which either or all the five senses indicate. Mind is neither sight, sound, feel, taste, or smell, nor is it a combination of any two or more of these. Is "mind" then a word without meaning.

Again Johnson complained that Adams had failed to understand his aim, but wrote in his autobiography that "on continued reflection, I deemed the book defective in not taking cognizance of the intellect and the emotions, as yielding an ultimate meaning to words that referred to no sensible revelations." To remedy this defect Johnson in 1854 wrote *The Meaning of Words: Analysed into Words and Unverbal Things, and Unverbal Things Classified into Intellections, Sensations, and Emotions* which, he states, "conveys my ultimate thoughts on the subject and is, I suppose, the best elucidation of human knowledge that has yet been produced." The reader of *The Meaning of Words* will have to judge whether it is indeed an advance over the *Treatise on Language,* or a compromise of the strong position taken in the earlier work.

In an age of some religious orthodoxy, a few critics saw Johnson's argument as undermining revelation and the life of the spirit. In commenting on the *Treatise on Language,* the theologian Horace Bushnell argued that "to language in its more comprehensive sense, as a vehicle of spirit, thought, sentiment, [Johnson] appears to have scarcely directed his inquiries." [3] Fanny Wright, on the other hand, vainly urged Johnson to "rescind the remarks touching the knowledge by revelation which appear misplaced in a work treating only of knowledge by sensation." John Quincy Adams observed that "the course of argument throughout your lectures, and the primary position upon which it seems to be founded, would have led me to class you among the philosophers who deny all spiritual existences," but was reassured by Johnson's declaration that it was not his intention "to dispute the truths of Divine Revelation, or the doctrines of Christian faith."

Timothy Flint, editor of the *Western Monthly Review,* was similarly concerned by the implications for both revealed and natural theology in his interpretation of Johnson's rigid empiricism. In his lengthy review,[4] which is virtually an outline of *The Philosophy of Human Knowledge,* Flint was effusive in his praise of the man and his work: "We opened the book before us without any uncommon expectation of interest; little calculating, that a series of metaphysical lectures would chain our attention from beginning to end, and lead us on from point to point, as a romantic girl clings to a novel, till it is finished." Flint had a firm and appreciative grasp of the theme of the book; his misgivings were more theological than epistemological. In Flint's view, Johnson's reform of language would, if carried out uncompromisingly, undercut all rational theology. Much can be said for such an inference, but Flint was unable to believe that such a consequence was Johnson's intention (as indeed Johnson frequently claimed it was not):

> We trust, that this strong reasoner and clear thinker, who manifests a sober reverence for religion, wherever that theme has come in incidental discussion in this work, did not fully meditate the extent of the influence, it would have upon a rational believer, to be convinced, that the principles of rational theology are all baseless. . . . It seems to us, that all the utility of the scriptures would be a nullity on this supposition, and all the instruction of revelation a matter of immediate and direct communication from above.

Flint concluded his criticism with a suggestion Johnson must have found very congenial:

> We cannot but think, that it is this very ambiguity of language, against which he writes, that has led him to denounce natural theology in this lecture. We regret the obligation of duty, which has impelled us to enter our dissent to one speculation, contained in this mass of disquisition of a character, generally, of so much reason, and evincing such uncommon keenness of mental vision.

In retrospect, one could wish that Flint's account—which may have been the longest, sustained review of Johnson's thought by one of his contemporaries—had broadened the critique beyond the objections of theological pietism. Johnson was quite capable of learning from criticism and surely would have profited from a critical and attentive audience. In view of the fact that Johnson's philosophic work received so little attention from his contemporaries, one could also wish that Flint's extensive review had not appeared in a relatively obscure literary journal which expired in the following year.

NOTES

1 Students of Johnson's thought and times will find rich resources in his several notebooks on deposit at the New York State Library, Albany, and in the unpublished autobiography and other documents in the Hamilton College Library. The Editorial Board of the Alexander Bryan Johnson Papers, Hamilton College, would welcome information regarding primary sources not found in these two collections.
2 Compare Adams' interpretation with the discussion in the Symposium of these *Proceedings*.
3 *God in Christ* (Hartford, 1852), p. 44.
4 *Western Monthly Review,* March-April 1829.

ALEXANDER BRYAN JOHNSON'S TREATISE ON MORALITY

♦ ♦ ♦ ♦ ♦ *DAVID RYNIN*

I

TWENTY YEARS AGO, after publishing my *Alexander Bryan Johnson's "A Treatise on Language,"* a conflation of his *The Philosophy of Human Knowledge* of 1828 and its revision of 1836, *A Treatise on Language,* together with an extended critical expository essay on his philosophy of language, I sat back with confidence, expecting that the discovery of this important unknown thinker, which we owe to Stillman Drake, would shortly come to the attention of and affect at least the linguistically oriented philosophers—at that time, and perhaps still, constituting the majority of the most gifted and active philosophers in the English-speaking countries. Although several thousand copies of the work, both in hard-cover and paperback versions, were sold, a number of favorable reviews appeared, and occasionally quotations or references found their way into the literature, the net effect was about nil. Nine out of ten, or even a higher proportion, of philosophers have still never heard of Johnson, almost nothing has been written about him, and to my knowledge his name does not yet appear in any history of philosophy.

◇ ◇ ◇ ◇ ◇ *Professor of Philosophy, University of California, Berkeley. Editor,* A. B. Johnson's "A Treatise on Language," *1947; author,* The Logic and Semantics of Argument, *1952; translator,* Problems of Ethics (*from the German of M. Schlick*), 1939 and 1962. Contributor to American and European journals. Professor Rynin's most recent work on Johnson is his article in the 1967 edition of the Macmillan Encyclopedia of Philosophy.

While a whole academic industry has grown up around the writings of Wittgenstein, attempting to preserve and unravel the obscurities of his every thought; while there is much talk of and several books about the language-oriented revolution of philosophy of our time —almost giving the impression that linguistic philosophy began at the turn of the century with the philosophies of G. E. Moore and Bertrand Russell, and came to full flower with the publication of Wittgenstein's *Philosophical Investigations* and in the writings of J. L. Austin—the achievements of this American, which anticipate by a hundred years or more a large part of this revolution, remain until today almost completely neglected. This is a most remarkable fact of nonhistory. The only explanation that I have been able to find is that advanced by a historian of American philosophy, who, when asked why Johnson, whom he had heard about if not studied, was not even mentioned in a recently published revision of his book, reportedly answered that as Johnson had had no influence on American philosophy, he did not constitute a part of its history.

I leave this curious principle of historiography to those best qualified to judge it; it resembles the well-known and painfully paradoxical view which considers a person ineligible for a job until he has gained experience in it. Another theory almost too cynical to mention is connected with an alleged remark of Bertrand Russell, according to which he is supposed to have said that when people read him they find his thought easy to understand and consequently consider him a superficial thinker, whereas when they find themselves unable to comprehend the obscurities of Whitehead's thought they deem that writer profound. If some skeptic is of the opinion that the neglect can best be explained by the assumption that Johnson's genius is of a much lower order than I take it to be, let him read the relevant works and then I shall be happy to accommodate him in debate on the issue.

When I realized that the anticipated growth of interest in Johnson's philosophy was a bit slow in coming, it occurred to me more than once that I should bestir myself and again begin crying in the wilderness until somebody heard. But I shared the faith expressed by Johnson in speaking about his own philosophical works: if they were of worth they would eventually be appreciated; and in any case it appeared to me a bit unseemly and likely to be ineffectual if I were to become insistent. I was hoping, having done what I could, that others would take up the task of seeing that historical justice was done—not to speak of the very much more than historical interest to be found in Johnson's works.

One voice was indeed raised, that of the English writer on science L. L. Whyte, who has spoken on several occasions of the neglect of Johnson as a scandal of British scholarship; how much more so of American! A quite unexpected indication of growing interest prior to the organization of this meeting, for which we are so much indebted to the indefatigable Professor C. L. Todd, was the recent appearance in an avant-garde German literary magazine, *Kursbuch,* of several pages of translations ("Aus dem Amerikanischen"!) from the *Treatise,* with parallel passages in English; as well as a highly appreciative blank verse poem on Johnson by the Swedish poet, philosopher, and critic Dr. Lars Gustafsson.

This memorial meeting, I am happy to say, confirms me in my faith that before long Johnson will be acknowledged as one of our most original and interesting philosophical thinkers, and that his work on language and meaning will find a place in the small list of classics in the field.

When the time came for me to make a decision as to the nature of my own contribution to these sessions, I considered several alternatives, including that of once more subjecting to analysis Johnson's main contributions to the philosophy of language, together with citations showing their astonishing up-to-dateness, and, as I believe, definite superiority in many respects over the best work that has been done on these topics in our own day. But having had my say on these matters once, it seemed to me better that I should turn to other aspects of his philosophic thought not hitherto discussed and even less known, if that is possible. I was encouraged in this decision on learning that Professor Max Black had accepted an invitation to take part in these discussions and had chosen as his topic "Johnson's Language Theories in Modern Perspective."

My intention now is to acquaint you with and offer some preliminary evaluations of Johnson's contributions to ethics, as revealed in his little book of 1841, *Religion in Its Relation to the Present Life,* or, as he entitled it in a second edition of 1862, *Morality and Manners.* This work, largely based on psychological insights which I believe show him to be a profoundly original thinker in this domain, well worth serious study by experts in the field and its history, presents aspects of his philosophy of language not revealed in his main works on the subject, *The Philosophy of Human Knowledge, A Treatise on Language,* and *The Meaning of Words.*

II

ON A HILLSIDE a few miles distant from this spot [in Utica], lies Johnson's grave. Inscribed on his tombstone are the following words, which, in view of Johnson's lifelong concern with them, we may assume were placed there in accordance with his instructions:

> ALEXANDER BRYAN JOHNSON
> BORN MAY 29, 1786
> DIED SEPTEMBER 9, 1867
> BORN IN ENGLAND, FROM 1801 HE LIVED
> IN UTICA, THRICE MARRIED, SEVEN
> SONS AND FOUR DAUGHTERS
> AND HIS WIDOW SURVIVED HIM.

> THE AUTHOR OF MANY BOOKS:
> A LAWYER BY EDUCATION.
> A BANKER DURING ACTIVE LIFE:
> A STUDENT OF PHILOSOPHY ALWAYS:
> THIS FOR THE WORLD
> THEY WHO LOVED HIM KNOW THE REST.

I have quoted the epitaph in order to indicate the role philosophy played in Johnson's life. I shall now give in his own brief words,[1] set down at the end of his autobiography a few months before the end of his life, the summary account of what he thought were the essentials and results of his philosophical teachings.

> And now in taking a review of my various writings that have engrossed a large portion of my active and long life, I feel that I have laboured in vain so far as my teachings have been accepted by the world or influenced the thoughts of reflective men. Teachings which, like mine, require an eradication of existing notions labour under disadvantages which may be well deemed insurmountable, while teachings which harmonize with prevailing opinions are readily accepted. My studies have been intellectually beneficial to myself and to that extent they solace me for the time I have devoted to them. In artistic construction I believe they are unsurpassed for brevity of expression and perspicuity of meaning.
>
> Though my life may well be deemed a miscarriage of the main object for which I have cast before the public the thoughts and studies of life that affluence at all times gave me the opportunity to pass in ease, I will condense briefly the object I have sought to accomplish in my philosophical speculations, that no man may deem I have laboured without an object that I thought worth the sacrifice I made therein:

What my philosophy accomplishes:

It divides all knowledge into sensations, intellections and emotions. These constitute all we know or can know apart from words.

By appropriate names, my teaching discriminates from one another, sensations, intellections and emotions, so that we can speak of each understandingly and recognize each in ourselves.

My teachings seek the meaning of every word not in other words, but in some sensation, intellection or emotion and when we have ascertained that the word means some sensation, the sensation referred to is the meaning; and when the word refers to an emotion—the emotion referred to is the meaning and when any word refers to any intellection, the intellection is the meaning. . . .

All speculative philosophies precedent of mine are like tunes, which skillful musicians play on a piano forte. Each philosopher plays with words such a tune as he deems best; but my philosophy plays no tune, but refers every tuneful note to the internal machinery of the piano from which the tuneful note proceeds. I am the first philosopher that has thus gone deeper than language, and has sought to discover the meaning of words in man's internal organism, a meaning that is not words. The verbal systems of speculative philosophy are as interminable as the different tunes that can be formed out of the notes of a piano, and realizing how barren such philosophies have ever been for the settlement of the questions for which such philosophies are employed, I have essayed the new system as an ultimate and fixed limit of all speculative knowledge; and which will in time, I fondly trust, cause an abandonment of the old and endless speculations of the verbal philosopher.

How wholly inadequate these words are to convey anything like the nature, extent, and flavor of Johnson's achievement will be realized by anyone who has ever looked into his philosophical writings. The wonderful insights and striking aphorisms that abound so richly in his thought and on every page of his work are completely lost in this abstract summary by a dying and disappointed man of eighty-one. I give it not to point out its inadequacy, which of course Johnson best of all understood, but to draw your attention to the interesting fact that nowhere in this most general account of what he conceived his philosophy to be concerned with do we find the slightest mention of his work on ethics, of which he had a sufficiently high opinion, as indeed of his other philosophic works.

In view of his very contemporary linguistic approach to so many philosophical problems, one might indeed expect that for Johnson ethics is to be identified with what is nowadays called "metaethics," i.e., explanation of the meanings and uses of ethical terms as they occur in moral discourse or as analysis or insight might demand that they should. But such expectation would be wholly mistaken. Nowhere in the work we are about to examine does Johnson deal with any such matters. In fact he takes it as self-evident, so much so as not even to require pointing out, that ethics is precisely what almost all philosophers in our time deny that it can possibly be: a systematized body of factual knowledge, an empirical science.

The view that there is no ethical *knowledge* but (to use the term without any pejorative overtones) only ethical *rhetoric* is the main stock in trade in this line of goods for most contemporary American and British philosophers. I well remember the amused condescension with which the late John Austin asked me, during a conversation on the subject, whether I *really* was prepared to tell people how they ought to act—and I do not think he was thereby showing any very special concern over my inadequate insights, or implying that an abler thinker than I might well have some knowledge on the subject.

It is an interesting fact, and perhaps more than a coincidence, that the only important recent writer on ethics known to me (other than John Dewey) who like Johnson treats ethics as a factual science and indeed as a branch of psychology—not however as practiced by academic psychologists—was Moritz Schlick (the leader of the Vienna School of so-called Logical Positivists) in whose philosophy the problem of meaning played as central a role as it ever did for Johnson, and who in fact under the influence of the early Wittgenstein came to *identify* philosophy with the activity of meaning clarification. The oddity is of course compounded when it is recalled that the positivists have been widely reproached for allegedly claiming, on the basis of their *verifiability principle,* that ethical statements are cognitively meaningless; a reproach made also by those thinkers referred to above who agree that there can be no science of ethics, but who wish to maintain that the putative ethical statements possess another mode of meaning, a *use,* and are therefore not to be eliminated or, for that matter, removed to the realm of merely expressive or evocative utterances, as proposed by some adherents of the nihilistic view.

But be that as it may, Johnson did not, as Schlick did not, consider such a position. Both take it for granted that there is ethical knowledge, which in fact is the most important kind there is. Both go back to the ancient traditional concern of ethics—the nature of the good life and how to achieve it. And for both it is assumed that all men know well enough what the good life is, and that the prime question of ethics is *how* one must live to live well; or, if one puts it in the time-honored and wholly proper language of religion: What shall a man do to be saved?

In the prefatory remarks to his lectures to the Young Men's Association of the City of Utica, which constitutes the substance of *Religion in Its Relation to the Present Life,* Johnson says:

> The title is intended to discriminate my subject from what is discussed in churches, and which is, perhaps too exclusively, Religion in its Relation to a Future Life.

The Bible, on the contrary, is for the most part if not altogether concerned with the present life.

> Churches occupy the same relation to morality as common schools occupy to literature; hence, they should present morality under all its aspects. With unimportant exceptions, they are our only schools of morals: the science which regulates health, peace and prosperity.

It is this science with which Johnson's book is concerned. About the work he writes in the autobiography as follows:

> Early in 1841, Harper and Brothers of New York published for me "Religion in its Relation to the Present Life.". . .
> The work was not controversial, but declarative, and like all my writings, the purport cannot be stated in a summary; the whole text being nothing more than a summary of general morality stated in the smallest compass in which the substance can be compressed. The book was intended to be a complete system of ethics, and hence in a later edition, I caused the volume to be labelled "Morality and Manners." Most authors write to communicate what they know, but usually I write to discover what I ought to know. I commence divested of all prepossessions but to elicit the truth, whatever it may prove to be; and when my judgment teaches me I have found it, I endeavour to make the discovery apparent to those who may become my listeners. This mode of composition is excessively laborious, and each of my books bears but a trifling proportion in bulk to the manuscript from which I elaborated it. An author who writes for a living cannot afford thus to consume his time, but as I never wrote for pecuniary compensation (and indeed always published at my own cost) [I] expected no reward but the inherent value of my product; hence, as I perfected my work, I received the only pay I sought, and for the same reason, I

never copied thoughts and conclusions already published by other writers, but presented those only that were newly originated by myself. . . .

The Harpers of New York who published the book wrote me that they would like to publish it as a volume of their Family Library, whereby it would obtain a large circulation, but they submitted it to a clergyman to whom they were accustomed to submit works intended for their Family Library, and he had objected to some expressions in the book. They wanted me to consent to the expurgation of the objectionable tenets, which were the doctrine that the readiest mode of obtaining any desired state of feeling was to speak and act as though we already possessed the desired feeling, and that the feeling thus evoked would naturally soon harmonize with our words and actions. He insisted that my doctrine inculcated hypocrisy, and that men should not act and speak benevolently, till the feeling of benevolence was first possessed. A French Proverb says "Eating excites an appetite," and my doctrine was analogous. My book simply inculcated the practice of a physiological feature of our organization and so did the French Proverb, and I would not consent to expurge any part of it. The book therefore remained excluded from the Family Library. When the book was first published, the Harpers intended to label it "Lectures to the Young Men's Association," but for want of space, they abridged the title to "Lectures to the Young." This rather implied that the book was designed for children and thus belittled its contents to those who judge books by their title. The book was designed by me for men, and as a treatise on Morality, of quite an original character in matter and form, and it never received the attention it merits in these respects. . . .

I shall now attempt to summarize, often in his own words, Johnson's science of morals, which is from a certain point of view but a vindication or rationalizing of the moral teachings of the Bible in terms of a science of human nature. The work consists of five lectures.

Every Department of Nature Obeys Determinate Laws

Johnson recognizes four realms of nature, each governed by its special laws:

a. The inanimate realm of material bodies; the disciplines that deal with its laws are the mechanic arts and sciences.

b. The animate realm of organisms: its laws are those studied by surgery, *materia medica,* and their subordinate branches.

c. Thoughts: on the general laws governing thoughts depend the arts of reading, writing, and speaking.

d. Feelings: i.e., passions, emotions, appetites, and desires, which as relating to conduct comprise the moral domain. Morality is the science of this domain.

The net effect of these laws is beneficial; thus the moral realm is likewise governed by determinate natural laws which make for the temporal good of mankind. The doctrine that the order of nature is such as to conspire toward human good is not, however, to be confused with the doctrine of optimism—that everything that happens is for the best. It is not in general for the best that a man should die as a result of a fire or explosion or poisoning, but the natural laws which make possible such disasters are the same that make possible the many goods that flow from the proper use of these natural forces. In general, the possibility of evil is a necessary condition of the good in the world as we know it. Whether God could have

> constructed a world in which every event would have been an unalloyed good is a question too profound to be discussed understandingly (p. 21).[2] The evils of life seem to me rather unavoidable consequences than immediate creations of Providence (p. 23). . . . I possess faith enough . . . to believe that . . . changes [involved in making arsenic innoxious] would be greater evil than the occasional death from arsenic that the changes would obviate (p. 25).
>
> The vehemence which gives to anger its power of mischief, is the very quality that constitutes its usefulness (p. 26).

Vanity is the source of most writing of books:

> To all of us existence would be deprived of more than half its enjoyments, were our words, thoughts, and actions as unimportant in the estimation of the actor, as they must be in the estimation of the rest of mankind (p. 27).

Fear is,

> the essence of moral courage, which, without much paradox, may be resolved into nothing but a fear of the consequences of yielding to fear (p. 28).

In general,

> . . . human nature cannot be improved, as some persons suppose (and as some have attempted), by eradicating from it any passion, appetite, or feeling. The imbecility of age results more from the decay of our passions, appetites, and feelings, than

LANGUAGE AND VALUE

from decay of our physical and intellectual organization (pp. 28–29). . . . Even death could not have been averted without depriving man of the social benefits which result from the relation of husband and wife; parent and child; infancy and maturity; for if man were not mortal, the earth would long since have attained the extent of its habitable capacity, and with the termination of increase would have terminated the relations which increase originates (p. 22).

Johnson's main concern is not, however, with these generalities but with "an investigation of the natural laws by which the moral world is governed" (p. 34). Human evil is, he claims, the result of ignorance or neglect of the laws that determine the conditions and circumstances of man's well-being; and it is with these that morality is concerned.

The Conduct Which Results Injuriously

In general, evil, illness, strife, and poverty are the result of our disobedience to moral laws, and their opposites are the normal outcome of action in accordance with those laws.

> . . . when experience has discovered that any practice is injurious, the practice is stigmatized as vice. When any conduct will engender vice, it is stigmatized as an immorality (p. 44). Hurtfulness is the essence of vice and immorality. A harmless vice or immorality would be as much a solecism as a healthful disease, a pleasurable pain, or a beneficial crime. The science of morality is nothing but a knowledge of the natural consequences which certain actions produce, just as the science of medicine is a knowledge of the natural effects which certain drugs produce (p. 45).

And as we do not require personal experience to teach us the harmfulness of certain drugs, so we do not require personal suffering or tragedy to teach us the harmfulness of certain actions. Such harmful actions are stigmatized by society as immorality so as to warn unwary persons who may be tempted to engage in them, for usually the practices themselves give little warning of danger and often seem to promise much apparently innocent pleasure.

> From this absence of apparent danger, many persons believe that vice and immorality are terms established by austere religionists from mere prejudice or caprice; while other persons admit the injuriousness of vice and immorality, but attribute it to special interferences of Providence or conventional interferences of men. The injuriousness is, however, as much the estab-

lished order of Nature, as the injuriousness of theft, the infectiousness of small-pox, or the deleteriousness of arsenic (p. 45).

Since our feelings influence our actions, "morality forbids us to revel complacently on vice in our thoughts." While Johnson would no doubt agree with the literal truth of the remark attributed to the late Mayor Jimmy Walker, of New York, that "no girl was ever seduced by a book," he has quite a different view so far as concerns the consequences of conduct aroused by feelings stimulated by reading certain books:

> A celebrated French author who well knew the tendency of our nature in this particular, prefaced a pernicious book which he was publishing with the precautionary prescription, "Any female who reads this book is ruined." I will not affirm that the prophecy would be confirmed, for a person may read to condemn as well as to approve; but a female who should read the book, and receive delight in the contemplation of it, would, I doubt not, reap in some way the bad fruits of her immoral contemplations (p. 53).

It may be doubted whether the truth behind this view of Johnson's is seriously affected by our much-relaxed conception of sexual morality, what with the advent of the pill and the extinction of innocent maidens and ladies.

> As a general rule, the tendency of every vice is to defeat the good which it seemingly ensures. Gambling leads to ruin, while it promises wealth; intemperance to pain, while it promises pleasure; . . . a merchant may obtain a customer by misrepresenting his merchandise; a lawyer a client by exciting false hopes; . . . but such practices are like a false move in chess: it may capture a castle or a queen, but, by the constitution of the game, it must result in defeat (p. 58).

Moral disapprobation is one of the barriers that nature establishes to safeguard us from injurious conduct, since "a conscious loss of the regard of our fellow-men is intolerable." Another is the natural concatenation of events and attributes that enable crime and vice to be readily detected.

> Who can counterfeit even a banknote that will escape the scrutiny of a practiced observer? A lie is therefore usually known as soon as uttered, but is sure of subsequent detection by the absence of congruous accompaniments; for every action bears a relation to a whole series of other actions. To supply these, we

32

must lie again; hence "one lie occasions many." But, if one can rarely be concealed, the more we utter (and more must be uttered to support the first), the more inevitable is the detection. And not our flagrant actions only are thus discoverable to our fellow-men, but all our actions, and the general tenour of even our thoughts (p. 60).

Nature ensures the publication of our secrets, for to know what others do not know gives us a feeling of superiority over them. But to enjoy this feeling of superiority, we must impart our knowledge.

> The secrecy of a matter ensures, therefore, its diffusion, by a process which is designed for such purpose as evidently as the down which wings the seed of a thistle is designed to diffuse thistles (pp. 60–61).

Further, every trait of man occurs in conjunction with others as a member of a cluster of related traits; thus lying gives rise to cowardice, which in turn generates treachery.

> To estimate any vice, crime, or immorality, apart from these its natural consequences is to estimate it fallaciously (p. 64).

While a vicious and criminal character may occasionally achieve wealth, reputation, and power, as well as health, these will not bring him happiness, which does not depend on them. A vicious man may even possibly be happy and a virtuous man unhappy, but there is no causal connection; generally vice reduces these goods and virtue mitigates the evils.

These truths, so important to man's well-being, are found preeminently expressed in the Bible. And since many of the modes of conduct it interdicts seem on first glance innocent and even highly attractive, and their deleterious nature learned with danger and difficulty, its teachings may well appear as revelations.

The Conduct Which Results Beneficially

Nature achieves her goals, i.e., maintenance and enhancement of life, by the infliction of pleasure and pain. Nature (or Providence, which comes to the same) disciplines us as we our children. But pleasure is merely an incitement to do what morality demands of us; it is not morality's end or purpose. When man reverses this relation and acts as morality demands for the sake of pleasure he defeats himself. Hypocrisy, which cannot be effectively dissembled, generates hatred and contempt in those before whom it masquerades as morality. Pleasure is not an end but a means, and when sought for its own sake generates its opposite. It is obtainable only as a consequence of acting as our nature, and hence morality, requires:

> . . . neither physical, moral, nor mental pleasure is procurable except from the discharge of our moral, mental and physical duties; and whoever attempts to procure it in any other way is sure to be disappointed (p. 77).

Nature and society conspire to reward with pleasure, happiness, health, and wealth those who perform useful services, provided such useful services and not pleasure constitute the ends of their actions. And as society rewards actions and characters useful to it, so do individual men; hence if I am arrogant others become vindictive in turn; if I am selfish, I shall be repaid in kind; if I am censorious or unsocial, I am repaid by isolation. "Scorn for scorn, blow for blow is the discipline of the world" (p. 92). Since he is vastly outnumbered, the odds are fearfully against a contumelious individual. These are of course but the teachings of the Bible, expressed on countless occasions in countless ways.

The Bible enjoins only what nature and society require, and to act contrary to it is to reap the natural rewards of harmful actions. The teachings of the Bible are based on natural and moral truths, not on bigotry.

> . . . though you may refuse to act as the Bible enjoins, you must submit to the consequences that the Bible predicts (p. 97).

The Bible enjoins that we have respect for our rulers, not for their sake but so that they may have the power to confer the benefits of government.

> Submission [to the will of the Lord] was enjoined for our benefit under the inevitable evils of life, and not for the gratification of Deity (p. 99).
>
> If, then, the religious injunctions of the Bible are thus practically connected with the moral injunctions, a disregard of the religious injunctions by reason of doubts in relation to the retributions of a future life . . . is as irrational as to disregard the precepts against stealing, adultery, and drunkenness by reason of like doubts; a utility in the present life being equally discoverable in both cases (pp. 100–101).

Johnson holds that the Bible enjoins no conduct that is not beneficial and that there is no beneficial conduct not enjoined by it. It furnishes us with fixed principles beforehand to guide us to such well-being as is achievable in life. Although he admits that this position is too general to be proved, he claims that

> sufficient for the utility of the Bible is the extent of our conduct that admittedly falls within its cognizance. To rely on experience alone for a knowledge of what is injurious or beneficial, would in many cases be as fatal as to rely on experience to teach us the properties of arsenic; the knowledge would not be attained till we had lost the capability of being benefited by it (p. 101).

The Art of Controlling Others

A large, perhaps the largest, part of our well-being depends on the feelings and actions of others in relation to ourselves:

> Providence in creating us with keen sensibilities towards the sentiments and feelings of our fellowmen, has not tantalized us with wants which we cannot influence; nor . . . has Providence intended that men shall feel as they please towards any individual, regardless of his moral qualities, and possess towards him the sentiments which they please regardless of his conduct (pp. 105–106).

We cannot, however, command the love and respect of others but must earn it by appropriate behavior. As the senses and intellect are governed by laws, and we cannot see and think what we will, so the feelings of others in relation to us are also governed by laws.

> A man of sound understanding need not solicit mankind not to deem him insane or idiotic. They possess no discretion in the matter, for our intellect is compelled to note correctly the properties of mind. . . . [We] rely with confidence, while we are not criminal, that crimes will not be imputed to us; and while we are not vicious, that vice will not be imputed to us. So unnatural is any other conduct, that when a man gratuitously attempts to prove himself not guilty of any crime, he excites suspicion of guilt; and when he gratuitously rebuts the presumption of any vice, as when he boasts of courage, we suspect him of cowardice (p. 106). We have, therefore, only to avoid conduct which we wish not imputed to us, and mankind cannot impute it (p. 107).

Attempts at dissimulation are finally vain:

> . . . a man cannot deceive men. You are masquerading before others who have masqueraded themselves. They know every

turn of the game as skillfully as you. . . . If what you utter proceeds from envy, no disguise can prevent your envy from being detected. If your actions result from penuriousness, no ostentation of liberality can hide it, no protestation of munificence conceal it (p. 109).

The organization which thus precludes men from imparting to you any quality which you possess not, compels them to impute to you every quality which you possess; hence, while you are endeavouring, by artful professions of religion, to conceal irreligion, you compel the world to impute to you hypocrisy in addition to irreligion. While you are endeavouring, by professions of courage, to conceal cowardice, you force the world to deem you a braggart as well as a coward (pp. 109–110). . . .

But we can, if we please, employ this principle beneficially. If we desire to be deemed religious, we have only to be religious, and we must be thus deemed. If you desire to be deemed veracious, speak the truth habitually, and you must be thus deemed . . . your reputation must conform to what you are. . . . Nor need you be anxious to make men observe your good qualities. Any agency which you thus exert will transform your reputable actions into disreputable. It will convert learning into pedantry; religion into pharisaism; humility into ostentation; condescension into arrogance; praise into flattery (p. 110). . . .

Having thus shown how we may control the opinions of the world with reference to our character, both negatively and affirmatively, I will show how we may control the feelings of the world with reference to our persons. While the senses and intellect of mankind are so organized that men must, as we have seen, impute to us the qualities which we possess, the moral feelings of mankind are so organized that men must feel towards us according to the moral qualities which we possess. If we are lovely, we must be loved; if hateful, we must be hated; if contemptible, we must be contemned; if despicable, we must be despised (p. 111) . . . and as we usually behave as we please, each of us can predetermine the feelings which the world shall entertain towards him, though, from the occasional complaints of men, you would imagine that the world dispensed its feelings either fortuitously or by favouritism (p. 113).

As a preliminary, however, to a control of the feelings of the world, a man must know what conduct will excite in other men the feeling he desires; and, providentially, Nature, in giving us wants which require the concurrent feelings of other men, has not failed to suggest the means of obtaining such concurrence. . . . [A]s anger clinches our fists, and dictates infliction of blows on the object of our anger . . . so love, which requires in its gratification the concurrent affection of another being, dictates to us the looks, words, and actions that will obtain the desired affection (p. 114). If you feel confidence in any person, it will dictate conduct that will excite in him confidence towards you. If you feel friendship for him, it will dictate conduct that will excite in him friendly feelings towards you. Sympathy will excite sympathy, respect will excite respect, liberality will excite liberality, forgiveness will excite forgiveness. In short, "as ye would that men should do to you, do ye to them likewise." This scriptural rule we are accustomed to estimate as a measure by which we are only to dispense favours; but it is equally applicable as means for obtaining favours (pp. 115–116).

But the above rule must be properly understood: to perform any action under the hope of an equivalent return deprives it of its beneficial influence.

Why should you be exalted for humility, if you are humble for exaltation? Why respected for disinterestedness, if you are disinterested to gain respect? . . . If you do good to your enemy, as a result of your benevolence, the enemy must reproach himself for having injured so beneficent a person; but if you do good to him for the purpose of exciting his self-reproach, and thereby figuratively heaping coals of fire on his head, you are no more deserving of his gratitude than if you feasted him on poisoned sweetmeats, or gave him a house which you expected would fall and bury him in its ruins (pp. 116–117).

But we are not content to let the feelings of other men towards us arise incidentally as a consequence of the feelings which we bear towards them. We want to be loved, without obtaining it as an incident of our loving others, but as an incident of our desire to be beloved. . . . Nay, we strive to diverge still farther from the established moral order of Nature, and to be loved though we hate, respected though we are mean, trusted though we are treacherous . . . which are all moral impossibilities (p. 121).

To the extent that clever dissemblings may for a time succeed, they

are a fraud on the processes of Nature, and like other frauds, are only partial in their success, and restricted in their operations. . . . [I]ncongruities attend a feigned character. Forgiveness, when it results from benevolence, is always accompanied with congruous qualities throughout the whole man; and which accompaniments will be wanting when forgiveness is only assumed to create self-reproach in an enemy (p. 122). Conduct that lacks sincerity is deficient in the quality that constitutes its efficacy; . . . our feelings dictate not merely the actions which we perform and the words which we utter, but the expression of our countenance and the intonation of our voice. . . . [I]n common life, we cannot counterfeit Nature accurately, we can only caricature it (p. 124).

So unvarying is the operation of the rule, in both the good feelings and the bad, that, if any person will tell me accurately the feelings which he cherishes, I can, without further information, tell him how men feel towards him, just as a mathematician can tell you the last angle of a triangle when you tell him the first two angles (p. 126).

Society is like a spacious hall hung with mirrors around and above. You may address yourself to any mirror; but if you contemptuously yawn before it, all the others will return the yawn (p. 127). . . . [I]f we will control our own feelings we can control the feelings which other men shall bear towards us, and be loved or hated as we shall elect, but if we will not control our own feelings we cannot thereby prevent them, whatever they may be, from exciting in other men the feelings which are correlative to ours (p. 128).

But can we control our own feelings? To this question Johnson devotes his final lecture.

The Art of Self-Control

It is generally held that we have no control over our feelings, that our passions are independent of our will. If this were so, says Johnson, the Biblical injunction: "Thou shalt love the Lord thy God with all thy heart, and thy neighbor as thyself" would be a "sarcasm." But the most obvious facts show that the common view is not correct.

Like the sounds of an organ, our feelings must burst forth if you press the proper key; and, among the objects which can thus press us, none is so effective over a man's own feelings as his own words, thoughts and actions; hence a man can excite in himself any feeling if he knows the words, thoughts and actions with which the feeling is associated (p. 131). . . . These natural associates of every feeling are so familiar to our experience, that we tell by a glance the feeling which is present to any person, be it love or anger, pride or humility, hope or despair. . . . [A]ll of us, when we meet a friend who is in distress, know how to adapt our countenance, language, intonation, and actions so as to express sympathy, though perchance we feel it not, except as our effort to represent sympathy causes us to feel it: for we are so constituted that the feeling of sympathy will arise in us when we assume the look, language, tone, and actions that belong to sympathy. I assert the like to be the general rule, and that a man can excite in himself any feeling if he will speak, look, and act as if he already possessed the feeling. The principle is among the most important, benevolent, and beneficial contrivances of Providence, as it indirectly subjects all our feelings to our control (p. 132). . . . If you will act and speak patriotically, you will soon possess the feelings of a patriot. If you speak and act as though you are persecuted, you will soon feel that you are a martyr. If you will speak and act avariciously, you will soon become a miser (p. 133).

In general, act and speak as you would if you had certain feelings, and your feelings will soon harmonize with your words and actions.

You may ask whether I intend to recommend hypocrisy, since I require a man to act and speak differently from what his feelings may dictate; I answer, no, I wish him to profess all that is virtuous, and act conformably to the professions. This is his duty and he possesses the power of compliance; for his words and actions are subject to his will. But he possesses not the feelings which the word and actions indicate. This he cannot help, for his feelings are not subject to his will. But they are controllable, and will conform to his words and actions; hence, to insist that he will not speak as duty requires, by reason of his not possessing the congenial feelings, is as unreasonable as for a sailor to insist that he will not hoist his anchor by reason of his not first being underway (pp. 141–142).

But since our words have less influence over our feelings when we are dominated by the opposite feelings, we should avoid when we can

the excitation in ourselves of any feeling which tends to produce conduct that we desire not to practice. The means of such avoidance are much within our power, and can be stated in a general rule: refrain from every word, thought and action that would naturally proceed from the feeling that you desire not to excite (p. 145). Even loud speaking is unfriendly to calmness of feeling . . . by reason of an exciting power which loud speaking seems to possess naturally (p. 150).

And Johnson adds the interesting observation that

This natural effect of loud speaking is a great obstruction to theatrical acting in cases where gentle feelings are to be expressed. The actor must speak loud, or he cannot be heard; but he cannot speak loud without destroying in himself all illusion of gentleness, and hence increasing the natural difficulty of his imitation (p. 150).

Our thoughts . . . are less influential over our feelings than our words. Yet, let no man estimate thoughts as powerless. The Bible says, "Curse not the king, no not in thy thought." No injunction is more judicious; and not for the reason that the king may hear us, but to prevent the excitation in ourselves of the feelings which produce cursing. . . . Both good thoughts and bad will arise in us without premeditation and even against our will; but their continuance with us depends much upon our will. A thought is like a timid stranger. He shows himself at your door, but will not walk in unless you invite him, nor tarry unless you evince a wish to detain him; but, after being cordially entertained, you may not get rid of him without difficulty (p. 151).

Feelings thrive on the expression of them. They are naturally "as evanescent as lightning, unless we keep them alive by words, thoughts and actions." We are thus able to strangle undesirable feelings by refusing to give them expression, to the degree it is within our power. But it is preferable to vanquish them, for this tends to prevent their recurrence. The manner of so doing is to utter words and perform actions that normally express their opposites.

"Do good for evil," "Render blessing for cursing," "If thine enemy hunger, feed him; if naked, clothe him." We often estimate these precepts as merely the wishes of the lawgiver; but they are elucidations of a profound principle of our nature, like the prescriptions of a physician, who, when our hand is frozen, commands us to thrust it into cold water, or rub it with snow, and not to obey our inclination by placing it before a fire (p. 159).

The indulgence of malevolent feelings creates, for one subject to them, a world that appears to him as everywhere malevolent; everything offends the petulant man, the jealous man sees guilt in every action, and for the melancholy man everything is covered in gloom. On the other hand,

to the man who indulges benevolence, everybody and everything will continually meliorate under the kind influence of his increasing benevolence. Viewed through the medium of his increasing friendliness, everybody will seem more and more friendly; through the medium of his increasing patience, everything will seem more and more calm; through the medium of his increasing resignation, events will seem more and more seasonable (p. 162).

The events of life are common to all men; the same havoc by death, the same hopes frustrated, the same fears realized;

yet from these similar occurrences the patient man extracts patience, the impatient man rage, the pious man hope, the impious man despair, the cheerful man tranquility, the melancholy man madness.

These opposite effects prove that happiness and misery, despair and hope, depend not on external differences, but on different states of feeling; hence, if our feelings are as much under our control as I have laboured to show they are, we can accomplish what is equivalent to controlling the events of life: we can control the effect which the events of life shall produce on us (pp. 163–164).

To attain, however, this result we must accustom ourselves to think, act and speak under the guidance . . . of our intellect. The eye tells us what pleases sight, the taste what gratifies appetite, but intellect must determine whether the eye shall be permitted to look and the taste to enjoy. . . . Our feelings, too, must be subordinated to our intellect. Anger tells us what action will yield it delight, pride what answer will yield it gratification; but intellect must determine whether anger shall be permitted to burst forth and pride to retort. The answer that thrills us with gratification while we are uttering it, and the action that delights us while we are performing it, may lead, ultimately, but irresistibly, to the most disasterous consequences. Intellect possesses the power to control our words, thoughts and actions; hence, we may reasonably infer that such was the function that Nature designed it to perform (pp. 164–165).

Our feelings cannot prevent this supremacy of the intellect. At the command of intellect, the limbs of a man will quietly submit to the tortures of amputation; and his hands will submissively adjust his neck, so that his head may be severed from his body (p. 165).

Intellect, however, has no intuitive knowledge of what it should enjoin; to learn and communicate this is the duty of morality, of which the Bible is the summary. And it communicates its truths not as generalities

whose meaning, like a riddle's, is anything and everything to which ingenuity can affix it. It abounds with examples, in detail, of both good practices and evil, through the whole compass of words, thoughts, feelings, and actions; prohibiting the evil and enjoining the good (p. 167).

Many people deem the whole merit of the Bible dependent on the question of its divinity; but if my estimate of its tenets be correct, the Bible, whether human or Divine . . . is precisely such a guide as our intellect needs (p. 169).

But, finally, whether I am correct in my estimate of the Bible as a safe guide in the business of life, and whether I am correct in the rules which I have given for the government of our feelings and the feelings of others, are experimental propositions easily tested; and, in truth, each one of us is every moment testing them. To your own experience, therefore, I refer you for either the refutation of these propositions and their rejection, or for their confirmation and adoption (p. 170).

Thus ends Johnson's treatise on morality.

III

I SHOULD LIKE to make a few comments and observations.

1. It is only in our own time and in Anglo-American culture that philosophers have on a large scale abandoned any pretensions to being lovers of wisdom. Just as many of the best contemporary logicians indignantly repudiate the aspersion that what they have to teach is or could be an aid to thought, so few if any contemporary moral philosophers would care to be caught giving moral advice, at least in their official capacity, or be thought capable of supposing there was any wisdom which an honest man might transmit by way of guiding the perplexed. The alienation of so many of our best students, and no doubt of some of the worst, is, I am confident, largely the result of our failure to respond to their need of spiritual and moral sustenance. Truly, they come to us asking for bread and we give them a stone: the answers to questions they never asked and have no need of knowing. While once they tended to move from literature to philosophy in search of answers to fundamental questions about values and life, now they reverse their path. An exclusive diet of analytical philosophy, while for a time stimulating, eventually palls, and disillusionment and disgust often follow. Students then turn to the Wisdom of the East, to the Art of the Absurd, to the pseudoprofundities of continental metaphysical philosophies, and finally to Happenings, Hippyism, and drugs.

It was not always thus. Plato's search in *Gorgias* for the sister arts to gymnastics, dietetics, and medicine, which were to maintain and restore the health of the soul, as these preside over the health of the body, was an expression of a belief that man has a nature and that the art of life was discovering how to live in conformity with that nature so as to live well. Spinoza, too, sought the key to human blessedness. If he found it in the rather too exalted intellectual love of God, which perhaps he alone understood and was capable of reaching, at least he was on the right track: not paralyzed by the paradox of analysis or so fascinated by observing how words work as to lose sight of what words were about and why.

The philosopher who makes central a study of meanings need not restrict his study to the meaning of words, important though such investigation may be. Men, and not the least profound philosophers among them, have even dared to raise questions as to the meaning of life (without quotation marks); and some of them have come up with answers one may take as seriously as the question deserves. We would do well not to permit certain current preconceptions to blind us to this fact. Among these preconceptions, to which some philosophers are subject, is that which holds philosophy herself to be barren. This view, with which the ironic Socrates amused himself, is capable of misleading less wise men to suppose that philosophy is merely conceptual analysis, and that if anyone makes a claim to positive knowledge, especially knowledge that is either established or refuted by observation of what goes on in the world, he is not, as such a claimant, speaking as a philosopher. So much for the view that there is no ethical knowledge or, if there is, that ethics is not a part of philosophy. We could do worse than go back to Johnson for whom the problem did not exist.

2. A few words now about Johnson's conception of religion. Properly understood, religion is not for him a theory of the universe or of another life, but rather a this-worldly theory of human happiness or well-being.

> What can revelation teach? A revelation must necessarily be adapted to our capacity. What we could not understand would be no revelation. It was given for the regulation of our conduct, and not for the gratification of our curiosity. We are told the conduct which is pleasing to God, and the conduct that is displeasing. We are instructed how to obtain His favour, and how to become obnoxious to His displeasure. All that belongs to life is revealed in intelligible language, and what belongs to another life could not be intelligible in any language (*Treatise*, p. 210).[3]

This passage goes far to explain Johnson's conception of religion, and if read in conjunction with his fundamental principle of statement meaning, suffices to explain both itself and Johnson's position on Biblical teachings in general. His doctrine is that in any given case we shall understand the factual content of an utterance insofar as we take note of the evidence a speaker adduces in support of it. That the Bible is the word of God is vouched for, he tells us, by

> the happy tendency of its morality; its insight into the human character; its adaptation to every period and every nation, and

to every vicissitude of life. All tend to bow the understanding and the will, not only to admit its doctrines, but to cling to them as the counsellor in the cares and pleasures of life, and the comforter in affliction, pain and death (*Treatise*, p. 210).

In short, the evidence for the truth of revelation is the effect of its moral teachings; and this remarkable effect is what constitutes the sensible and emotional meaning of the doctrine that it is the word of God. It has in addition what Johnson calls verbal (syntactical) meaning and conceptual or intellectual meaning, but these are all distinct and not convertible one to another.

Therefore when Johnson speaks of Providence, as he often does in the work we have been examining, we must apply the same hermeneutic principle. The evidence for Providential arrangements consists of the natural regularities, especially in the moral domain, which constitute the basis of the science of morality: hence they constitute the sensible or empirical meanings of his statements about the actions of Providence. These remarks if taken seriously may remove much of the oddity and apparent old-fashioned quality of Johnson's ethical ideas, and perhaps render them more acceptable to those of us affected negatively by this way of speaking.

3. It is an important point (and in my view much to his credit) that in Johnson's whole treatment of the theme that every domain of nature, including the moral, is subject to laws, the subject of free will and determinism is never once mentioned. It is for him a matter of faith that nature is regular, and the effect of its laws on the whole beneficent. That there is much evidence in support of this belief he thinks obvious; but, as his closing passage quoted earlier indicates, it is a matter for empirical determination, not for a priori stipulation. That nature should be everywhere governed by laws he thinks not merely compatible with man's freedom, but in fact essential to it. It is by intelligent action in terms of the laws governing his own and others' feelings and conduct that man is able, by controlling the events of life and especially his feelings in relation to them, to control the effects which the events of life shall produce.

As to the nature of these supposed laws, whether strict or statistical, Johnson has nothing explicit to say. Yet he understands perfectly well that the moral laws describe practically inevitable, underlying, long-term tendencies—which, however, in view of the incredible complexity of human society and character, allow for much variety of specific effect in different cases, much delay, and (on occasion) apparent or even genuine exceptions. But this complication in no way alters the correctness of his view of the adequacy for all practical purposes of the knowledge and power which acquaintance with the laws of nature gives us.

4. There are for Johnson almost metaphysical grounds accounting for the beneficence of the order of nature, or Providence, despite numerous appearances to the contrary. While he makes no use of evolutionary principles which might be adduced to account for the fitness of the environment (i.e., for the dependence of man's well-being on the laws of nature—if they were not supportive of it he could not long continue to exist) he puts great stress elsewhere in his writings, especially in *Deep Sea Soundings*, on the polar character of concepts and on what may be called the "dialectical" basis of conscious life. The contrast principle, the "figure-ground" relationship of Gestalt psychology lies at the very basis of awareness and thought. The negative aspects of experience thus constitute the background against which the positive becomes recognizable as such. The essential dependence of life upon death, light upon darkness, pleasure upon pain, sound upon silence, feast upon famine, all show the necessity for every positive of its corresponding negative. This tendency in his thought may come as a surprise to those whose acquaintance with Johnson is restricted to his earlier books, which might give the impression that he is a nominalistic empiricist and nothing more.

An interesting example of the role that the figure-ground pattern plays in his thought is to be found in the explanation Johnson somewhere gives of the fact that as we grow older time seems to flow faster. His explanation is that a given unit of time, say a year, has the felt duration corresponding to its ratio to the whole of one's conscious life. For a child of three, his third year constitutes one third of his whole life, while for a man of thirty a year constitutes but a thirtieth of that life, and for a man of sixty but a sixtieth. Thus each successive year in its quality of felt duration grows regularly shorter than its predecessor.

5. The view, which plays so central a role in Johnson's science of morality, that feeling and its normal modes of expression in action, including speech, are dialectically related, so that on the one hand a feeling has a constant tendency to express itself in action and conversely that actions normally expressive of feelings have a tendency to generate those feelings, is reminiscent of and supported by the

James-Lange theory of emotions. With respect to the "coarser emotions at least," James says the correct view is that ". . . we feel sorry because we cry, angry because we strike, afraid because we tremble, and not that we cry, strike, or tremble, because we are sorry, angry, or fearful, as the case may be ." [4] Johnson has or at least offers no theory of the essentially physiological nature of feelings like that on which James bases his position, nor does he explain why if we cry, strike, or tremble we feel sorrow, anger, fear; he simply recognizes the fact that feelings express themselves in appropriate actions and that actions tend to arouse their corresponding feelings, and he relates these facts to his science of morality. Oscar Wilde's paradox that nature imitates art is often interpreted to mean that men come to see nature as it has been depicted by great artists. Perhaps this is what he meant; but I would consider a more profound interpretation Johnson's teaching that we tend to become in fact what we habitually pretend to be.

6. Johnson's very important insight in connection with the above, that speech itself is a most decisive type of action, as being maximally under our control, has profound implications for the problem of freedom. For speech if suitably chosen is capable of arousing feelings in the speaker, which in turn produce actions in him which have the power of generating corresponding feelings in others, and these have as their outward expressions actions desired by the speaker. All this goes in its implications far beyond what one finds in James' physiological theory of the emotions. The only thinker known to me who has understood something of this is Professor Harald Ofstad of the University of Stockholm, who in his important but little-known work, *The Freedom of Decision,* makes central to his discussion of freedom-as-power the notion of degrees of freedom and stresses the maximal power we have of uttering certain words, which when properly exploited may bring within our power the generation of certain feelings, and ultimately in some cases lead to decisions and actions. But his treatment is concerned mainly with the question of freedom of decision, not with moral science or the art of life.

The role which (according to Johnson) our utterances play in influencing our feelings and thereby our actions and the feelings of others can be brought into illuminating relationship with two other historically important doctrines: Hume's teaching that "Reason is and ought only to be the slave of the passions," [5] and Spinoza's maxim that an emotion can only be controlled by another emotion (see *Ethics,* Prop. VII, Part IV). What Hume may have meant by "ought" in this passage we need not inquire; but it is clear that he thinks reason impotent, so far as being able to affect our feelings. Whether this view of his be accepted depends of course in part on what he meant by "reason." If it is not a reification of some putative power expressing itself in acts of reasoning but essentially these acts themselves, it is clear that reasoning consists of certain kinds of sequences of usually subvocal, meaningful utterances, typically of statements. Now if Johnson is right, such acts normally express certain feelings, possibly of belief in causal or logical relations holding between certain types of events or in the statements asserting them; or perhaps of certain feelings expressed in assumptions hypothetically entertained, together with the expectation of logical or causal consequences. According to Johnson's doctrine, these same feelings tend to arise when we utter the sentences typically expressing them. Thus reasoning, if not reason, has the power of generating feelings and (accordingly) actions, and consequently need not be the slave of the passions (i.e., feelings), but may in fact be instrumental in controlling them. Such at least is the import of Johnson's teaching, which I think is very much worth taking seriously in this connection.

It may be interesting to note that Johnson clearly holds that certain types of thoughts essentially involve verbal utterances, a view having profound relevance to the by now rather overworked problem of the knowledge of other minds. The following passage from his *Treatise* should strike a familiar chord in those acquainted with the related passages in Wittgenstein's *Philosophical Investigations:*

> We cannot think the word George, while we are speaking the word Thomas; nor can we pronounce Thomas while we are thinking George. Speech is limited to an utterance of successive syllables. Verbal thoughts require a similar succession of syllables. The phrase "our father," we can no more condense into one thought, than we can pronounce the words in one articulation (p. 93).

Concerning Spinoza's recipe for controlling the emotions, it may well be correct; but the more important question is, what, if anything, controls the controlling emotion? If Johnson is right, much of the force and interest of Spinoza's remark is lost.

7. One of Johnson's views developed in the *Treatise* is that we often quite mistakenly impute certain thoughts to earlier thinkers because of the similarity of their words to those we should ourselves have used to express those thoughts. On rare occasions we can guard

ourselves against this tendency, namely when we have overwhelming grounds for assuming that they cannot have intended what their words seem to mean to us, because of the undeveloped state of some science or technology of their day. But otherwise the tendency can hardly be avoided, for we can understand a thinker only when we have had similar ideas or, when stimulated by his words, we rise to a new level of insight on which what was earlier incomprehensible becomes to us intelligible. We have then, in the end, no other way to try to understand a thinker than to impute to him meanings which we ourselves make use of or adopt in connection with his words.

Now the greatness of a thinker for one who considers his thought as expressed in his words must be measured by the illumination derived from them. Most of this illumination will be a reflection of one's own incipient insights, warmed into life by the generative words of a genius, who is indeed simply a person having exceptional powers of drawing forth from others a higher level of understanding or awareness. With this quality I think the subject of our commemoration was endowed to a remarkable degree. I would be most happy to think that all agreed with me, but the next most happy thought would be that those who disagree or have doubts might apply themselves to a study of Johnson's philosophy. I have much confidence in the eventual outcome.

NOTES

1 Indented passages in reduced type are, throughout, quotations of Johnson's own words. Condensations and deletions from the original are not always indicated, although page references will usually be given.

2 Page numbers in parentheses refer to location of quoted passages in Johnson's text.

3 This page number refers to the 1947 edition, published by the University of California Press.

4 William James, *Principles of Psychology* (1st ed., 1896) Vol. II, p. 449.

5 David Hume, *A Treatise of Human Nature,* Bk. II, Section III (Selby-Bigge ed.), p. 415.

JOHNSON'S LANGUAGE THEORIES IN MODERN PERSPECTIVE

◆ ◆ ◆ ◆ ◆ *MAX BLACK*

ON THE EVIDENCE of his writings, Alexander Bryan Johnson was an original and vigorous thinker dealing with extremely important matters with characteristic independence and determination. No reader of his books can doubt that he is in the presence of a genuine philosopher, whose views deserve the attention he asked for them. Whether one agrees or not, one certainly is provoked to that "species of fermentation or elicitation in the reader's intellect" (*M*, p. 9)[1] that, according to Johnson, is "the most which verbal communications can accomplish" *(ibid.).*

I say this much by way of introduction, because I shall have occasion to be highly critical of Johnson's method and conclusions. But no writer as serious as Johnson would wish for less. Any first-rate thinker deserves to be treated as more interested in the truth of what he is saying than in the vanity of remaining uncorrected. I shall try throughout to follow Johnson's own maxim that "where a reader finds that his interpretation of an author contradicts the author's comments

◇ ◇ ◇ ◇ ◇ *Susan Linn Sage Professor of Philosophy, and Director, Society for the Humanities, Cornell University. Author,* Critical Thinking, Language and Philosophy, The Nature of Mathematics, Problems of Analysis, Models and Metaphors, A Companion to Wittgenstein's Tractatus; *editor,* The Philosophical Review.

and conclusions, the reader should amend his interpretation, and make it conform to the author's comments and conclusions" (*M*, p. 11). Unfortunately, this advice, taken at face value, would imply that the author in question is free from inconsistency. Given what we know about the difficulty of philosophical argument, this is too much to expect. Johnson, no less than his illustrious predecessors, lapses into inconsistency. I shall try to salvage his positive insights and to discard those features of his thought which seem to me mistaken.

I

BEFORE I TRY to assemble Johnson's ideas about language and its relation to reality in a systematic way, it may be as well to provide a preliminary sketch of what Johnson was up to.

I think of him as a man very much struck by the gap between language and reality, and equally struck by what seemed to him certain inescapable disparities between the two. He was very sensitive to what he called the "sophistries of language" (*M*, p. 11). It seemed to him that in much scientific and philosophical writing there was to be found an extraordinary insensitivity to the defects of language and, accordingly, much philosophical argument which only close attention to the "structure of language" (*M*, p. 11) might dispel.

His remedy for this pervasive disorder of thought and writing was a return to nature. He was constantly impressed by the contrast between what he called "the paucity of language" and the "extent and variety of creation" (*T*, p. 49). Such remarks as the following occur again and again and must be regarded as the very heart of his practical teaching: "We must contemplate creation apart from words" (*T*, p. 47); "All that the book contains is the elucidation of but one precept: namely, to interpret language by nature" (*T*, pp. 27–28); "The object of my analysis is to teach you to subordinate language to nature" (*T*, p. 161); "Instead of contemplating creation through the medium of words, men should contemplate creation itself" (*T*, p. 299); "We must turn to 'Nature's unverbal dictionary' (*M*, p. 97) [and learn to study the] 'natural, unverbal, and unconventional language' " (*M*, p. 96).

We shall have to pay close attention to this program for a return to nature. For the moment, it will be enough to notice that Johnson stands squarely in a tradition of empiricism, which has been prominently associated with England and America. It is perhaps not implausible to think of his philosophy as reflecting the plain common

sense of a man of affairs to whom words must seem at best a poor substitute for experience. I should add that in Johnson's case his innate
thrust toward empiricism was somewhat checked to the detriment of
consistency by his earnest but somewhat heterodox religious views. I
shall say no more about this, since I have not sufficiently studied Johnson's writings on religious topics.

II

I TURN NOW to a more systematic sketch of Johnson's theories. It will be necessary to say something about his main opinions
concerning the external universe, "internal consciousness" (*T*, p. 166),
thoughts, the nature of language, and the nature of theories. I shall
deal with these topics in the order in which I have announced them.

Let us begin with the "external universe" (*T*, p. 47) which
Johnson also at various times calls "creation" (*T*, p. 47 and *passim*)
and "nature." He thinks of this as an "objective" reality, independent
of human action and contrasting, as we shall see, with a "subjective"
realm of thought and feeling.

Objective reality, as I shall call it, consists, at least in the
Treatise, of "sensations" (*M*, p. 20) or phenomena. He also speaks of
"sensible realities" (e.g., *T*, p. 123). In the *Treatise* he specifies in
some detail that he is thinking of "sights, sounds, tastes, feels, and
smells" (*T*, p. 48). Indeed, in the earlier book he goes so far as to say
that fire, oranges, grass, tobacco, and so on, *are* simply "groups" of
such phenomena (*T*, p. 48). So far as I can see, he does not officially
withdraw from this radical phenomenalism even in the later book. Although he there uses the term "physical things" (*M*, p. 20), he goes on
to say that "Physical, wherever used by me, will be as a synonym of
sensible" (*M*, p. 20), and explains that he intends phenomena in one
or other of the five sense modalities. This leads him to make an odd
but quite characteristic remark:

> To an uneducated deaf-mute [Johnson adverts repeatedly to
> this touchstone] sensible things must appear in entire separa-
> tion from words. He sees in the heavens neither sun, moon,
> stars, clouds, nor firmament, but he sees the unverbal things
> which the words name; and he sees on the earth neither trees,
> grass, men, women, houses, streets, nor water, but he sees the
> unverbal things that those names designate (*M*, p. 20).

I think Johnson was in the position of holding that what the deaf-mute
does not "see" does not really exist either. Or, rather, we make a mis-

take if we think that trees, grass, and so on are anything but groups of phenomena.

The groups of phenomena, which, according to Johnson, comprise the external world, are composed of completely independent "particulars." "Creation is a congregation of individual existences" (*T*, p. 79). Thus, in the technical jargon of philosophy, Johnson is an atomist as well as a phenomenalist. He insists again and again upon what he calls "the multiformity of nature" (*T*, p. 74). Indeed, this is one of the main reasons why he holds language to be necessarily imperfect as a representation of nature. Language bunches things together, but "the particulars which we can discover in nature, are all which truly pertain to nature" (*T*, p. 75).

Yet Johnson is not really as much of a nominalist as this last quotation might suggest. I have already pointed out that, according to him, sights and feels and the like are "associated" in nature (see, for instance, *T*, p. 48) and in the second book he even speaks of one phenomenon being an "unverbal sign" (*M*, p. 98) of others. He certainly seems to think that phenomena are not presented higgledy-piggledy, but are arranged in natural orders, though to be sure he says very little about such orderings. Furthermore, there are also certain internal relations between the phenomena: they show similarities (*T*, p. 74) varying in degree (*ibid.*). Johnson somewhat perversely takes such similarity to be partial identity (*T*, p. 80) or "approximation to a sensible oneness" (*T*, p. 74). He also suggests that the similarity varies from case to case.

Let us notice in passing that Johnson complains that we confound "verbal identity" with the merely "approximate identity" to be found in nature. He concedes that we can do no other when we speak:

> Still we need not confound the verbal identity with the realities of nature. In nature, the identity is just as we discover it to be. It must not be measured by names, but ascertained by observation. We reverse this rule: we interpret the natural identity by the verbal (*T*, p. 81).

I think this means that we ought to be satisfied with observable similarities between the things that are instances of a general term. The prime mistake induced by inattention to language is to insist that there must be some hidden identity, just because we have the single word, and to suppose that behind the grouping there must be some occult principle of organization. Here I think Johnson is perfectly right and is making a very important point.

This about concludes my summary of what Johnson has to say concerning the external universe. It is something like a vast mosaic of individual items, all capable of being perceived by the senses and separable in thought. There are some associations between the items, varying in character from one case to the next, and also some internal resemblances. But that is all. We are far from the kind of existence and the kind of relational structures that reliance upon language would suggest. This metaphysical position of Johnson's is, of course, strongly reminiscent of Hume, whom he had studied closely. It also reminds one of Berkeley, though I fancy that Johnson was far less influenced by him, if at all.

III

I TURN NOW to what might be called the subjective universe of "internal consciousness" (T, p. 166). Here we find "feelings," which "I am conscious of experiencing within myself" (T, p. 173). Johnson gives a list of such feelings which includes love, anger, joy, hope, faith, hunger, pity, sympathy, judgment, reverie, etc. (T, p. 159). Clearly he is using "feeling" in a somewhat extended sense. He thinks of the subject as obtaining "information" by means of his "consciousness" (T, p. 161). As we might expect, he stresses the diversity of "feelings" behind the superficial simplicity of the language that we use to refer to them. Indeed, he thinks that the language of internal feelings is even more deficient in this respect than the language of the external world. On the whole, however, Johnson says very little about feelings.

He says rather more about thoughts, which he regards, in the *Treatise,* as "phenomena." Some thoughts are sights, sounds, etc. (T, pp. 93, 94) and some are words (T, p. 92). For example: "Think the word million. The thought is a word. When we pronounce million audibly, it is a word; when we pronounce it inaudibly, it is a thought" (T, p. 92). In the *Treatise* Johnson seems to attach little value to what he calls "verbal thinking" (T, p. 96).

A fairly obvious objection to Johnson's rather crude conception of thought is that he fails to distinguish thought from sensation, on the one hand, or from silent speech on the other. In *The Meaning of Words,* we find a radical change and development in this point of Johnson's doctrines. He is now prepared to think that there are what he calls "intellectual unverbal things" (M, p. 21) which need to be assigned to a third realm.

A key passage is the following:

> The intellect conceives in *words,* and thus the intellect seems to possess no *unverbal* utterances. A very important question therefore arises, whether our intellectually conceived words possess any unverbal meaning—any meaning ulterior to the conceived words. I, at one period, supposed they possess no ulterior meaning, and that all abstract speculations are mere words (*M,* p. 200).

Johnson makes it clear that one important reason why he abandoned what he calls "this short-sighted belief" (*M,* p. 200) was that it would involve scrapping a good deal of theory and especially theology. As to what these "intellectual things" are, Johnson speaks somewhat unclearly. As examples, he gives memory, thought, and reflection (*M,* p. 22); he says that "our causal knowledge is intellectual" (*M,* p. 53); he says that "the relations of father and son are intellectual conceptions" (*M,* p. 56); according to him, "time is only a conception of the intellect" (*M,* p. 57) and "next week exists in only the intellect" (*M,* p. 59). Other examples are "power, quantity, quality, number, infinity, omnipotence, omnipresence, omniscience, etc." (*M,* p. 58). My impression is that anything that cannot plausibly be regarded as a directly observable feature of a phenomenon, and anything that cannot plausibly be called a feeling, is now assigned to the realm of "intellectual things." The intellect begins to look like a vast Lost Property Office.

Johnson locates the "unverbal" basis for "intellectual conception" in what he calls the human "organism." "The organism is within us . . . the organism of the intellect that conceives any given words is the unverbal meaning of the verbal conception" (*M,* p. 202). Johnson's main reason for accepting some unverbal backing for words having no direct sensible signification seems to be the supposed uniformity of human organization. "The organisms are part of every man's nature, hence the conceived words possess an unverbal meaning as truly as the words horse or orange" (*M,* p. 203). This all sounds somewhat Kantian, though I have been unable to find any reference to Kant in Johnson's writings.

IV

THUS FAR I have been attending to Johnson's ontology, his conception of the global features of reality. In understanding and evaluating the position of any thinker such as Johnson, whose attitude toward language is severely critical, it is obviously of capital importance to become clear about how the critic conceives of that "reality" with which language, in its unavoidable imperfection, is contrasted. "Nature" or reality, for Johnson, as for other "semanticists," is the touchstone: but our use of such touchstone can only introduce gratuitous confusion to the extent that our conception of the standard of objectivity, or conformity with reality, is itself insufficiently critical. I do not think that Johnson's own conception of the nature of reality can resist careful examination. But I will reserve my criticisms on that score for later. It is time to turn to the other term of the language/reality contrast and to consider in as much detail as time will allow how Johnson thinks about *words*.

Johnson regularly thinks of words as *names* of things. One of his summarizing subheadings runs as follows: "We should endeavour to regard words as merely the names of things" (*T*, p. 54). This remark, with its stress upon something that we should "endeavour" to do, suggests that Johnson does not intend to use "name" merely as a synonym of "word," though his practice sometimes suggests otherwise. I think it fair enough to say that Johnson thought of *all* words, at least those that were not merely noises, devoid of "signification" or meaning, as mere labels arbitrarily attached to nonverbal things in the universe.

At first sight this may seem sufficiently harmless, at least when applied to the kind of words we call proper names: that "Utica" is an arbitrary noise, conventionally attached to a certain city, seems conformable to common sense. It is harder to make this idea plausible when we come to general terms such as "water" or "number"; and harder still when we consider such "syncategorematic" words as "if" and "not." It is a weakness of Johnson's theories about language that he seemingly felt no need to undertake any examination of the great variety of ways in which words are actually used in a language. (He does have something to say, however, about how the meaning of general terms is to be construed.)

Johnson's conception of words as names, conventional labels for the things to which they are attached, leads him to a further and highly dubious doctrine, that the things in question are what he calls the *signification* of their names. He states this quite explicitly: "Words signify the objects to which they are applied" (*T,* p. 114).

Now it is important to understand that Johnson throughout uses "signification" as a synonym of "meaning." Speaking of the word "red," on the same page at which he makes the statement I have just quoted, he says, "The precise *meaning* of the word in each application is the sight itself which the object exhibits" (*T,* p. 114, italics added). To be sure, Johnson distinguishes between the "sensible signification," or sensible meaning, of words and what he calls their "verbal meaning." On this point too he is quite explicit: "Nearly every word possesses a verbal meaning as well as a sensible meaning" (*T,* p. 149). But, for reasons that will become plainer as we continue, he takes a disparaging view of "verbal meaning." His efforts are nearly always directed to establishing the presence or more often the absence of *sensible* meaning: unfortunately, he falls into the trap, unwarranted on his own showing, of identifying lack of sensible meaning with lack of meaning *simpliciter*. (This could be justified only in the case of those words, if they exist, that do not purport and do not need to have any verbal meaning.)

Such remarks as the following are quite typical, in their emphasis and sweep:

> [It is a] general principle that words have no signification but as they refer to some phenomenon. The principle is applicable to every word. It is as broad as language, and has no exception, but when words refer to revelation [an interesting caveat] (*T,* p. 111).

More succinctly, "Words have no signification but as they refer to phenomena" (*T,* p. 104). And again, "language cannot enable us to penetrate beyond the range of our senses. . . . Language cannot enable us to pass the barrier of our senses" (*T,* p. 250). It follows that whenever the "sensible signification" is lacking, meaninglessness results:

> When we subtract from a word its sensible signification, the word returns (so far as relates to the external universe), to the pristine insignificance which the word possessed, before it was applied to the purposes of language (*T,* p. 105).

We can view this, if we please, as a primitive precursor of later attempts to apply a "principle of verifiability" to exhibit the meaninglessness of certain well-formed, grammatically acceptable sentences.

Johnson applies the principle that identifies the meaning of words with the sensible particulars to which they apply to propositions and to questions as well as to words. "The sensible signification of a sentence is the sensible existence to which the sentence refers" (*T,* p. 168), and again, "A question which the senses cannot answer is insignificant" (*T*, p. 242). Notice here the unobserved slide from "sensibly insignificant" to simply "insignificant."

But perhaps the most important application of the principle of what might be called the reduction of meaning to sensible reference is in its application to general propositions: "No general proposition is significant of more than certain particulars" (*T*, p. 131). This has paradoxical consequences. If when I say that all dogs have tails my meaning is limited to features of the dogs I have encountered, it is most unlikely that you will have had the same experiences, and so most unlikely that you will understand the same as I do when I speak. Johnson says "Two men, who assent to the same general proposition, may possess very diverse meanings" (*T*, p. 91). This is an understatement: given the inevitable variety of human experience, he ought to have said "will," not "may." But how then do we ever succeed in making ourselves understood to another? And how could we ever succeed in agreeing or disagreeing with another? On Johnson's principles, the remark about dogs should have the same meaning as "All the dogs I have encountered have had tails"; and then if *you* say "Some dogs do not have tails," you are not disagreeing with me, since all that you can properly mean is that some of the dogs you have encountered have had no tails. And how am I or anybody else to make a remark about dogs I have *not yet* seen; i.e., how can I truly *generalize* beyond actual experience in the past?

Such difficulties as these may have led Johnson to speak of the "objective indefiniteness of subjective general propositions" (*M*, p. 171) and to say, more explicitly, that "The generality of a proposition is subjective, not objective" (*M*, p. 170). But here the comfortable word "subjective" is a mere placebo that produces only the illusion of a remedy. The difficulty, if it is a difficulty, is an endemic one, since language, as Johnson recognizes, is irretrievably committed to the use of general terms; "In every tongue the same word is applied to many phenomena" (*T*, p. 113).

It is surprising that Johnson should be relatively untroubled by such direct consequences of his restrictive conception of meaning, and should be willing to swallow such absurdities as the idea that a negative statement like "There are no unicorns" must count as "insignificant." He says flatly, "If a negation refers to no sensible particular, the negation is insignificant" (*T*, p. 140). And yet he is willing to treat the negations of such negations, i.e., universal affirmative propositions, as not only having meaning but even as being true. "Affirmative propositions possess a universal application, when the negation of their universality refers to no sensible particular" (*T*, p. 139). In other words, affirmative generalizations are true, because their negations are meaningless. On the most charitable interpretation, this would require us to treat empirical generalization as linguistically a priori. Johnson, when he nodded, could conjure and mystify as well as any classical metaphysician.

We should now glance briefly at Johnson's doctrine of "verbal meaning." The tale is a short one, quickly told. Words, says Johnson, "possess a further signification: they name words also" (*T*, p. 150). His examples show that he intends to refer to the *definition* of such words as are definable. For instance in *T*, p. 151, he refers to "definable words, though generally the name of other words . . ." and in such passages as *T*, p. 164, he speaks of words as often possessing "no signification but as representatives of other words" (his example being that of the French word *oui* as representing the English word "yes" for somebody ignorant of the French language).

This helps us to see why Johnson sets so little store by the verbal meaning of words: if we trace the verbal meaning of a word, we are led only to other words that define it, and thence to still more words; unless we terminate in sensible signification at last, we shall never break out of the linguistic realm and so arrive at genuine meaning, i.e., genuine connection with something unverbal. Here Johnson's refusal (at least in the earlier book) to admit of genuinely conceptual reference forces him to regard the verbal connections between words as a mere dispensable artifice for facilitating economy in expression.

Little more needs to be said in this brief survey about Johnson's conception of language. I have already mentioned his view that language necessarily distorts reality by grouping together particulars that are separate in nature, and by presenting the appearance of "identity" where nature only supplies various degrees and kinds of similarity. I should add that Johnson fully recognizes that such defects, if we are to call them such, are irremovable. He is no iconoclast, absurdly demanding the abolition of language: "We must discriminate between the question which relates to the appropriateness of a word, and its signification" (*T*, p. 118). The former "depends on custom; but whether the expression is significant or not, and what it signifies, depend on nature" (*ibid.*). He wants us merely to be constantly vigilant, to remain always alert to language's power of deception—and especially not to confuse the useful contrivances of language with the objective features of reality.

V

IT IS RATHER surprising to find Johnson having a good deal to say about the nature of scientific theorizing in general and also about the proper interpretation of particular examples, such as Newton's theory of gravitation. His ideas on these topics are of considerable interest, considering the close alliance between subsequent positivistic views and the criticism of science. It is more than coincidence that Johnson's ideas about scientific theorizing should seem at times so close to the later positions of Ernst Mach and Percy Bridgman. Johnson's remarks about particular examples of scientific theorizing also have the merit of helping us to see more clearly than we otherwise might the strange consequences that follow from applying his conception of language to any doctrine that purports to extend beyond the direct evidence of the senses.

Johnson regards scientific theories as human artifacts: "Theoretical agents are of man's fabrication, and partake of the mutability of their creator" (*T*, p. 227; cf. also *T*, p. 238, Sec. 26). He grants that "theories are useful. We are acquainted with no mode of creating a science, but by embodying facts in some theory" (*T*, p. 237) and he proceeds, quite in the modern spirit, to stress the predictive power of a theory: "When certain conclusions are deducible from a theory, we resort to experiments for their realization, and thus many new facts are occasionally developed" (*ibid.*). On the other hand, he restricts the significance of theories, in effect, as we saw him doing with regard to general propositions, to the known *evidence* for the theory: a theory "is significant of nothing but the data which are adduced in proof of the theory" (*T*, p. 236). And so we have the old question, which does not seem to have bothered Johnson at all, about how a theory, so cribbed and confined, *could* be used for the anticipation of further experience.

So far we have a mildly instrumentalist conception, which seems harmless enough, even though it leads Johnson in the later book to say that "the unverbal meaning of all theories is *subjective* (in the intellect, not in the objective universe)" (*M*, p. 73). (Here again, one wants to ask, How can anything referring only to the intellect have any bearing at all upon external reality?) Indeed his remarks about theories as embodying fictions have a remarkably modern air:

> I desire particularly to remark in relation to theories—and I solicit for the remark much attention—that every theory is a fiction to the extent that we employ it to materialize a modus operandi that is only intellectually conceived (*M*, p. 215).

Where he goes wrong, I think, is in supposing that theoretical terms must have unique "sensible" correlates on pain of insignificance otherwise. This is what he means, I think, when he continues the passage I have just quoted by adding the words, "and such a materialization is the object of every theory."

Johnson's idea seems to be that in the presence of unfamiliar or surprising phenomena we are powerfully drawn to postulate some imperceptible agent, whether gravitation, magnetic attraction, or the like, which will assimilate what is observed to what we actually experience. But in so doing, we spin a verbal web: we pass from words to words, mistakenly supposing that we are saying something about reality.

This attitude toward theoretical terms, with its insistence that they shall have sensible correlates, leads Johnson to some strange conclusions. He seems to think that sphericity, when predicated of the earth, means only the phenomena by which we argue in favor of the round earth and *not* what we mean when we call a tennis ball spherical. He is prepared to say, about causes, "We think a cause must exist, hence we see not the absurdity of attributing verbal causes. Cause and effect are, however, mere words" (*T,* p. 257). He is very skeptical about scientific talk about the vast extent of space, or the tremendous compressibility of air, and so on.

> Let no man confound such answers with the realities of the external universe. Ingenious they may be, and they may refer to certain sensible experiments; but beyond the sensible existences to which they refer, they are words; and besides words, they are nothing (*T,* p. 260).

In at least one instance this strongly reductionist interpretation of scientific theory leads him actually to deny the existence of relevant empirical experiment:

> I entertain no doubt that some fallacy exists in relation to the late pendulous experiments at Paris, and which seem to materialize unverbally the intellectually conceived diurnal motion of the earth—a conception as little likely to be realized physically as the once intellectually conceived residence of the soul in the pineal gland is likely to be realized physically (*M,* p. 216).

What assurance—and what an unfortunate choice of an example! I wonder what Johnson would think about the views of the earth enjoyed by our orbiting astronauts. I think he might be as shocked as Zeno was, in the apocryphal story, by seeing actual runners overtaking one another.

It seems clear enough that Johnson was misled by accepting an unnecessarily restrictive conception of meaning—and that this part of his theory of language is certainly inapplicable to science. Any view of language that is forced to chastise scientific theory as severely as Johnson dared is suspect, to say the least.

I have now completed my necessarily inadequate sketch of Johnson's main view about language and its relation to reality. The one topic that would require attention in a fuller treatment is Johnson's somewhat peculiar views concerning logic. About these I will simply say that Johnson held it possible to reason with words devoid of signification, a position that is in harmony with modern views about the formality of deductive reasoning. The point has some importance as reinforcing Johnson's insight that apparently cogent argument, whether in science or in philosophy, can be conducted in the absence of reliable semantic connections between the words or symbols used and external reality. We can draw conclusions from nonsense! Here Johnson draws our attention to something important, though today the point is more familiar than it could have been at the time that he wrote.

I shall turn now to criticism, in order to show certain serious inadequacies in Johnson's conception of the nature of words and of "nature," and I shall raise some questions about the status of Johnson's insights, when measured by his own criteria of semantic adequacy.

VI

LET US BEGIN with a fundamental point, the way in which Johnson regularly conceives of the nature of words. We have seen that his leading idea here is remarkably simple: a significant or meaningful word is simply a label arbitrarily and conventionally attached to a "thing." He subscribes, in short, to what is nowadays called a "bearer theory" of meaning.

On this fundamental issue, Johnson unconsciously violates his own wise maxim to search always for underlying multiplicity and variety behind the superficial unity imposed by verbal appearances. It does not seem to have occurred to him, obvious though the point really is, that the word "word" itself deserves at least as careful and critical scrutiny as such words as "red" or "gold" or "shape" that he refused to accept at face value. Had Johnson *looked at* language as sharply and as candidly as he urged everybody to look at "nature," he could hardly have failed to see that the bearer theory of meaning is too crude a distortion (one might almost say a caricature) to be acceptable. I suspect that, unconsciously, Johnson never regarded language as a part of nature and therefore failed to give it the empirical examination it needs.

The notion of a "thing," with which Johnson operates uncritically, is itself highly suspect. I am inclined to think that we have here a linguistic category projected upon the world, so that a thing, roughly speaking, is *whatever can be named*. However this may be, the notion of a word deriving its meaning by having a thing conventionally attached to it is plausible only when applied to nouns or noun-substitutes. But language is not composed of substantives alone. Once we notice, what is obvious immediately, that language is a patterned system, necessarily including connecting and binding words (adjectives, verbs, conjunctions), the bearer theory reveals itself as patiently inadequate. And even in the case of proper names, the idea that the "meaning" of the name is the man or thing to which it is attached clearly will not do. In order to be able to use such a name, in thought or communication, in the absence of the name's bearer, it is obviously necessary to have in one's possession some criteria of application—the kind of thing that writers have variously referred to as "connotation" (Mill) or "sense" (Frege). Even the simplest theory of language must recognize this dual aspect of words and sentences—their capacity to mean as well as to refer. Of course, such a two-dimensional theory is only the crudest beginning of a satisfactory theory of the varieties of meaning.

Now, I have already said, in the course of outlining Johnson's views about language, that he systematically confuses meaning with reference—and, indeed, with sensible reference. Here are two serious and perhaps fatal flaws. For the point I am making is not merely a verbal one. Johnson could accept it in part, by agreeing to say that he is concerned only with that aspect of the relation between words and things which I am calling "sensible reference." And he might say, quite correctly, that it is important and useful to consider, wherever appropriate (but the qualification is important), whether and how words have sensible reference. So far so good. What cannot be accepted is the surreptitious conflation, to which Johnson repeatedly succumbs, of lack of sensible reference with lack of meaning. We can have lack of sensible reference without absence of reference, as when we use numerals as names or quasi-names of numbers; and we often have lack of reference without attenuation of meaning. When I say, "There is no elephant in this room," I am not referring to any particular elephant. But it is quite preposterous to say, as Johnson does, that my utterance is therefore insignificant or meaningless. Johnson's paradoxical remarks about negative statements and his less obviously mistaken, but still quite unacceptable, remarks about general statements are a reductio ad absurdum of his general conception of language.

This flaw plays havoc with Johnson's criticisms of other writers. His favorite argument is, in effect, "Look how this word ('cause', 'gravitation,' or what you please) is being used here. It refers to nothing." Usually he is right about this. But the step to "Therefore, what is being said is only words" is quite unjustified. Criteria of significance, as we have learned to our sorrow after fifty years of abortive attempts to construct such criteria, must necessarily be more complex than this. Indeed, it is plain that the accusation of insignificance or "nonsense" can be sustained against a writer only after a thorough examination of his intentions, the linguistic system he is using with its built-in conventions, and much else. Johnson looks at language with the innocence of a child looking at the puff of steam issuing from a locomotive, without any inkling of the enormous complexity concealed behind the appearances.

VII

JOHNSON'S CONCEPTION of "experience" or "nature" is also grossly oversimplified, though here the simplicity is one imposed by a metaphysical preconception of what reality *must* be like. Experience, *pace* Johnson and Berkeley and other phenomenalists, is not obviously composed of sights and sounds and feels. What we see consists of persons and trees, bodies and spaces between them, all given in a single framework. As a contemporary psychologist says:

> The phenomenal world is not composed of colors, sounds, touches, tastes, and smells as we have for so long assumed, but of such properties as surface, edge, slant, convexity, concavity, of rising, falling, beginning, ending, moving and changing. Sensations are the occasional symptoms of perception, not the cause of it.[2]

And the attempt to view the external world phenomenologically, or aesthetically, demands a very exceptional and difficult "set" of the observer.

> Although compromise occurs, it does seem that the more one notices the patchwork of colors in the field the less one sees objects in the world, and the more one observes objects the less one sees the patchwork of colors.

The term refers to a rare and sophisticated kind of experience, not a basic one.[3]

More serious, perhaps, than this radically inadequate conception of experience as a mere mosaic of separable phenomena is Johnson's naïve view of experience as at once wholly passive—"out there," just what it is—and at the same time somehow an "interpreter" or "revealer" of meaning. This won't do at all. Nature, after all, can teach us nothing if we ask it no questions; and in order to ask a question, we have to know in advance what we mean by the question. It is all very well to say as Johnson does: "Look to external reality for the meaning of gold." But what are we to look *for*? First, we must know the meaning of the word, or our search will be quite pointless. Suppose somebody asked me to look for the meaning of "dlog." How ridiculous it would be for me to accept this meaningless word and hope to discover its meaning by looking at the world!

Our conclusion must be, I am afraid, that the kind of primitivism that holds that we can approach experience "without words," which is tantamount to saying without ideas, can only work mischief. That experience must function as some kind of control, even for words that are linked with experience very indirectly, is true enough. But how such control is properly to be exercised is a far more difficult question than Johnson realized.

I must add a word about Johnson's nominalism. The label is at least partly appropriate, considering Johnson's reiterated stress upon reality as a congregation of "particulars." But, as we have seen, although he thinks that nature never exhibits instances of perfect "identities," he does grant the presence in nature of *similarities,* that is to say of certain abstract features of order. It ought to have bothered Johnson, if he had pursued the matter further, that similarity or resemblance was, according to him, experienced directly without the intervention of words or ideas. If this is the case for similarity, why not for other less abstract universals? For one thing, we never perceive *mere* similarity. Whenever we say one thing resembles another, it is always proper to ask "Similar in respect to *what*?" So, after all, qualities and relations do emerge directly in our experience. And these are hardly "things," except in some strained and misleading sense of that word.

Johnson's nominalism and atomism, both somewhat half-hearted at best, I think, would need drastic revision in a systematic defense of his position. Had Johnson accepted the point I have been making about similarity, I think he might have been tempted to embrace the more radical view that even similarity is not found as "given" in nature, but must be conceived as imposed through the intervention of thought and language. This more radical nominalism might in the end have driven him to a kind of mysticism that would surely have been uncongenial.

VIII

I MUST NOW INQUIRE, if only briefly, concerning the source of Johnson's sweeping conception of the three separate and independent realms of sensation, feeling, and thought ("the intellectual realm"). Where does Johnson get this? And how, and on what ground does he *know* that they are segregated from one another as he claims? These fundamental questions are, so far as I know, nowhere discussed by Johnson. He seems to think that experience suffices to show that the realms are separate and inviolable. But how could experience show that experience is only one of three distinct and severally autonomous realms? Or are we to suppose that there is some kind of global and superordinate experience of sensation, feeling, and thought indifferently? The truth is, of course, that experience shows nothing of the sort. The threefold division is a product of metaphysical reflection, for which Johnson would need to make room in his philosophy. How he would do so I have no idea.

But even if this could be done, one would still remain uncomfortable about the great gulf set by Johnson between the three realms. To anybody who believes, as Johnson officially represents himself as believing, that there is an unbridgeable chasm between thought and sensation, the relevance of thought to experience must remain an insoluble mystery. An obvious feature of some thoughts is that they are, or at least seem to be, *about* "external things." How is this possible? This question, to which Wittgenstein, like so many of his greatest predecessors, devoted agonizing and unrelenting attention, seems not to have worried Johnson at all. Yet to suppose that thought and experience are inviolate realms between which no traffic is possible is to render thought completely ineffective, a mere play of words and images in a void. Viewed in this light, human experience would be truly mindless.

The best that Johnson can do, in his ripest reflections upon these themes, is to say that thoughts refer to something "organic"— that is, I suppose, something uniformly characteristic of mental structure and constitution. But this somewhat Kantian idea is insufficiently elaborated by him. I doubt that Johnson had any clear idea of what he really meant by the "organic structure" that he postulated. Here I am afraid a comforting word took the place of the hard work of philosophical thought.

IX

MY STRICTURES ON Johnson's views will seem harsh only to anybody unfamiliar with the severities of philosophical debate. It might be held unfair to subject an amateur, even one so obviously gifted as Johnson was, to the standards of adequate philosophical argument. But I would not agree. When we are dealing with matters as fundamental as the nature of reality and the nature of language, with the structure of thought and the imperfections of the symbolic systems in which thought is embodied, all considerations of politeness and respect must be subordinated to an unflinching search for reasons and grounds. I am afraid that my final judgment must be that, by these criteria, Johnson's philosophy (for it is nothing less than that) was somewhat rickety.

But, it may be asked, does nothing survive from the wreckage? Had Johnson nothing to say from which we can learn something of value for our own time? Yes. When we make sympathetic allowance for the state of knowledge about these matters in Johnson's times, and the difficulties under which he labored, we must still admire the flashes of penetration he showed. To be as critical as he tried to be, of the language in which philosophers and scientists try to formulate their most basic insights is wholly admirable. If Johnson failed to provide us with a usable praxis of semantic criticism, he was at least a voice crying in the wilderness when he proclaimed in pungent and eloquent phrases the need for such a praxis. May his example teach us to do better.

NOTES

1   Throughout this paper I shall use "M" to refer to The Meaning of Words, edited by Irving J. Lee (Milwaukee, Wis., 1948). I shall also use "T" to refer to Alexander Bryan Johnson's A Treatise on Language, edited by David Rynin (Berkeley, Calif., 1947).
2   James J. Gibson, "Perception as a Function of Stimulation," in Sigmund Koch (ed.), Psychology: A Study of a Science (New York: McGraw-Hill, 1959), Vol. 1, p. 460.
3   Ibid., p. 461.

A NOTE ON THE CONCEPTS OF "VERBAL SIGNIFICANCE" AND "SENSIBLE SIGNIFICANCE" IN ALEXANDER BRYAN JOHNSON'S TREATISE ON LANGUAGE

♦ ♦ ♦ ♦ ♦ *LARS GUSTAFSSON*

1

THE DISTINCTION between "verbal significance" and "sensible significance" constitutes the very core of the philosophy of language in Alexander Bryan Johnson's *Treatise*.[1] It is in the light of this distinction that his program for a radical empirical therapy of philosophical problems has to be seen: "We must make our senses the expositors of words, instead of making words the expositors of what our senses reveal" (Lect. I, par. 14).

This distinction is the very instrument by which his reasoning proceeds in *A Treatise on Language,* and he is quite concerned to stress the importance and originality of this conceptual tool: "To this distinction I wish to direct your particular attention. It has never been noticed, and produces dire confusion in every disquisition that relates to human knowledge" (Lect. X, par. 12).

However, at first neither the very nature of this distinction nor its originality becomes very clear, and in spite of the fact that reference is made to the distinction on almost every page of Johnson's *Treatise,* the reader remains uncertain for some time as to the exact nature of the two concepts.

Here, as in many other respects, Johnson proves to be a

◇ ◇ ◇ ◇ ◇*Swedish poet and philosopher. Editor,* Bonniers Litterära Magasin. *Currently preparing a monograph on Alexander Bryan Johnson's philosophical works.*

representative of that particular breed of philosophers to whom his predecessor George Berkeley and his successor Ludwig Wittgenstein are to be referred: philosophers whose thought seems governed by one central complex of ideas whose consequences penetrate every part of their thinking.

The present paper attempts to sketch an interpretation of these two concepts, an interpretation which seems to make good sense and at the same time supports Johnson's claim to originality.

2

IN CONSIDERING questions of meaning, according to Johnson, we have to make a very firm distinction between the *sensible* significance of a word, phrase, or sentence, and its *verbal* significance.

Consequently, he speaks about the sensible and the verbal *significations* of words, phrases, and sentences, where the signification is the ontological component different from itself to which the significant word, phrase, or sentence refers. The elements of this doctrine are illustrated in the following statements from the *Treatise:*

> Nearly every word possesses a verbal meaning as well as a sensible meaning (Lect. 10, par. 11).

> The senses alone can reveal to us the sensible signification of words (Lect. XII, par. 2).

> The sensible signification of a sentence is the sensible existence to which the sentence refers (Lect. XII, par. 5).

> Words can yield us nothing but the verbal signification of words (Lect. XII, par. 3).

From other passages in the *Treatise* (e.g., Lect. X, par. 11), it seems clear that Johnson holds that nearly all expressions have either one or the other kind of significance, but—and this is one of the major points of his philosophy—having one kind of significance is independent of having the other one.

At the source of this doctrine are the philosophies of the early British empiricists, but Johnson's originality consists in the fact that at a crucial point he takes a stronger empirical position than that of either Locke or Hume. While he seems to take this position under the influence of the Scottish common-sense philosophers, especially Reid and Berkeley, Johnson goes much further than these philosophers at the crucial point.

In paragraph 49 of his *A New Theory of Vision,* George Berkeley observes that the data of different fields of sensible experience are logically independent of each other. This is the same point that Molyneux makes in stating his famous problem in the correspondence with John Locke: If a person blind from birth is accustomed to differ by means of feel between a cube and a sphere, would he be able on suddenly gaining sight to make the same distinction by sight alone? Berkeley states his conclusion thus:

> But if we take a close and accurate view of things, it must be acknowledged that we never see and feel one and the same object. That which is seen is one thing, and that which is felt is another. If the visible figure and extension be not the same with the tangible figure and extension, we are not to infer that one and the same thing has divers extensions. The true consequence is that the objects of sight and touch are two distinct things. It may perhaps require some thought rightly to conceive this distinction. And the difficulty seems not a little increased, because the combination of visible ideas hath constantly the same name as the combination of tangible ideas wherewith it is connected: which doth of necessity arise from the use and end of language.[2]

It is to this opinion that Johnson subscribes in the opening paragraphs of the second lecture of his *Treatise,* and even without an explicit reference to Berkeley it seems reasonable to presume that at least some of his inspiration comes from the *Theory of Vision.*

The first part of Johnson's doctrine may be stated as follows:

I. From the object of a sensible experience within the possible experiences of one sense no information follows concerning the object of a sensible experience within the possible experiences of another sense.

Strong as this statement is, it is only half of Johnson's claim. For in fact (and this is the decisive step which makes his empiricism more radical than that of Locke and Hume) he not only maintains I, but he generalizes the independence to hold even between sensory experiences within the same sense. Thus he clearly denies Locke's statement that it is possible to describe the actual appearance of a rainbow to someone who has only seen the various particular colors which constitute it (Lect. X, pars. 12–13). More radically, he answers Hume's famous question in the negative:

Suppose a man is acquainted with every colour except a particular shade of blue. Let now all the shades of blue, except the above, be placed before him in an order descending gradually from the deepest blue to the highest; will he not be able, by his imagination, to acquire a knowledge of the absent shade?

According to Johnson, the task imposed by Hume is as impossible as it is for a blind man to know any color (X:3), for "so rigid is nature on this subject that the most intimate acquaintance with two sights will not enable us to know the appearance which they will present when blended" (Lect. X, par. 16).

The first part of Johnson's doctrine must therefore be followed by:

II. From no particular sensible experience does there follow any possible information concerning any other, actual or possible sensible experience.

From I follows the doctrine that with respect to sensible experiences, language is systematically and unsystematically ambiguous, for the meaning of a word varies not only with respect to what senses it refers to but also with respect to the total experience of the individual who uses the word.

From II (being stronger than I) follows the doctrine which forms the very *leitmotif* of Johnson's philosophy of language: From words, phrases, and sentences, being sensible existences themselves, there does not immediately follow any information as to the nature of sensible existences different from themselves. "Words can *supply* the place of no sense. They can simply refer us to what our senses have disclosed" (Lect. X, par. 1).

Thus if a sentence should have any informative force which carries beyond linguistic convention, it must be found in the designatum itself: "The sensible signification of a sentence is the sensible existence to which the sentence refers" (Lect. XII, par. 5).

The theory of the two kinds of meaning has to provide an explanation of this fact. Johnson's main interest, however, lies not so much in studying the relations between words and their designata, as in a very special semantical situation: when a word, phrase, or sentence is applied in a context where it is apt to lose its original meaning. Most of the space of his *Treatise* is used to describe different examples of this situation.

But it still remains a matter of fact that words, phrases, and

70   LANGUAGE AND VALUE

sentences, the signification of which we are not immediately able to refer to sensible experiences of our own, *do* make perfectly good sense. This fact, which does not cause any considerable difficulty for Locke and Hume, becomes for Johnson an issue requiring explanation. He gives us a number of examples. For most people the word "decapitation" refers to something which they have never seen, as does the word "bonfire" for a blind man and the word "melody" for a deaf man. These three words make good sense by description exclusively.

The point of departure of his analysis is formulated very well in one of the opening paragraphs of the *Treatise*: "Language may be formed into propositions whose results, though incontrovertible by logick, are irreconcileable with our senses" (Lect. I, par. 8). This results in a dilemma which is the classical focus of so much philosophy of knowledge: either we have to disbelieve our senses or disbelieve the best demonstrated conclusions. Johnson makes the attempt to demonstrate the existence of a third alternative:

> . . . Hence the importance of ascertaining whether language, when thus employed, possesses not a covert signification that will save us from the alternative of either disbelieving our senses, or disbelieving the best demonstrated conclusions. I will satisfy you that it possesses such a signification, and I will teach you the signification of language which is thus sophistically employed (Lect. I, par. 8).

The third alternative is introduced by the distinction between two different kinds of significance, the sensible one and the verbal one. The philosophical dilemma is born in the moment the two kinds of significance are confused with each other. In this context we shall not go into the details of Johnson's account of the different ways in which this can be done. The most frequent source of confusion is, according to Johnson, that the verbal significance of a sentence is mistaken for a sensible one.

But words alone, i.e., words which do not refer to a sensible particular directly, "can yield us nothing but the verbal signification of words" (Lect. XII, par. 3). This of course is not a definition, and as a matter of fact no attempt to define the concept in a strict way is made within the *Treatise*.

That the distinction could be interpreted in a way which is apt to give at least some of Johnson's statements a contradictory character is shown by David Rynin in the very informative "Critical Essay" which concludes his edition of the *Treatise*. Taking as his point of departure Tarski's well-known condition of adequacy for a definition of the truth of empirical statements, Rynin concludes that a statement has to be simply false if it refers to no sensible particular, in the sense intended by Johnson. A sentence has sensible significance in Johnson's sense if and only if it refers to a sensible particular. Thus if no such particular exists, the sentence must be sensibly insignificant. But this, on Tarski's criterion of truth, is exactly what is the case when a sentence is false. Rynin concludes:

> We see, then, that from evidence that at best shows that some statement is false or improbable Johnson concludes that the statement is without sensible signification. Except for those important but special cases in which the statement refers to no sensible particular in the sense that it is unverifiable, we find that what Johnson means by "insignificant" is what we and most men mean by "is false," or "is not known to be true" (p. 392).

Thus according to Rynin—and I think to other students of Johnson as well—it might seem as if this philosopher tends to narrow the concept of meaning to a point where it coincides with the concept of reference, "meaning" and "reference" here taken in the sense in which Frege uses them in stating his well-known distinction. This narrowing is rather apt to make Johnson's views unacceptable, for the assumption that all empirical sentences which lack reference are senseless would corrupt the entire notion of falsity in empirical statements. From quite a number of passages of the *Treatise,* however, it seems clear that Johnson did not intend this consequence of his philosophy of language, or at least never realized that it did follow. (The latter seems to be Rynin's opinion.)

In commenting on a passage by Hume, Johnson explicitly makes the concession that a proposition may be untrue so long as it has any "signification":

> Hume says, "Our senses inform us of the colour, weight and consistence of bread; but neither sense nor reason can inform us of the qualities which fit it for the nourishment and support of the human body." So long, however, as the proposition of Hume has any signification, it is untrue (Lect. XXIV, par. 6).

Further, in the 1828 edition of the *Treatise,* Johnson makes the following observation:

> If then the object of definition is to reveal any sight, sound, taste, feel or smell, that our senses have never experienced, the

attempt is vain; and it is no more vain in simple ideas than in complex; in the word white, than in the word rainbow. But if the object of a definition is to teach us the verbal signification of any word, the instruction is useful and adequate (Lect. X, par. 16).

It seems, after all, very puzzling that Johnson should regard the instruction by means of definitions "useful and adequate" if he considered it completely unable to convey any meaning of words whatsoever.

Johnson's doctrine on questions is also informative in this respect; he states that "the question How? refers usually to a theory, —the question What? to a definition: we mistake both for physical inquiries" (Lect. XXII, par. 9). Johnson here seems quite clearly to state the distinction between questions as to the meaning and questions as to the reference of a word.

On the other hand, Johnson's use of such phrases as "lacks sensible significance" and "lacks significance" is rather confusing. He is not completely consistent in his use of terminology, and the terminology actually used, at its face value, may seem to conform much more with modern semantical terminology than may actually be the case.

Perhaps at this point some words have to be said about a subject which has not been very much discussed, but certainly has relevance—Johnson's style. Certainly every reader will agree that the prose in his early philosophical works is remarkable in its vigor, concentration, and candor. At the same time, nobody will fail to perceive some rather peculiar properties of this prose—the extensive use of metaphor, the aphoristic trends, and most of all the repetitions.

These trends do not become quite clear until we consider the philosopher's situation. The repetitions as well as the metaphors are the obvious results of that type of wrestling with the material in which a man gets entangled when addressing an audience which lacks the requisite knowledge and philosophical training for absorbing and comprehending what is said. This was exactly Johnson's situation lecturing in the Utica Lyceum in 1825.

Many of the peculiarities of Johnson's style seem to be completely explained by the situation in which his thoughts were made public, and certainly would not have appeared if he had had the opportunity to convey his thoughts to a public of philosophically trained listeners, who would have been able at the same time to absorb as well as to provide resistance to his thoughts. Therefore it seems to be important that in interpreting Johnson we do not make too rash an identification of his use of words like "verbal," "significant," and "insignificant" with the use of the same terms today or even among his philosophical predecessors. If we do, it might well be that we arrive much too fast at an interpretation which seems to make his conclusions absurd.

It seems reasonable to avoid as long as possible committing Johnson to a too definite ontology or semantic system. It may be that he wanted to express one very important observation rather than to construct a complete semantical theory. And it might well be that such a word as "verbal" in his rather personal terminology has a different sense from that of ours.

3

IN STRESSING THAT all meaning ultimately depends on sensible experience, Johnson's philosophy corresponds with the program of empirical reduction in early twentieth-century philosophy. Thus Johnson would certainly agree with that central principle which Bertrand Russell formulated as: "Every proposition which we can understand must be composed wholly of constituents with which we are acquainted." [3]

What, then, is the difference between Johnson's approach and the commonplace empirical reductionism? As a matter of fact, this is a much more delicate question than it perhaps seems at first sight. According to the classical view every empirical sentence, in order to have meaning, must be translatable into a statement about immediate experience. Thus expressions which are not logical connectives and whose meaning cannot be known by immediate experience must be shown to contain as constituents of their meaning concepts that are already known by acquaintance—or, as in Bertrand Russell's theory of singular descriptions, must be transformed into descriptive phrases, the constituents of which are understood by acquaintance.

The commonplace empiricist doctrine, however, does not make any distinction between definable and indefinable words with respect to their cognitive content. It is assumed that the meaning of one word could be contained as a part within the meaning of another word. But this is exactly what Johnson denies as far as "sensible significance" is concerned. This is the point of his insisting that the word "decapitation" lacks sensible significance for everybody who has never witnessed such an event, and that the word "bonfire" lacks meaning for a blind person.

For Johnson all knowledge is simple, whatever complexity its linguistic expression may have. This is a consequence of his doctrine of the mutual cognitive and logical independence of all sensible particulars. A very important passage in the original edition of the *Treatise* seems to be the following:

> It is curious that so simple a distinction in the meaning of words should be unknown in the disquisitions of our most acute metaphysicians. They constantly disregard the simplicity of our knowledge, and look for truth either above the surface of things or below it. They have therefore again attributed to nature a property which exists in language only: that is, they have observed that some words are reducible into other words, while some cannot be reduced; for instance, murder can be translated into a sentence: "a felonious killing with premeditated malice." The word white cannot be thus translated; it names a sight only. This difference, which is purely an artifice of language to condense a sentence into a single word, has been supposed a mysterious mental process; and the words which affect such condensations, have been termed complex ideas, abstractions, &c. (Lect. X, par. 12).

Thus it seems as if Johnson wanted to maintain that the distinction between simple and complex meanings of words does not correspond to a similar difference between simple and complex constituents of our knowledge. All empirical knowledge for Johnson is a knowledge of something unique and indivisible: a sensible particular, a sight, a feel, a sound, a smell, or a taste.

Johnson draws the attention to a difference between two sorts of questions—those that relate to the appropriateness of a word and those that relate to what he calls signification:

> Every word refers for signification as scrupulously to the existence to which it is applied, as a pronoun refers for signification to the substantive whose place it supplies. I may say that two sounds look alike. Whether the expression is appropriate or not depends on custom; but whether the expression is significant or not, and what it signifies, depend on nature:—the expression will signify any sensible relation to which it refers; and if it refers to nothing, it will signify nothing (Lect. VII, par. 8).

According to Johnson, the application of a word could be appropriate in two different senses: (a) it could be appropriate to linguistic custom; or (b) it could be appropriate to reality.

The question whether a word is the right one or not thus has two aspects, one purely linguistic and one purely cognitive, and—

this is the point Johnson wants to make—these aspects have to be treated as completely independent of each other: "Words can *supply* the place of no sense. They can simply refer us to what our senses have disclosed" (Lect. X, par. 1).

4

IN THE HISTORY of philosophy there is a very frequently recurring situation in which some central concept, say "motion" or "time," is found on detailed analysis to contain contradictory notions, and that as a result of this discovery (whether right or wrong), the conclusion is drawn that time, or motion, does not exist. This seems, for example, to be the type of argument intended by Zeno in stating his paradoxes of motion.

It is to the credit of George Edward Moore (1873–1958) and the Swedish philosopher Adolf Phalén (1884–1931) to have shown that this type of argument is not conclusive. For it may be the case that time or motion does exist, despite the fact that our concepts of these phenomena, on a detailed analysis, may prove to be inaccurate. For obviously the existence or nonexistence of a natural phenomenon is not dependent on what concept we have of it. Thus, with a terminology suggested by Anders Wedberg, a distinction has to be made between "the intending connotation" and "the confirmatory connotation" of a word.[4]

An explication of a concept can be inaccurate for two different reasons. (I intentionally avoid the word "analysis" because of its associations to analytic truth.) It may be the case that the purported explicans does not really get the point of what we conceive of when we conceive the explicandum. And it could be the case that the explicans is accurate to our way of conceiving an object but that this concept is inaccurate to reality. (This is analogous to what Johnson means by the two kinds of appropriateness above.)

In recommending us to ". . . make our senses the expositors of words, instead of making words the expositors of what our senses reveal" (Lect. I, par. 14), Johnson refers us to the reference *(bedeutung, denotatum)* as the only source of information which could tell us whether our explication is appropriate or not in the sense of (b) above.

This means that the reference of the word is the only source of our information as to the accuracy of its connotation, but it by no

LANGUAGE AND VALUE

means has the consequence that meaning and reference have to be confused. Our knowledge of our own concepts, i.e., the connotations of our words, can neither extend nor diminish our knowledge of something different from these concepts. And the denotata obviously are something different. Even if this may seem confusing, it is perhaps after all not so strange an opinion as would be supposed.

In his well-known paper "On Denoting," which has a very interesting affinity with Johnson's *Treatise on Language* ["This difference, which is purely an artifice of language *to condense a sentence into a single word*" (Lect. X, par. 12)], Bertrand Russell makes the observation that one important consequence of his theory of definite descriptions is that "when there is anything with which we do not have immediate acquaintance, but only definition by denoting phrases, then the propositions in which the thing is introduced by means of a denoting phrase do not really contain this thing as a constituent, but contain instead the constituents expressed by the several words of the denoting phrase." Russell draws the following conclusion:

> What we know is "So-and-so has a mind which has such and such properties" but we do not know "A has such and such properties," where A *is* the mind in question. In such a case we know the properties of a thing without having acquaintance with the thing itself, and without, consequently, knowing any single proposition of which the thing itself is a constituent.[5]

A consequence of Russell's theory, which strangely enough seems to be overlooked from time to time, is that no word which appears as an ultimate constituent of a descriptive phrase could lack denotatum, and that the description thus does never even purport to refer to a particular object.

The appropriateness (b) of a descriptive phrase to an object could thus only be checked independently, by observation of the particular object itself. Perhaps it may be useful to the reader to keep this in mind when we try to understand Johnson's distinction.

> The word "heap" signifies a sight and a feel, and hence possesses an existence and an oneness without reference to the separate grains of which the heap is composed;—while the unit gravity possesses in nature no existence independently of its constituent parts. Gravity, as a unit, is a verbal aggregation; while the heap, as a unit, is a sensible aggregation. Language disregards the distinction; the verbal oneness being equally complete in both cases (Lect. IV, par. 16).

This passage seems to give a rather clear idea of Johnson's intentions.

In the case of the word "heap," the ultimate test of the accuracy of an explicans of the connotation of "heap" would be a particular visual experience: the different grains form a unity in the visual field. And an explicans of the connotation of "heap" which did not take account of this experience would certainly not be accurate.

With the word "gravity," on the other hand, the situation appears to be different. Johnson seems to mean that we conceive of gravity as a unit. And this unit forms a part of our intending connotation of the word. The word certainly also has a reference; a number of particular experiences such as the sights of falling physical objects, feels of weight, or sights of different instruments.

But in contemplating the concept of gravity in order to give an explicans of our explicandum, we shall not find, by inspecting the different experiences which are the reference of the word, a sensible unity of the same type as we find in the sensible experience of a *heap* of stones. Thus if the question should arise whether our concept of gravity is accurate in making a unity behind the different phenomena referred to by the word part of its connotation, no investigation of the phenomena will give us any guidance. For the phenomena referred to by the word would not differ if the concept of gravity as a unit was inaccurate, while on the other hand they would differ if the concept of a heap as a unit was inaccurate.

The concept of gravity as a unit is exclusively verbal because it does not seem to follow with necessity from our observation of the sensible phenomena whether the unit ought to be part of the concept or not. Therefore to Johnson, the question of whether an unsupported stone would fall or not has a sensible significance only if the question is related to an actual experience.

The unity of gravity, like other concepts which Johnson supposed to lack sensible significance, is, so to speak, something which takes place exclusively *within* the conceptual or verbal machinery of our language. It could be disposed of in the same manner as Wittgenstein's beetles in the boxes.

In its remarkable anticipation of such modern theories of the nature of science as Bridgman's operationalism and Wittgenstein's later discussions of the concept of "seeing something as something," Alexander Bryan Johnson's philosophy seems to deserve much more attention than it has received for the past one hundred years. In his stubborn insistence on a strictly empirical concept of knowledge lies his lasting importance.

NOTES

1   In this paper all reference to Johnson's work is to the text of David Rynin's 1947 edition of *A Treatise on Language*.

2   George Berkeley, *A New Theory of Vision*, par. 49, here quoted from Berkeley, *A New Theory of Vision and Other Writing* (London, 1963).

3   Bertrand Russell, *The Problems of Philosophy* (London: Oxford University Press, 1946), p. 58.

4   Anders Wedberg, *Filosofins historia. III. Från Bolzano till Wittgenstein* (Stockholm, 1966), pp. 390–391.

5   Bertrand Russell, "On Denoting," *Mind*, Vol. XIV (1905), pp. 479–493.

SYMPOSIUM

♦ ♦ ♦ ♦ *MAX BLACK   Cornell University*
RUSSELL T. BLACKWOOD   Hamilton College
STILLMAN DRAKE   University of Toronto
K. T. FANN   Cleveland State University
LARS GUSTAFSSON   Bonniers Litterära Magasin
DAVID RYNIN   University of California

BLACKWOOD: An important criticism of Johnson, made some time ago by Mr. Rynin, and pressed today by Mr. Black, has been that Johnson fails to distinguish between the referent of a word (what it is that the word "table" points to—for example this table) and the meaning of the word "table" (what characteristics something would need to have if it were to be properly called a table).

On first inspection, this would seem no more than the sort of useless speculation to which Johnson was opposed. But if one substitutes for "table," "angels," "tomorrow's weather," "a perpetual-motion machine," or "the general happiness," one might face certain problems in holding that a word meant what it pointed to. If there are no angels to point to, does the word "angel" lack meaning? And what of the word "Mohican" if the last Mohican is gone? Still more, what of "tomorrow's weather"?

Yet a word in use would not seem to be about nothing at all. The word "Mohican" points, and in a way so does the word "angel." One might maintain that if a word did not point it would not be a word at all. The question I would ask this panel and this audience is the following: Is there a real gain in distinguishing the meaning of a

◊ ◊ ◊ *Condensed and edited by Russell T. Blackwood from a tape recording of the* Proceedings.

word from its referent—or does this distinction only introduce a needless confusion, a confusion which Johnson perceived and properly avoided?

RYNIN: Among contemporaries the difference between sense and reference is important. It is a distinction that one can make. It plays a role in an adequate theory of language as we understand it, and I think that if Johnson in some sense did not take account of it, this is a count against him from our point of view.

Now, there is the question: did he or did he not take account of it? I don't think one can deduce from the fact that he used the word "meaning" to refer to what nowadays is called "denotation" or "referent," that anything follows with respect to this issue. He himself was acutely aware of the difference between "propriety" (a proper or socially proper or historically proper locution) and whether a question, a statement, or a term had "meaning." So I think what we have to do if we want to be fair to him on this particular issue is to see how he handles this problem or whether he is even aware of it.

With respect to one of your examples, there is a passage in which he says that he doesn't know what the meaning of the word "decapitate" is because he hasn't witnessed a decapitation. As we would now say, so far as his experience goes, that subject is not denoted by any term that enters into his vocabulary. But he says "if I were to witness a decapitation tomorrow, then of course, that decapitation would be the meaning." It is clear that he is using "meaning" in the sense of "denotation." That's his privilege, whether we like it or not. Perhaps we can do better with a different terminology, but he is not bound by our terminology. We are bound by our duty to try to understand him in terms of his own principles, and not catch him up on what are verbal infelicities from our point of view, not his. If so, I think it is perfectly clear that what one wants there is there. He does not have a separate term. He had "verbal meaning" which gives meaning although there is no sensible meaning. He has "intellectual meaning" and "emotive meaning."

So in passing I take exception, if I may, to Professor Black's implication that when Johnson now and then says a word refers to no sensible existence, it is therefore without signification. Now it is perfectly obvious, it seems to me, that he is talking about sensible meaning and he makes that distinction and qualification *ad nauseam*. And none of us wants to bore our audience with constantly making senseless qualifications that are evident to everyone.

Mr. Blackwood is quite right in stating that when we say that it will rain tomorrow, there is some sense in which we must understand what is said. Otherwise we wouldn't know how to prepare for it or say that we were right or we were wrong. It is perfectly clear that Johnson has, in his own way, allowed for this. He is not a fool after all; he got around in the world, and took account of the weather here in Utica. It's all there. What is missing is that particular word. Now I don't want to lean over too far defending him. It may be that he was occasionally misled by not having that word. It is a useful word and much is made of it in our time, and rightly so. But I don't think we can impute to him all of the blunders which we would think inhere in a man's talk if he doesn't happen to know our pet vocabulary and know what philosophers one hundred years later find it useful to say.

BLACK: I think I would like to say a little about this, because I think my friend David Rynin and I are not seeing eye to eye here. To start with the last point. We are not talking about a technical term at all. The term "to refer" is part of the English language. The term "to mean" is part of the English language. Johnson uses both words. If he wants to say that the term doesn't refer to anything, he knew enough English to say it. He says quite explicitly that the term doesn't mean. It doesn't signify.

It's all very tolerant to say that a man has the right to use language as he likes. But Johnson himself was perfectly clear that there were standards of what he calls appropriateness. If you use the word "horse" and privately say "cow," you are going to mislead the audience. We are not dealing with a technical question. We are dealing with a straightforward question about whether, if a term does not sensibly refer, it is to be said to be meaningless. With all deference to Mr. Rynin, who probably knows more about the content of Johnson's writings than anyone else in the world, I still stick to my opinion, which I think I can sustain with detailed evidence, that in the absence of a systematic distinction between reference and meaning, Johnson constantly made this very mistake. That is, he would show that a term used in a particular way did not refer to anything at all, and then conclude that the statement in question was insignificant.

But Mr. Rynin wants us to say, "Well, when he said, 'insignificant,' he really meant 'without reference,' which is the same as uttering a tautology. He was just saying it doesn't refer, and it is uncharitable to interpret him in any other way." My interpretation is that Johnson, like many great men including Hume, Berkeley, Mach, and so on up to our time, including Russell, made this mistake—which seems incredible when you spread it out very plainly. But it is quite intelligible when you consider what leads to it. If you have an oversimplified theory of meaning, if without realizing it you identify meaning with reference, then the step from no reference to no meaning is very easy to make. There is no question of blaming anybody. It is a very natural error. The evidence is very plain in his discussion of negative statements. I mean those passages some of which I have already read—but I have many more—where Johnson says very explicitly that the negative statement is meaningless. He actually uses that expression.

DRAKE: What does that mean?

RYNIN: That means "without denotation," and then he still is correct.

BLACK: No sir. He is saying very clearly that it is insignificant, meaningless. He is not saying that it doesn't refer to anything—because he uses an argument. He says it doesn't refer to anything, therefore it is meaningless. You are putting him in the position of offering the argument that because it doesn't refer to anything, therefore it doesn't refer to anything.

DRAKE: Professor Black, do you know any specific instance where A. B. Johnson uses the word "meaningless"? I know many in which he uses "insignificant," and you quoted one or two of those.

BLACK: And there are also passages where he says explicitly that by "insignificant" he means the same as "meaningless."

DRAKE: Not quite. "Insignificant" he does not define. He does define, by this sort of cross-reference, the verb "signify," but not the adjective "significant." And that is a little jump that a professional philosopher is almost sure to make. If he defined "signify," then "significant" must be precisely the same, but I think not. I think Johnson was writing for an ordinary audience. In the cases you quoted—where he said that a negation which refers to no sensible particular is insignificant—I am pretty sure the context shows he meant that we need not take any account of this, we need not change our opinion or modify our belief in the universal proposition. "Insignificant" has the sense of "of no moment" or "trifling." "Wait until someone comes up with a particular stone that doesn't fall and then we will reconsider our universal." So I think that here the attempt to apply professional, philosophical, terminological standards to Johnson merely results in a sort of punning criticism, where you work from "mean" through "refer" to "signify." Then you run on to the word "insignificant" and conclude that that was to be the complement of the others. And I believe that is not so. If you run into Johnson's use of "meaningless," I certainly would reconsider this opinion.

BLACK: I must repeat that we are not dealing with professional philosophical uses, whatever they are. We are talking about the interpretation of a man writing English and I simply cannot accept the suggestion just made that "insignificant" means "trifling." It doesn't. It's used in a more pregnant sense. There are many, many passages to show it. For example, I see one right here, "is significant of nothing but the data which are adduced in proof of the theory." Now, that would never bear a gloss of "trifling."

DRAKE: No. That one won't.

BLACK: What is the opposite of "trifling"? I mean, it's just not going to fit. If you say "is significant of nothing," you can paraphrase that, if you like, as it "refers to nothing" or "means nothing"—either one is a plausible candidate. But you may not give it the interpretation which is being offered, namely the popular sense of "insignificant" as meaning "trifling."

DRAKE: Just a minute. I am simply saying that he uses the words the way we use them—sometimes meaning one thing and sometimes another. In the case of the salvo, or the empty negation, of general propositions, I say the context there shows that he means "insignificant" in the sense that "we need not take any account of it." I don't mean by that, that whenever he uses the word "significant" he means "we must take account" or "not significant," "we must not," or anything of that sort. But I do think that you can't take the word "insignificant," with respect to the assertion that perhaps some stones untried will not fall, apart from his whole theory of meaning.

BLACK: We are not going to settle this without more detailed reference to the text than we have time for. I will simply repeat that I have read these texts, those two books at least, with very great care and am perfectly persuaded as of now that when Johnson said that negative statements are insignificant he meant that in the pregnant sense of whatever you take significance to mean, reference or meaning. With respect to Professor Rynin, there is a further question—whether he was just saying "has no reference" or "has no meaning." I think that is a little more difficult. But as to the idea that he was saying that negative statements are simply unimportant or trifling, I just cannot see that in the text at all. It would have been, by the way, a very odd thing for him to say, since he takes the affirmative propositions to be the negations of the negative propositions. If he thought the negative proposition was trifling, I suppose he would have said that the negation of a trifling proposition was still trifling. It just won't fit the text, I am afraid.

DRAKE: No indeed. And I would never assert anything of the sort. I think his theory of universals is perfectly clear. You are entitled to assert any universal proposition so long as the attempt at refutation is only the assertion of a possibility that something might exist which hasn't been found yet. This he says is "insignificant," and I take that to mean "trifling." He calls it a salvo, an empty salvo. But he does not say this of negative propositions in general; merely of the attempt to question a universal for which no exceptional particular is known. Johnson's rule is perfectly clear, namely: "don't bother me until you bring me the exceptional case and exhibit it to me."

BLACKWOOD: Mr. Fann, would you like to comment on this issue?

FANN: Not directly. I would like to make a general remark and it may touch upon some of the issues. I think the most important point is to first see what Johnson was doing. I am most struck by his conception of philosophy and I think his most valuable contribution is his method of attacking or approaching philosophical problems. In this I think he has anticipated the contemporary movement typified by Wittgenstein. He was mainly interested in dissolving philosophical problems. He sees the perplexity and paradoxical nature of philosophical utterances, especially metaphysical statements. He wanted to show why those statements are so mystifying. To show that, he analyzed the structure of language. But to criticize him for not having come up with an adequate philosophy of language may be to misunderstand his intention. He was interested in showing clearly the nature of philosophical statements, metaphysical statements which are presented in empirical form, but he wanted to show that they are not empirical in fact. It is a verbal, or, in our contemporary terminology, a conceptual question, not an empirical, factual question. Johnson held that the mystifying feature of metaphysical statements can be dissolved and will vanish if we understand the structure of language.

With respect to the nature of language, he concentrated on the sensible meaning, the sensible signification, of language. To criticize him for not taking account of words like "if" or "or," which have no sensible signification, would be irrelevant to his intention. His theory of language arose from his work on epistemology, namely his *Physiology of the Senses*. He said, "We can know sensible things only through our senses." So he wanted to find out the limits of our sensible faculties. We must array in the senses our statements in the form of empirical sensible propositions, but in fact we do not. It was Johnson's intention to show that. And that seems to me his purpose. Therefore much of the criticism may be missing the point of his original intention.

BLACKWOOD: Mr. Gustafsson?

GUSTAFSSON: I do sympathize very much with what Mr. Fann says. I do think there is a certain danger of completely missing the point with Johnson if you regard him as too much committed. You could easily find out that he is to some extent committed to the ideas of his time. For example, as Mr. Black clearly observed, he is committed to some extent to a bearer theory of meaning. But Johnson does not make any attempt to analyze this relation, the bearer relation, and that of course is simply because he is not interested in a detailed sort of ontological analysis of that relation. His main interest is something quite different. It is to formulate a sort of vision, a sort of methodic vision, which is closely connected with something he has observed in the role of a particular in human knowledge. And I think it may be his concept of sensible significance can be seen as a sort of parallel to Frege's "reference," and it may even be that this has led to some inconsistencies. But still there is something more in this concept than just the concept of reference, and that is his idea of the ultimate simplicity of everything which is given to us by means of acquaintance.

BLACK: I think that Mr. Johnson, like any serious thinker, would wish to be protected from his friends when they ascribe to him a vision. I don't know what a vision would be. Johnson was a serious thinker who by his own account spent fifty years on this subject. It wasn't a matter of vision. He was trying to investigate language just as thoroughly as he could. And of course he was interested in just the things that Mr. Gustafsson says he wasn't interested in. Of course a man cannot do everything. He can't invent an entire new science, even if he is a genius. And I have no interest at all in awarding good marks or bad marks to Johnson. He escapes any such ridiculous business. But on the substantive issue, there is a risk of misunderstanding what the whole thing is about. I don't think for a moment that Mr. Fann's idea, which comes from recent philosophy, that Johnson was interested in showing that philosophers were not scientists—which is what it amounts to—was anything central to him at all. He speaks constantly in the most general terms. He doesn't address himself to philosophers particularly. He is at least as critical of scientists as he is of philosophers. He is talking about language. He has a grand theme and he applies it to everyday life. It's not this very specialized theme Mr. Fann has described. As for the idea about the simplicity of experience, which is Mr. Gustafsson's point, again I simply don't see it. I think the aim is a much grander one. It isn't a narrowly technical one. It is really an attempt to display the grand plan of language and its relation to reality. It's a tremendous, grandiose project, beautiful in its audacity. But you can't do it, unfortunately, without having a metaphysical position. I think that if Johnson had been in contact with a first-rate, sympathetic, professional philosopher, the point would have been brought home to him and he might very well have developed a systematic metaphysics to parallel his views on language.

FANN: But it seems to me quite clear that Johnson did not have a metaphysics or ontology, a view of the nature of experience, the nature of the world. He disclaimed having anything to say about it.

BLACK: No, he says quite explicitly things like, "reality is a congregation of particulars." That is a straightforward statement about the nature of reality, and one simply can't get around it. I don't know any place where he disclaims having a theory about reality.

DRAKE: I think that Mr. Fann is quite right in saying that Johnson attempted no system, that he stayed out of trouble, and that all the trouble one might see in him is in one's own viewpoint. I take it that Johnson's real point was not to construct a theory of language at all, but to tell his listeners here in Utica that language was liable to certain defects that undoubtedly remained unknown to them, that these defects were moreover irremovable, and that the most we can do is to make them known, even "as we erect a beacon on a shoal that cannot be removed." Now beacons on shoals are useful to mariners and that's similar to the usefulness of Johnson. He helps ordinary people detect rather monstrous errors they have made in their own thinking or that they see in their newspapers. After that they think a little better. If he didn't erect a beacon on every shoal, including unexplored oceans which you philosophers have since then explored, you can hardly blame him for not putting beacons on shoals in oceans that never came into the knowledge of his own navigation. Nor, I think, even if he marked sixteen shoals where nobody was accustomed to sail, or left sixteen shoals unmarked that were right in the paths of commerce, should I blame him too much, so long as he saw clearly that what you do with shoals is not just go on getting shipwrecked, but put beacons up wherever you see them. And this is what he has done well.

RYNIN: It's obvious that whatever he said, and whatever we impute to him, he knew as well as the next man how to tell whether there would be a decapitation. Now, he attended one. It was an execution of an Indian. That's where one of the founders of Hamilton College gave such an eloquent speech. The real question is the relation between statements we make, whose truth or falsity we are not now in a position to determine, and may never be in a position to determine, namely those about the past and those about the future. Of some of them we understand perfectly well how we would tell whether they were true or false if we were in the suitable situation. If this is what one wants the notion of sense or connotation for, I am certain Johnson would quite agree. I am sure he would answer that he knows perfectly well how to determine whether a man will be decapitated. But suppose someone says "But wouldn't it be a good thing if you distinguished between two senses of meaning, and then you could say that this has meaning, only now we are not talking about denotation or referent, we're talking about sense or connotation?" I think he would say, "If that means, 'would you know how to tell?' (which is very close to his view) why, yes, of course." It never occurred to him that this was a real issue or problem, and I'm sure that the deductions we make from it would only have amused him. I haven't the slightest doubt that he would say to our criticisms "obviously, who would have ever thought otherwise, and why did you think that I wasn't talking about what I said I was talking about, and it is clear what I was talking about from my theory of meaning, namely, what you gentlemen, oddly enough, call denotation or referent."

BLACK: But he does say, for example on page 114 of the *Treatise,* "Words signify the objects to which they are applied," and then immediately afterward he says, "The precise meaning of the word in each application is the sight itself." And there you have the two, "signify" and "meaning," tied together. In short, I'm content to say that in the absence of an automatic, systematic way of making the distinction, the slide from one to the other will occur. It occurs in Russell, it occurs in Berkeley, and it occurs in Aristotle. It's an old and elementary point that if there is an important distinction and you have nothing in your language that marks it, you will, without knowing what you are doing, slide from one to the other. If you don't distinguish between men and women, but use a single word, fallacy will result.

Finally, I would like to say something about the interesting point that Mr. Drake raised about beacons. I'm dubious about the analogy, because in the case of the shoal and the beacon on it, the danger is clear: the danger is one of shipwreck. But in the case of language, half the problem is to know what the danger really is. Both Mr. Fann and Mr. Drake speak as if somehow the philosophical or scientific arguments that are "disposed of" by Johnson are just obviously bad. I don't share this opinion. I don't regard Johnson's remarks on Zeno, for example, as of any value at all. And I think in general, treated as philosophical discussion of specific philosophical issues, Johnson's attempts, though interesting, are not terribly good. What interests me is the general view of language. Now whether you call it a theory or not, if you have a man who is quite properly making general remarks about language, for the sake of dealing with the whole thing and not just with examples, you have a theorist. And what's wrong with that?

ALEXANDER BRYAN JOHNSON'S PLAN FOR A "COLLATED DICTIONARY"

♦ ♦ ♦ ♦ ♦ *ROBERT SONKIN*

ONE ASPECT of Johnson's interest in language that has received comparatively little attention is his plan (abortive, as it turned out) for "a new species of dictionary," which he first announced in a pamphlet published in 1830. It was to be entitled a "Collated Dictionary, or a Complete Index to the English Language; designed to exhibit together all words which relate to the same subject, for the benefit of persons who are not acquainted with the whole compass of the language, and to assist the memory of persons who are acquainted." [1]

The plan was next presented in the form of a lecture to the New York State Lyceum in Utica on August 10, 1831, and printed as part of the Proceedings of the Lyceum for that year.[2] It was also printed separately in the same year under the title *A Method of Acquiring a Full Knowledge of the English Language* [3] (quotations are from this version), presented to the American Lyceum in New York in May 1834,[4] and finally printed in shortened form in *Our American Union* (1857).[5]

Johnson begins his lecture by commenting on the copiousness of our language, "rich with spoils from every other," but "uncollected except in the Babel of an alphabetical arrangement." Webster,

◊ ◊ ◊ ◊ ◊ *Associate Professor, Department of Speech, The City College of the City University of New York. Coauthor (with L. Levy and E. W. Mammem) of* Voice *and* Diction Handbook; *author of articles in* American Speech *and* Quarterly Journal of Speech.

whose definitions and etymologies he admires but whose innovations in orthography he deplores, lists 70,000 words.[6] "These all men are supposed to know. On this false supposition is founded the alphabetical arrangement of our dictionaries. To teach us the words themselves lexicography has never made an attempt" (p. 4).

This is obvious once it is pointed out: one can only look up a word if one already knows it or has previously encountered it. That a word may exist, related to other words which one does know, the ordinary alphabetical arrangement of a dictionary will not tell us. "If irony were suited to so grave an evil, a lexicographer might say to students, with reference to his definitions, what a celebrated cookery book says of cooking a hare—first, 'catch it' " [7] (p. 6).

The "energy" of our language "consists chiefly in possessing words in sets; a substantive, adjective, verb, and adverb constituting a set: as, *knowledge, knowing, know, knowingly.*" When these parts of speech are, as in this case, clearly related in form,

> alphabetical precedence places them so nearly together that a reference to one of them discloses the other. But in very numerous cases the different parts of speech are not thus derived, and we have no systematic means of learning their existence: for instance, can the verb, *to vanish,* be expressed adjectively [sic]? . . . Why should we not find under the word *vanish* . . . that its adjective is *evanescent* (p. 5)?

What, for example, he asks, are *cobweb, summer, spring, tree, son,* adjectively? [The answers are: *araneous, estival, vernal, arboreal, filial* (p. 6).] "Can the adjective *tender,* be expressed verbially [sic]? Can the substantive *pauper,* be expressed verbially? Few of our youth, I fear, can tell me that *intenerate* and *depauperate* are the verbs" (p. 7).

What are the verbs for *doctrine, naked, abscess, climate, timid, arithmetical tables?* [*Indoctrinate, denude, imposthumate, acclimate, intimidate, tabulate.*] What are the adverbs for *chance, money, praise, war, shyness?* [*Casually, pecuniarily, eulogistically, belligerently, coyly* (p. 7).]

First, then a "collated dictionary" would group together those words that form a "set" so that they could be presented simultaneously. In addition, it would give for each word all of its synonyms, and distinguish their meanings:

> In the abundant copiousness of our language, a word has usually several adjectives. *Copper* has the English derivative *cop-*

pery, and the Latin derivative *cuperous* [sic], consisting of copper; and *eruginous,* partaking of the nature of copper. *Iron* has the adjective, *irony;* also *chalybeate,* impregnated with iron; *ferruginous,* partaking of the nature of iron, and *ferreous,* consisting of iron.

Bark (the rind of a tree) has, in addition to *barky, corticated,* resembling bark; *corticose,* full of bark; and *cortical. Cold* has *gelid,* very cold; *frigid,* which is cold when applied to the feelings; and *frigorific,* producing cold; also *algific* and *algid* (p. 6).

The dictionary would also bring together words that have some association in various areas. For example, under *color:* "possessing one color only, as a painting or object—*concolor";* of the color of mud—*lutarious";* "of the color of lemon—*citrine";* "of the color of a dry leaf—*feuillemort* [sic]"; "of the color of straw—*festucine"* (p. 12).

> To say that a man is a sinner, signifies that he has committed sin; but have we a word which signifies merely, that he is liable to sin? We have no means of knowing unless we accidentally meet with *peccable.* Have we a word that signifies a hatred of women? I admit that the word should be stricken from our vocabulary, but while it is in all our dictionaries, we ought to find it under the word, *woman,* that we may at least show our gallantry by reprobating its existence (p. 8).

Another important relationship between words is that which they bear to their antonyms (or, as Johnson calls them, their "correlatives"), and these, too, should be collated. So: *war/peace; potent/impotent; desecrate/consecrate; analogous/anomalous; dissonant/consonant; patent/latent*—"How else would a youth know that the correlative of *symmetry* is *asymmetry?"* (pp. 8–9).

Johnson then discusses yet another relationship between words which is of great interest: that between "affirmatives" and "negatives" (or "privatives"). This is the relationship between a word indicating a state or quality and one indicating the absence thereof (as distinguished from its opposite or "correlative"). For example, *unwearied* is the negative of *wearied; unconsecrated* is the negative of *consecrated* (the correlative, I assume, is *desecrated*); *remembered* of *unremembered* [the correlative is presumably *forgotten* (p. 9)].

He stresses the importance of this relationship with a philosophical speculation:

> Man is so constituted that he can recognize no quality till he can recognize also its privative. The blind cannot recognize

darkness, because they cannot know what "not darkness" is. The deaf cannot recognize silence, because they cannot know what "not silence" is.

If light was as unintermitted to us as darkness is to the blind, we should be unable to recognize light, because we should not know what "not light" is (p. 9).

There follows what seems to be a rather daring theological flight:

The Scriptures teach us that God is omnipresent. Were his omnipresence as apparent to all our senses as light is to our eyes, and temperature to our feelings, his unintermitted presence would prevent us from recognizing his presence. Should he withdraw his presence, so as to let us know what his "not presence" is, we should be able to recognize his presence (p. 9).

And finally:

We may suppose that life has an individuality, but we recognize it not, even in our own bodies. Could we, however, become conscious of what "not life" is we should immediately attain a knowledge of life (p. 9).

But Johnson quickly drops his discussion of this principle ("too novel and abstruse to be discussed thus incidentally"), to give a few further examples of words and their negatives: *one*/"more than one" or *multiplicate; laudable/illaudable; evident/inevident;* "capable of being set on fire"/*uninflammable;* "capable of weeping"/*illachrymable;* "capable of being broken"/*infrangible;* "capable of decay"/*indefectible;* "devout"/*indevout;* "capable of being tasted"/*intastable* (p. 9).

There are certain other kinds of groupings that Johnson would like to see. Under, for example, *digestion: peptic, eupeptic, dyspeptic,* etc.; *death: euthanasia, posthumous, demise, defunct,* etc.; *day: ephemeral, diurnal, triduan, diary,* etc.; *murder: patricide, sororicide, deicide, infanticide, tyrannicide,* etc.; *transparent: opaque, pellucid, translucent,* etc.; *visible: sapid, tangible, audible, odorous,* etc.; *shoe: calceated, discalceated,* etc.

In short, I desire a complete index [8] to our language, so that a person who refers to any word may see all the words with which it is connected in signification;—may see also how the word can be expressed substantively, adjectively, verbially, and adverbially; and may see its synonyms, its correlatives, its negatives, and affirmatives (p. 11).

Johnson's originality lies in his scheme of arranging words in groups according to their related meanings, so that words of associated sense but of different origin (Anglo-Saxon, Latin, Greek) can be brought into immediate proximity—as they cannot be in a strict alphabetical arrangement. As we shall see later, Johnson did not mean to abandon the alphabetical arrangement entirely, but probably intended to have major groups of words gathered under certan key headings, and a system of cross-indexing elsewhere.

Grouping together words of associated meaning for pedagogical purposes was by no means a new idea. In fact, the earliest "dictionaries" in English (or rather Anglo-Saxon) were "glossaries" (that is, collections of "glosses" or interlinear translations of Latin words), in which the Latin words and their translations were grouped under such headings as parts of the body, domestic animals, wild beast, fishes, trees, plants, names of relationships, tools, articles of clothing, etc.[9] And there is probably not a school grammar of a foreign language today which does not group vocabulary items under such heads as the family, the schoolroom, the railroad station, and so on.

Johnson's collations are different in that they are largely based on grammatical relationships, and would bring together, for example, noun, verb, adjective, and adverb. For countless words in English, the various members of such "sets" may be words derived from different languages, and not automatically derived from one another. A "Collated Dictionary" would be a most convenient source for learning these frequently difficult words—and it is clear from Johnson's examples that it was the unusual and literary words that he was most interested in.

In other respects, although we may be sure Johnson was unaware of it, some of his ideas were not at all new in the history of dictionary making. For example, his intention to introduce hard or learned words was itself in a very old tradition. Through the seventeenth and into the eighteenth century, the emphasis in English dictionaries had been on defining "hard" words (especially the "inkhorn" terms and technical borrowings and coinages from Latin and Greek) in simpler English terms. Some of these words were hard indeed: for example, in *The English Dictionarie* of Henry Cockeram (1623), one finds such words as *adecastick* "one that will do just howsoever"—i.e., do justly under any circumstances, and without being bribed; *bubulcitate* "to cry like a cow boy"—i.e., like a cowherd, not an American cowboy; *collocuplicate* "to enrich." Copied from one dictionary to another, some ghost words like these led very long lives.

But Cockeram introduced a new feature. In addition to his section of hard words, he had one devoted to defining "vulgar" words in "refined" terms. Thus, for "baked," *pistated;* "to bolt a door,"*obserate;* "to abound," *exuperate;* "too great plenty," *uberty;* "he and I are of an age," *we are coetaneous;* and "youthful babbling," *juvenile inaniloquence.*

Cockeram was, of course, followed by others. For example, the editor of the third edition (1663) of John Bullokar's *An English Expositor* also added an index of "ordinary English words" defined in terms of a more "scholastick" nature. Thus: "bashful," *verecund;* "howling," *ululation;* "huckster," *regrator.*

Also, Johnson's plan to provide all the synonyms of a word had been anticipated by many compilers of dictionaries. For example, to take a very early work, there was *An Alphabetical Dictionary* by William Lloyd, printed at the end of John Wilkins' *An Essay towards a Real Character, and a Philosophical Language* (London, 1668). "A patient and reasonably intelligent reader" of this dictionary, would find in the definition of the word *corruption,* for example, "the carefully discriminated words *defiling, destroying, infection, decay, putrefaction, unholiness, viciousness, unchastity, bribery,* etc.; and for each of these, in turn, he would find a long list of further synonyms, antonyms, and related words." [10] Later, during the eighteenth century, more and more attention was paid by dictionary makers to refining definitions and developing extensive and discriminating synonymies.

Johnson was, then, in purpose if not in method, continuing in an earlier tradition of lexicography: that of introducing learned words, through more scholarly translations of common words and through nicely discriminated synonyms.

A. B. Johnson makes the interesting observation that in Samuel Johnson's definitions of familiar words "there are constant evidences of a desire to reveal unusual words." Therefore, for example, the famous definition of *network* as "any thing reticulated or decussated, at equal distances, with interstices between the intersections," far from arousing ridicule (as it did) for its pompous Latinity, should elicit our gratitude for the new words it reveals to us. We look up *network* not to find out what *network* means (since surely we know this already), but to learn new words related to it (*network* adjectively is *reticulated,* and so on).

Indeed, many of Samuel Johnson's definitions of common words are of this type: *butter,* "an unctuous substance made by agitating the cream of milk, till the oil separates from the whey"; *cough,* "a convulsion of the lungs, vellicated by some sharp serosity"; *drunkenness,* "habitual ebriety"; *dryness,* "1. want of moisture; siccity; 2. want of succulence." Occasionally these Latinate definitions are not entirely Dr. Johnson's own, but may be found in some of his sources, such as Benjamin Martin's dictionary (*Lingua Britannica reformata,* 1749), or Ephraim Chamber's *Cyclopaedia, or An Universal Dictionary of Arts and Sciences* (1728).[11]

On the other hand, like many of his predecessors, Samuel Johnson frequently made no real effort to define simple words. Thus in most seventeenth-century dictionaries, for example, *dog* is merely "a well-known creature." In Bailey's dictionary (1721), which provided the basis for Samuel Johnson's work, it is slightly elevated to "a quadruped well-known." Johnson's own definition in 1755 is not much more copious: "A domestic animal remarkably various in his species; comprising the mastiff, the spaniel, the bulldog, the greyhound, the hound, the terrier, the cur, with many others. The larger sort are used as a guard; the less for sports."

The fact is that Samuel Johnson was fully aware of the difficulties in defining simple words. In his Preface he writes:

> To interpret a language by itself is very difficult; many words cannot be explained by synonimes [sic], because the idea signified by them has not more than one appellation; nor by paraphrase, because simple words cannot be described.

Here he may be echoing Ephraim Chambers who "had also drawn the distinction between simple words, which are inexplicable because the simple ideas attached to them cannot be communicated by language but must be had from sensation, and terms which *can* be defined, since they symbolize a combination of simple ideas. . . ."[12]

This distinction A. B. Johnson (whether independently, or following Chambers or Samuel Johnson) had made, too, in his 1824 *Address* on eloquence:

> In a rude age, language consists of such words, as denote sensible objects; but when a nation has meliorated, the language comprehends words that import sentences and phrases. The Saxon was far from its pristine state, when it was implanted in England; still, if we examine our language, we shall discover that the Saxon part includes but few terms, which do not name either sensible objects or sensible operations. *To eat, to sleep, to stand;* and *man, fire, water,* and *earth* are all Saxon. Nay, so

LANGUAGE AND VALUE

comprehensive is this characteristic, that you will seldom err, if you impute to the Saxon every similar word.[13]

Johnson returned to this idea in the 1828 edition of the *Treatise on Language:*

> Perhaps no language is so uncultivated as not to possess words of both the above classes [i.e., those that have a signification which refers to our senses, and those that refer to other words]; but rude languages are chiefly composed of words that name sensible phenomena only, that is words which are undefinable. If we examine the English language we shall find that our Saxon words are principally of the above character . . . and when we find an undefinable word that is not Saxon, we may generally discover that we have a Saxon word that is synonimous [sic]; for instance, *infant* is Latin; but we have the synonimous word, *child* which is Saxon.[14]

However, in the plan for the dictionary, A. B. Johnson seems no longer concerned with the distinction between undefinable and definable words. He apparently believes that all words can be defined, either through a Latinate periphrasis in the manner of Samuel Johnson, or through a synonym borrowed directly from a foreign "cultivated" language.

He had already pointed out in the *Address* on eloquence that these borrowings from cultivated languages are valuable in English in three ways: by contributing to the richness or copiousness of our vocabulary, by making possible fine distinctions of meaning, and by making for conciseness:

> At Babel, a moral convulsion severed the bond which united men in one community, and burst many a ligament that knit family to family in the officiousness of love; still from this hopeless calamity has originated the copiousness of expression, the nice distinctions which constitute the apparent boundaries of apparent synonymes [sic]; and the term that comprehends a sentence (p. 10).

For example:

> The terms *hundred* and *thousand* are . . . Saxon, but here terminated the ascending series; hence to denote *ten hundred thousand,* our ancestors were compelled to employ three words; but by resorting to Italian, we condense them into one—a *million.* What we denominate a *trillion,* they could not signify, but with several sentences, that would occupy some minutes to indite.
>
> Again, in an early period of literature, if I had wished to say

that there is an art, which, by the appearance of a man, determines his talents and dispositions, I must have employed a circumlocution as tedious as the above: but, by the adoption of a Greek word, the whole can be expressed in the single term— *physiognomy.*

To enable us so to consolidate sentences and phrases, our predecessors employed every known ancient language, and every modern . . . [with the result that] while we were studying foreign languages, a word, which required in its translation a number of native terms, came in time to supersede the use of the explanatory sentence.

[To disregard the advantages we have thus derived, and] . . . employ a plurality of words when our intention can be expressed by one, is not more unskillful than to utter a repetition of units, when we desire to denote a hundred. Dr. Johnson has been accused of using too freely, words of uncommon occurrence; but examination will satisfy us, that he was thereby avoiding the verbosity with which unskillful writers are overwhelmed (pp. 9–10).

He repeats this in the *Treatise* (1828):

When men acquire a knowledge of a foreign language, they enrich their own. A foreign word supersedes gradually the words which constitute its interpretation; instead of saying, "an arm of the sea," we now use the word *estuary,* and thereby condense a sentence into a word (p. 151).

And he repeats the point at greater length in the dictionary plan of 1830, and with further examples. To cite just one: "*Suicide* enables me to express with a word what, without that word, I must employ a sentence to express" (p. 8).

Johnson stresses the importance of conciseness again and again (although, for that matter, is *estuary* really more concise than *arm of the sea,* which contains just as many syllables?), and it is probably his own efforts to achieve conciseness that account for the terseness and aphoristic quality of his prose at its best.

In the *Address* on eloquence he applied the criterion of conciseness to Henry Clay, and took him to task for saying, for example, when talking about public distress: "It is like the atmosphere which surrounds us, all must inhale it:—and none can escape it."

One of the assertions is superfluous. Nay if I were severe, I might insist, that it is pleonastic to say the atmosphere surrounds us. Circumambiency is as inseparable from a definition of the atmosphere, as fluidity is from a definition of water (p. 8).

He objects to the use of an adjective to express something already conveyed by the noun it modifies ("hopeless despair"), and to the use of an adverb of time if it is already implied in the tense of the verb ("the languour which *now* prevails in our city")—both these examples being also from Clay (p. 8).

In the dictionary plan of 1830 he gave further examples

> . . . for instance, *pellicle,* involves in its meaning a superlative degree of thinness, the thinnest kind of skin;—hence, to say, a "thin pellicle," destroys the character of the word, by taking from it all that prevents its being synonymous with *skin.* . . . *Glance* is another example. It signifies the slightest view; hence to say a *slight glance* makes the word synonymous with view; thereby destroying a word which advantageously expresses a phrase. *Faint glimmer, petty pilfering, remote antiquity*, are also examples (p. 14).

He goes so far as to ask, "What, but a want of knowledge, produces the uncouth compound *side by side,* when we have the adjective [sic] *abreast?*" (p. 7).

This last example hardly seems to betray an abysmal "want of knowledge," but there is no doubt that Johnson felt his dictionary would provide a valuable fund of information about the English language not easily available elsewhere. He insists that the source of his proposal is "not the suggestion of knowledge but of ignorance."

Johnson had been painfully aware of the difficulties he had labored under as a youth due to a lack of formal schooling. The learning and elegance of expression which he commanded in his maturity had been achieved with great effort. "The discipline of regular instruction" might, among other things, have taught him to achieve conciseness of style much earlier in life. In the autobiography he tells us that he had been "sophomorically ornate at an age when regularly educated men are simple, natural, and mature."

He had been conscious of his lack of training in the very rudiments of the English language. Speaking of his mother in the autobiography (she had been born in Holland), he says that

> [S]he ultimately spoke English with scarcely any foreign accent, but mixing less with society than my father, her choice of words was less ample than his, and her general information more restricted. Thus indoctrinated while young to no very accurate phraseology I continually found, as I verged towards manhood, that I not only had much to learn, but also much to unlearn in words and pronunciation.

He says further:

> The greatest need that I felt in my attempts at composition, and they began early, was an ignorance of syntax; to say nothing of orthography, which compelled me continually to resort to a dictionary; and in such resorts I was embarrassed by my ignorance of etymology. A great fault in me, consisted in an unwillingness to admit my literary ignorance; and on the contrary a pretension to more literature than I possessed—a fault which was probably induced by my having read much for my age, and thus enabling me to appear more learned than I was; an appearance which pleased my vanity and was more attempted than restrained. Indeed the need of grammar is unfelt in proportion to a person's ignorance of grammar; and this was a great obstruction to my acquiring the knowledge, for the labour seemed great and the advantages of the knowledge were unobvious. I, however, procured a small Murray's grammar, and attempted to learn it; and I believe I should never have succeeded had not a lad, who was a shop boy in my father's store, expressed to me a regret at his ignorance of grammar. He had studied it somewhat at school, before he came into my father's service; and knew much more of it than I did. But he supposed I understood it, and asked me to teach him, and I consented. In endeavouring to instruct him, I made some progress in instructing myself; but I was twenty years old, and perhaps more, before I could apply the rules of syntax to my own composition, and properly understood the etymology of words, so as to consult a dictionary understandingly.

By the "etymology of words" I think that Johnson probably means that knowledge of foreign roots which would enable one to find the related nouns, verbs, adjectives, adverbs of "sets," and their correlatives, privatives, etc., as they have been described above. (How does one express *tender* verbally? What is *network* adjectively?) This is precisely what the "Collated Dictionary" would have given the reader.

In the lecture he gives one further instance of his "want of knowledge." He says that he knows that English has a word "which expresses adjectively a stepmother" (p. 13), but that he has forgotten it. A dictionary drawn up according to his plan would have supplied the word immediately under the entry *stepmother*.

Johnson's "Collated Dictionary," then, would have been just such a work as he had felt the need of in his youth, a "self-help" book intended for young people situated as he had been, or "for the benefit of persons who are not acquainted with the whole compass of the language," and which might even serve, as he puts it, "to assist the memories of persons who are"—or, one might add, who think they are.

LANGUAGE AND VALUE

Johnson also tells us in his lecture how he began the actual production of the dictionary:

> I procured two blank folio books. Each is the size of a volume of newspapers. On the outer edge of every second page, the book binder pasted a column, cut from an English dictionary [Johnson does not, alas, tell us which dictionary he used].
>
> Having a whole dictionary thus formed of single columns, with a blank margin of almost two folio pages to every column, I took another dictionary [which?], and with a scissors cut out for instance, the word, *abacus,* with its definition. This word purports to be a counting table. I pasted it in my dictionary against the verb *to count.* But *abacus* is also "the uppermost member of a column." I therefore cut another *abacus* with its definition, from a supplemental dictionary [!] and pasted it into mine, against the word *column.*
>
> After a little familiarity with the labour, and with the assistance of my children to whom it was a pleasant and instructive amusement, I could generally cut out two hundred words of an evening, and place them appropriately into my dictionary (pp. 11–12).

With this picture of fun-and-games in a Utica household in the late 1820's, Johnson ends his lecture. He adds that since the completion of the dictionary would be "mere mechanical labour," he is leaving that task to others. Many years later in his autobiography he says that he had hoped his son, William Clarkson Johnson, would complete it, "but he never did."

The 1830 version of the lecture from which quotations have been taken carries an interesting colophon:

> NOTE!—Some persons understood this address as recommending a dictionary that is not to be alphabetical in its arrangement. They are mistaken. The proposed dictionary is not to differ from other dictionaries, except in possessing the suggested collocations [Johnson uses *collocation* and *collation* indifferently] adscititiously to the ordinary matter.

Here, as I have suggested before, Johnson indicates that he did not expect to retreat entirely from "the Babel of an alphabetical arrangement," within which he still hoped to place his groups of words. (It may be, of course, that he had modified his thoughts about arrangement to some extent under the influence of comments on his lecture, and was not trying to make his idea of a dictionary appear less radical to his readers.) At any rate, as in the case of Samuel Johnson's definition of *network,* we should be grateful for having made the acquaintance of *adscititiously.*

Among the letters which Johnson received about his plan, he must have been especially pleased by one dated [15] August 30, 1831, from the distinguished patriot, lawyer, and philologist of Philadelphia, Peter Stephen Du Ponceau (1760–1844), urging him to undertake the work of completing the dictionary. The classification of words "by families," he says, "would certainly be useful to facilitate the study & the acquisition of the English language, which, on account of its Anomalies seems to require it more than any other." He points out, however, that "this plan was acted upon by Court De Gébelin. . . . The only difference is that he classed the words in families with respect to their Etymologies whereas you would do it in respect to the Sense."

The reference is to Antoine Court de Gébelin (1725–1784), for whom Du Ponceau had worked as secretary in Paris for a time before joining Baron von Steuben to serve as his secretary-translator and aide-de-camp in the Continental Army (but Du Ponceau deserves much fuller discussion in his own right somewhere). Gébelin's *Le Monde primitif* appeared in nine volumes in Paris between 1773 and 1784 (after his sudden death—through the malpractice of Mesmer, it was rumored [16]—his notes and manuscripts for nine further volumes were scattered and lost). Volumes 5, 6–7, and 9 are etymological dictionaries of French, Latin, and Greek respectively. But, as Du Ponceau pointed out, in these works the words are grouped according to the roots from which they are supposed to be derived, whereas Johnson's plan was to group English words according to their sense, whatever their etymologies.

Johnson also preserved in his letter-books a letter [17] from John Quincy Adams (dated from Quincy, September 10, 1831), addressed not to himself but to his wife, Abigail Adams Johnson, J. Q. Adams' niece. Adams, too, tried to belittle the originality of Johnson's scheme (but without the tempering effect of Du Ponceau's flattering remarks):

> The plan is not entirely new. The great and celebrated dictionary of the Latin Language by Robert Stephens is compiled upon the same principle, as is that of the Greek Language by his son Henry Stephens. The names of these two lexicographers are among the most illustrious in the history of letters; but there is not to my knowledge any such dictionary of the English language. I advise you therefore and your husband to pursue the occupation which has afforded you all amusement for six months.

Adams is referring to Robert Estienne (1502–1559) and his son Henri Estienne (1528–1598)—the name is sometimes latinized as Stephanus, and anglicized more usually as Stephans—two of the most important members of the dynasty of scholar-printers who, in Paris and Geneva, produced hundreds of handsome and valuable texts in Latin, Greek, and French during almost the whole of the sixteenth and seventeenth centuries. Robert Estienne's *Thesaurus linguae latinae* first appeared in 1531; Henri's *Thesaurus graecae linguae in* 1580.

Adams did not point out that in these dictionaries the arrangement is chiefly alphabetical. However, compound words are listed under the simple words from which they are derived. For example, *philobárbaros (bárbaros amans)* in Henri Estienne's Greek dictionary is listed under *bárbaros*. But Estienne did not have to deal with English words which may be related in meaning but derived from different languages. An arrangement of this kind would be rather like including after the *knowledge, knowing, know, knowingly* "set," such terms as *unknowing, all-knowing,* or *acknowledge,* but could make no provision for such related words from other roots as *unwitting* or *omniscient.*

Adams then proceeds to lecture Johnson, through Abigail, on linguistics (using, incidentally, almost the same words Johnson had used in his lecture):

> The English language borrows freely from all others; but the two great fountains of its wealth are the Teutonic, through the Anglo-Saxon, and the Latin through the French; the Latin itself being much enriched from the Greek.

He goes on at considerable length: *"Cold,* for instance, is a word of Teutonic derivation, but *gelid* and *frigid* are of Latin, and *algid* of Greek parentage." Adams' greatest triumph is that of sarcastically remedying the "want of knowledge" to which Johnson had confessed in his lecture:

> The word which Mr. Johnson says he cannot recollect and which turns the stepmother into an adjective is *novercal.* You will find it in your namesake's Dictionary with its derivation and its definition—and if your husband wishes to complete his set of words from this root he may introduce the verb to *novercalize* and the adverb *novercally,* or the substance *novercation* and *novercality.* All these words would be as good English as *novercal* although for this there is and for them there is not the authority of Samuel Johnson—none of them flow [sic] from the well of English undefiled. [There is small wonder that in the shorter version of Johnson's lecture which he printed in *Our American Union* there is no reference to *stepmother.*]

Adams seems merely to be echoing Johnson's remarks about Samuel Johnson's definition of *network* when he says of it

> that it is very exact; and they who censure it would do well to offer a definition of their own in its place. *Net-work* is a word of Teutonic origin. The words might be unintelligible to many who knew perfectly well what *net-work* was, but in what need were they of any definition?

And he concludes by wishing his niece and her husband "all success in this and every other laudable pursuit."

Johnson also kept a letter [18] dated August 31, 1831, from S. De Witt Bloodgood, offering the services of the Young Men's Association of Albany in the task of completing and publishing the dictionary ("I am satisfied that the work would revolutionize the lexicographical world"), and asking for a copy of the lecture to forward to the London Royal Literature Society.

But Johnson apparently found more promising an offer to complete the dictionary which now came to him from Lyman Cobb. Cobb (1800–1864), a resident of New York, was a prolific and industrious author of spelling books, readers, arithmetics, and dictionaries (he compiled one based on Walker's dictionary of 1791). Opinionated, narrow-minded, and conservative in linguistic matters, ever eager to promote the sales of his books, he is remarkable for the animosity he expressed toward his rivals. (Curiously, he retains a small place in the history of American education because of a work in which he denounced the use of corporal punishment in schools. [19])

For example, in a holographic letter preserved in the New York Public Library [20] dated February 19, 1830, to Azariah Cutting Flagg (1790–1873), at that time Comptroller of the State of New York and Acting Superintendent of Common Schools, he viciously attacked a *Common School Manual* by one M. R. Bartlett. He finds Bartlett's orthoepy "exceedingly contradictory . . . and, I unhesitatingly assert what from a thorough examination I believe, Mr. Bartlett's work contains more *errours, blunders,* and *contradictions* in orthography and pronunciation than *all* the other books now in use in the schools in this state! Pardon my strong language, I have just read the work."

Cobb is better known for his acrimonious feud with Noah Webster, whose spelling book (which first appeared in 1783) he began attacking in 1827 and 1828 in a series of letters to the Albany *Argus* over the signature Examinator (Cobb's own spelling book had appeared in 1821). His attacks, frequently reprinted and extended, culminated in *A Critical Review of the Orthography of Dr. Webster's Se-*

ries of Books for Systematick Instruction in the English Language (New York, 1831), in which he mauled all of Webster's books up to that date. He objected particularly to the spellings *music* and *physic* without *k,* and *favor* and *labor* without *u.* (Johnson's usage agreed with Cobb's on these points.) Cobb also found Webster's pronunciations objectionable whenever they departed from Walker's. Webster, naturally, replied in kind. The account of their controversy is long, complicated, and not particularly edifying, since clearly what was involved was not (or not merely) linguistic principles, but sales of books.[21]

According to the *Dictionary of American Biography,* Cobb had a similar feud in the 1840's with another New York State writer of schoolbooks, one Charles Walton Sanders (1805–1889), but the details of this controversy are now obscure.

In any case, Cobb's offer to complete the dictionary appealed to Johnson. In his autobiography, written some twenty-five or thirty years after the events, Johnson sums up his dealings with Cobb as follows:

> He was a veteran lexicographer and author of many school books as well as dictionaries. He was apparently poor and would not commence a dictionary on my plan without considerable pecuniary assistance which I was not willing to give. I was willing to give him my plan and all pecuniary gains to be derived therefrom; but as I never wrote for pecuniary gains, I was unwilling to hazard therein any pecuniary loss. He ultimately promised to take up the work on his own funds when he should be able which he trusted would occur; but he died without fulfilling these expectations.

The letters of Cobb which Johnson preserved do not altogether support this version of what happened. The story is not perfectly clear, since Johnson's own letters do not survive, but it might be interesting to follow it as well as we can, both as it relates to the dictionary itself and for whatever light it may shed on Johnson's personality.

In the first letter [22] from Cobb which Johnson preserved, dated October 17, 1831, Cobb refers to a meeting with Johnson at Utica on September 17. He continues:

> I have . . . read the pamphlet containing your views relative to the plan of a new dictionary, with very considerable attention and pleasure. I admire the plan exceedingly.
> I am very desirous to make an arrangement with you, relative to the compilation and publication of your contemplated dictionary, as I stated to you when I saw you. I am fully satis-

fied that it will supersede the use of all other dictionaries, and will be an invaluable acquisition to the library of every literary man and student in our country.

Will you have the goodness to inform me whether you have a copyright for your contemplated work, and also whether you have yet made an arrangement with anyone for its publication? Please to inform me also what arrangement you shall wish to make with me, if I shall be compiler of the work.

He concludes by saying that he is sending Johnson a copy of his critique of Webster.

Johnson was apparently favorably impressed by this letter (and by his previous meeting with Cobb). In Cobb's next letter,[23] dated December 5, 1831, Cobb acknowledges receipt of a letter from Johnson dated November 19 with Johnson's comments on his review of Webster. He writes:

I am exceedingly well pleased with your remarks relative to a change in orthography, &c. May I, dear Sir, have the privilege of publishing in the New York Evening Post, without name, an extract from your letter? I think the publication will be of great advantage to the cause of correct and uniform spelling.

He also acknowledges another letter of November 21 relating more particularly to the dictionary, which "numerous avocations" have prevented him from answering earlier:

. . . and, even now, I can not answer it as definitely as I could wish, particularly that part which says, "what benefits are to result to *me* [clearly Johnson], if you undertake this work?" My view has been this, and this only, thus far. To make an arrangement with some wealthy publisher who will pay me (while compiling the work) for the compilation. My pecuniary circumstances are such that I can not undertake it otherwise.

It would appear from Cobb's quotation of the excerpt from Johnson's letter that although Johnson may never have written for "pecuniary gains" he did expect some "benefits" from the dictionary, even if Cobb were to undertake the labor of completing it. Cobb himself seems only to hope that some publisher will pay him an advance while he is working on it (a not unreasonable expectation for a professional writer).

There is a curious gap of a year before Cobb's next letter,[24] dated December 8, 1832, in which he writes almost as though he were beginning negotiations all over again:

While in Buffalo on the first of Oct. last, I conversed with Mr. Williams of your city, in relation to the publication of a dictionary, the plan of which you have devised; and, as I understand him, partly or nearly executed. The plan has been highly spoken of by many of my literary friends and acquaintances in whose opinion I have great confidence; and I now think it will be advisable for me to undertake, in connection with some influential booksellers, the publication of it. I have written Mr. Williams in relation to it.

On January 3, 1833, Cobb writes again:[25]

> Your favour of the 11th Dec. was received in due time, since which, I have shown your lecture, delivered before the New York State Lyceum, Aug. 1831, to a number of the booksellers, stereotypers (they to *their* literary friends) and to a number of literary men, all of whom speak in the most favourable terms of your plan of forming a Dictionary of our Language.
>
> Mr. James Conner, an enterprising stereotyper of this city [New York], who has recently published the "Treasury of Knowledge", the Dictionary part of which I edited for him, proposes to publish a number of specimen pages of the work, to be distributed throughout the United States, among literary men generally, that an opinion of your plan may be obtained from them. I have not, at present, the least doubt, but that he will, in connection with some booksellers, stereotype and publish the work; as a favourable expression will be the turning point, of which I entertain no fears. I sincerely believe that the production of such a book as you propose, well executed, will form an era in the history of English Literature as important as that produced by the appearance of *Samuel* Johnson's Dictionary. Perhaps I am too sanguine, though I think not.
>
> I feel under the greatest obligation to you for your kind and generous offer to loan me your collations to the extent which you have proceeded, and also to give me your advice in relation to the work, generally.

These collations, the two folio volumes Johnson and his family had been working on, Cobb suggests should be sent to him in care of A. C. Flagg in Albany, unless Johnson knows of someone coming directly to New York soon. He promises that they "shall be carefully used and preserved, and returned to you." He himself is at present engaged in editing a work for Mr. Conner or he would be glad to come to Utica to collect them:

> With the specimen pages, a titlepage and general description of the plan shall be published, as given in your Lec. Aug. 1831, or if more agreeable to you, you may write a page or two expressly to accompany the specimen pages.

In his next letter,[26] dated February 26, 1833, Cobb acknowledges receipt of the "specimens of the new Dictionary." But Cobb now has more ambitious plans for the dictionary, which may be related to what was going on in the dictionary-publishing business in this country at the time.

It will be recalled that Webster's two-volume quarto dictionary had appeared in 1828. In 1829 Joseph E. Worcester (1784–1865) had prepared for Webster an octavo redaction of this. In 1830 he suddenly produced his own *Comprehensive Pronouncing and Explanatory Dictionary of the English Language*. (He was immediately accused by Webster of plagiarism.) Webster himself was working on his own abridgment of his dictionary, which appeared as a *Dictionary for Primary Schools* in 1834. The two large volumes of Charles Richardson's *New Dictionary of the English Language* came out in 1837–1839. Webster's final revision of his 1828 dictionary appeared in 1841.[27] Besides - Webster, Worcester, and Richardson, there were still various editions of Samuel Johnson (very popular was the revision by H. J. Todd, 1818), Sheridan, Walker—Cobb himself, after his plans for completing the "Collated Dictionary" broke down, produced one in 1834—such combinations as Johnson-Walker (Johnson for definitions, Walker for pronunciations), and many more. In short, the dictionary publishing world at the time was humming with competition. Cobb's idea now was to take advantage of this situation, and to make the "Collated Dictionary" a work able to compete in the market with the others.

> You have favoured me with a number of suggestions relative to the whole plan and contents of the Contemplated Dictionary. My views are these—that, independent of the "Collations", it should be a *full* and *complete* Etymological, Orthographical, Pronouncing and Defining Dictionary, equal, and even superior to Webster's and all others extant. In addition to all this, I intend to annex to the work, a list of all the words of variable orthography and pronunciation in the English Language, and a list of Verbal Distinctions comprehending *all* in the language. These additions are not to be found in any Dictionary.

He is back in his familiar vein of attacking other writers:

> I would also in this work aim at the accomplishing of one thing heretofore entirely disregarded by all lexicographers, not excepting Dr. Webster, viz.: that all words in the *definitions* shall be spelled as they are in the *text;* and that no words shall be used in *defining* other words, which are not in the *text,* themselves defined.

Another fault in Dictionaries is that a word is frequently defined by one other word reciprocally, so that the inquirer knows nothing definitely in relation to the word. Thus,, Bilberry, s. a whortleberry, Whortleberry, s. a bilberry. Diaphragm, s. a midriff, Midriff, s. a diaphragm, &c. &c. This evil I would attempt to remedy, by giving one or both such words a full, distinct, and clear definition.

My opinion is that all the anticipated good which might be reasonably hoped for and expected, from the "Collations" would be lost, or nearly so, if they were not connected with other matter which would make the work in all other respects equal or superior to Webster's Quarto Dictionary.

The specimens sent are very good. I shall probably, however, add a few more to them, of some good examples. Before the specimens are stereotyped, I will send you a proof-sheet, if you wish.

Before I can make very definite arrangements with the stereotypers and others who may conclude to engage in the publication of this Dictionary it will be necessary for you, inasmuch as you have taken out a copyright [we will learn from Cobb's next letter that Johnson had done this as recently as January 12, 1833], to make a legal and regular transfer in a pecuniary view. It is true in your letter to me Dec. 11, 1832, you have given me full permission to compile and publish the work on your plan [only a month, that is, before taking out his own copyright], and have proposed to give me the loan of your "Collations" to the extent to which you have proceeded, yet, I think this is not a sufficiently legal transfer to warrant me in being at the trouble and expense of preparing the specimens for the press, to stereotype and publish them.

There is, indeed, something rather odd about Johnson's giving Cobb "full permission to compile and publish" the dictionary according to his plan on December 11, 1832, and then taking out a copyright on the plan on January 12, 1833. (Cobb, as we have seen, had asked Johnson whether he had a copyright for the work in his very first letter to him, dated October 17, 1831.) Cobb seems not to be upset by this, but he is surely justified in his attempts to clarify the arrangements between him and Johnson:

I have, therefore, sent you two Indentures, executed on my part, which if agreeable to you, you may execute on your part, retain one, and return the other to me by mail.

You will perceive by the Indenture that your name as the author and inventor of the plan will appear in every copy of the work which may be published [Query: but possibly not on the titlepage itself?]. I think it advisable to publish the whole of your Lecture delivered before the New York State Lyceum,

Aug. 10, 1831, prefixed to the specimens and the Dictionary itself. What is your opinion in relation to that?

Then, in a passage which indicates that in undertaking the dictionary he will be giving up other work which might be profitable to him, Cobb continues:

> I have now proposals from three different establishments to edit a dictionary—from A. Pell & Co., Stereotypers, to edit Dr. Johnson's Royal Octavo Dictionary, and to add all new and useful words—From Rees & Co. Stereotypers, to edit an Octavo Walker's Dictionary, with the addition of new and useful words, and the participles, preterits, and plurals, &c. as in my school Dictionary. From Betts & Co., Booksellers, to edit an 18mo. Walker's Dictionary, with the new and useful words, with the Division of Words as in my School Dictionary.
>
> Should I engage to edit any one of these, I must abandon the idea of compiling the collated Dictionary. I choose to edit a Dictionary on your plan.

Cobb now comes to a crucial point:

> You will at once perceive the importance to me that my name should appear on the titlepage of the Dictionary; for, under no other circumstances can it benefit my other books now before the publick, which is the only inducement (except that of assisting to furnish [the] community with a useful and correct Dictionary), for me to engage in editing the work.
>
> My circumstances are such that I should be under the necessity of anticipating the payment for editing it, or nearly all of it, before the work will be completed; consequently, can expect no future benefit from the publication of the work, except what it may do in assisting to give publicity and character to my other works.

He concludes, rather pathetically:

> These are my views, and these are the facts in relation to my pecuniary circumstances, given to you confidentially; for, although it is not a crime in this or any other country to be poor, yet a man seldom gains friends by letting his poverty be known.

It seems reasonable that a man who has to live by the drudgery of his pen should hope for some advance payment to keep him going while he is engaged in a work of this kind, especially if it means that he has to forgo other commissions which promise immediate return. There is no evidence that he is asking Johnson himself for money. He presumably still hopes, as he mentioned in one of his earlier letters, that one or more publisher-booksellers will provide the funds. It is also reasonable that he should want his name on the title-page (to the exclusion of Johnson's?), if he is going to do the actual labor on the dictionary, and to think of this as a way of promoting and giving prestige to his other works. Finally, there is no reason why Cobb should not have contemplated making the dictionary a more ambitious work, fit to compete in the market with the other dictionaries of the time.

The next letter from Cobb in the Johnson papers, dated March 14, 1833, is the "indenture" itself.[28] In his previous letter he mentioned two copies of this document. Johnson has kept only a single copy, signed by Cobb alone. It is likely, therefore, that Johnson signed the other copy and returned it to Cobb.

The indenture is a very businesslike and legalistic paper. According to its terms, Johnson transfers copyright of "The Collated Dictionary, or a Complete Index to the English Language" to Cobb:

> The plan of the said book is more fully set forth in the title which was filed by the said party of the first part [Johnson] in the Office of the Clerk of the Northern District of the State of New York on the twelfth day of January last; and also more fully described and set forth in a printed Lecture pronounced at Utica by the said party of the first part on the tenth of August, one thousand eight hundred and thirty-one before the New York State Lyceum.

The indenture continues (I dispense with the parties of the first and second parts):

> In consideration of the assignment aforesaid and of having received of [Johnson] . . . two folio volumes, being the said "Collated Dictionary" in an incomplete state, . . . [Cobb] agrees to . . . compile, edit, print, and publish, *at his own proper charge and sole expense* [italics added], "A Collated Dictionary of the English Language," to conform to the said plan as nearly as may be found useful, and on which point . . . [Cobb] is to be allowed a liberal and large discretion both as to the extent of the Collation and to the kind—so however as to keep constantly in view the publick benefit proposed to be created by the original plan of the work as described in the said lecture and entry—the said Dictionary is also to be a good defining dictionary, but how far it shall include etymology and orthoepy is to rest in the discretion of . . . [Cobb] who is also to control the orthography and all other matters relating to the style and execution of said Dictionary.

Further, Cobb binds himself to begin the compilation of the dictionary on or before May 1, 1834, and to complete, print, and publish it on or before May 1, 1837. Johnson is to be given full credit as "author and inventor" of the plan of the dictionary, and his lecture is to be included, but he

> is to be entitled to no part of the merit which may be due to the definitions of the said dictionary, to its orthography, orthoepy, or to its etymology, or to the style in which the "Collocations" are executed, defined, and arranged, or to the extent of words the said Dictionary may embrace.

Finally, Cobb is to furnish Johnson "free of any expense to him . . . twenty-five perfect copies (bound in a handsome and workmanlike manner)" as soon as published.

The arrangements seem fair enough, in view of the fact that Cobb was to do all the work, add the definitions and other matter to make the work a complete defining dictionary, and in addition assume the financial risks.

It is not possible to be certain about what happened next. It may be that Johnson felt that his original plan was being submerged in Cobb's proposal for expanding the scope of the dictionary, or that he felt that he would not be receiving adequate credit and acknowledgment in the published work.

At any rate, Cobb's next letter,[29] dated April 17, 1833, apparently written in some agitation and with a certain ambiguity about pronouns, refers to a letter from Johnson dated April 11. From this Cobb quotes Johnson's "last proposition":

> to issue proposals, specimens, &c., and await the result of their reception by the publick; so that I [Cobb?] may decide understandingly, and in the mean time you [Johnson?] make no other disposition of the work, &c.

If we take the pronouns this way, Johnson's proposal seems to be that Cobb undertake the labor and expense of preparing and circulating a prospectus and specimen pages, and then await the response to them before going ahead. Johnson, meanwhile, promises only not to dispose of his plan elsewhere, and seems to assume that, in spite of the indenture, he still possesses exclusive rights thereto.

The alternative reading is:

> to . . . await the result of their reception . . . so that I [Johnson] may decide understandingly, and in the meanwhile you [Cobb] make no other disposition of the work. . . .

This reading would mean that Johnson acknowledges Cobb's right, as set forth in the indenture, to use the plan, but still reserves the authority to decide on final arrangements, perhaps even to prevent the publication if he chooses, while again allowing Cobb to assume the labor, expense, and uncertainty of preparing and circulating the proposal and specimen pages.

In either case, such an understanding was unacceptable to Cobb. He says that he has consulted his friends in relation to this proposition and

> they, as well as myself, think it not advisable for me to engage in it on those conditions. It will cost me in time and money, one thousand dollars, at least, to publish the prospectus and the specimens, and circulate them extensively throughout the United States. This I am unable to expend without a certainty of having the work, (should it be approved, of which I have no doubt), and at such length of time that I should be able to complete it without the forfeiture of $500 [Query: to the publishers if he should fail to meet his deadline?], which in addition to the $1000 necessarily expended, would, inevitably, reduce me and my family to beggary.
>
> I am therefore under the necessity of abandoning the project altogether. I hope, however, that either yourself or some other competent person will, ere long, compile and publish the work —a work intended and well calculated to be of incalculable benefit to the literary world.
>
> I rejoice that you are making arrangements to publish the second edition of your "Lectures on Language." They have, and will be highly advantageous to the community.

And so the plans for publishing Johnson's dictionary came to nought. There is an interesting contrast here between the contentious, Grub Street type of lexicographical drudge, strictly professional and conscientious, however, and, after all, absolutely dependent on his pen for his livelihood—and the wealthy amateur of letters, willing to let another man undertake a long and grueling work without the certainty of having the right to publish it. Cobb's letters do not, as I read them, bear out Johnson's statement quoted above from his autobiography that Cobb asked him for "considerable pecuniary assistance which he was not willing to give." It was surely true, as Johnson said, that "as he never wrote for pecuniary gains, he was unwilling to hazard therein any pecuniary loss." The conclusion seems inescapable, however, that in this instance he was not unwilling for someone else to hazard such a loss.

Neither Cobb nor Johnson bore any ill will in the matter. On January 12, 1835,[30] Cobb wrote to Johnson asking for "a piece or two" which he might include in "a Reading Book for higher classes." Johnson obliged him with three, two of which Cobb printed in his *North American Reader* (1835). Cobb also undertook, according to a letter [31] dated November 28, 1835, to act as Johnson's literary agent, and succeeded in placing the revised edition of *A Treatise on Language* with Harper & Brothers, who published it in 1836. There may be a touch of wistfulness in his statement to Johnson that "Messrs. H. & B. never throw the risk and responsibility of getting up and selling a new work, upon the author."

Our last glimpse of Cobb is a rather sad one. In 1859, having apparently suffered financial losses, he attempted to create a Joint Stock Association with a capital of $20,000, in 200 shares at $100 each, to enable him to continue his work. His son Lyman Cobb, Jr., was to be the trustee; an insurance policy on the life of another son, George Whitney Cobb, in the sum of $20,000, was to protect the investment of the subscribers. The funds were to enable Cobb to pay off debts against his copyrights, to increase the publication and sales of his books, and to enable him "to publish, as soon as practicable, a School Dictionary, and a Large Pronouncing and Defining Dictionary." Cobb seems not to have reached his goal of two hundred shares (apparently only 106 were subscribed for), but among the many prominent New Yorkers whose signatures appear on a manuscript in the New York Public Library, and who subscribed to (and paid for) one or more shares were Peter Cooper (three shares) and Horace Greeley (one).[32] This is a striking tribute to Cobb's honesty and professional reputation in the City of New York.

We are at the end of the story of Johnson's "Collated Dictionary," but there is one interesting sequel. Many years after Johnson first propounded his plan, he heard about the publication in 1852 of Roget's *Thesaurus of English Words and Phrases,* which seemed so close to his plan as to have been founded upon it. Since copies of the pamphlet printing of his lecture had been sent to England, he "naturally concluded," he writes in his autobiography, "that they had originated the work of Mr. Roget."

Peter Mark Roget (1779–1869), a native of London, was a remarkably distinguished and active physician, a Fellow of the Royal College of Physicians, and a Fellow of the Royal Society (he served as its Secretary from 1827 to 1849, when he retired). He was also active in founding the University of London. On his retirement he devoted himself to an idea for a philosophical arrangement of words under "categories" which had engaged his attention for nearly fifty years. According to the preface to his work, he had compiled his first "classed catalogue" in 1805, and he included a facsimile of the first page of this earliest attempt.

Actually, Roget's classification of words is based on a much more complicated and sophisticated system than Johnson's. According to Simon Potter,[33] in it is "partly materialized" Comenius's dream of a complete "picture of the universe of things" and ideas. "This universe of ideas is first ordered in six broad classes of abstract relations, space, matter, intellect, will, and affections. These are then divided and subdivided in their turn." Potter makes an interesting comparison between Roget and modern subject indexes to library catalogues, such as the Dewey Decimal Classification system, which also attempt to divide into categories all human knowledge.

Roget, in a footnote to his introduction of 1852 (reprinted in all subsequent editions), acknowledges certain sources and influences:

> The principle by which I have been guided in framing my verbal classification is the same as that which is employed in the various departments of Natural History. Thus the sectional divisions I have formed correspond to Natural Families in Botany and Zoology, and the filiation of words presents a network analogous to the filiation of plants or animals.
>
> The following are the only publications that have come to my knowledge in which any attempt has been made to construct a systematic arrangement of ideas with a view to their expression. The earliest of these, supposed to be at least nine hundred years old, is the *Amera Cósha,* or *Vocabulary of the Sanscrit Language,* by Amera Sinha, of which an English translation, by the late Henry T. Colebrooke, was printed at Serampoor, in the year 1808. The classification of words is there, as might be expected, exceedingly imperfect and confused, especially in all that related to abstract ideas or mental operations. This will be apparent from the very title of the first section, which comprehends *"Heaven, Gods, Demons, Fire, Air, Velocity, Eternity, Much"*: while *Sin, Virtue, Happiness, Destiny, Cause, Nature, Intellect, Reasoning, Knowledge, Senses, Tastes, Odours, Colours,* are all included and jumbled together in the fourth section. A more logical order, however, pervades the sections relating to natural objects, such as *Seas, Earth, Towns, Planets,* and *Animals,* which form separate classes; exhibiting a

remarkable effort at analysis at so remote a period of Indian literature.

The well-known work of Bishop Wilkins entitled *"An Essay towards a Real Character and a Philosophical Language,"* published in 1668, had for its object the formation of a system of symbols which might serve as a universal language. It professed to be founded on a "scheme of analysis of the things or notions to which names were to be assigned. . . ."

Professor J. R. Firth is surely guilty of an understatement when he says that it is "interesting" to find in this famous book the convergence of "such various cultural constituents" as seventeenth-century rationalism (Wilkins), modern science, and oriental thought.[34]

Roget's *Thesaurus* and Johnson's "Collated Dictionary" could not have been further apart in their purpose and conception. Strangely enough, Johnson had, as a young man, been engaged on a project which in some ways does resemble Roget's book. According to the autobiography,

> I . . . passed much of my time in reading instructive books, as they happened to casually become known to me; and unfortunately, I think, the books to which I most inclined were metaphysical . . . and I longed to know all the powers of the human mind; and I conceived that I could attain my object by extracting from a dictionary all words that named such powers; as for instance *judgment, reason,* with their definitions. I even made some attempts at such a collection of words; when I found that I was only attempting to compile a new dictionary; and that probably some powers existed to which no name had been given.

But Johnson had no actual knowledge of the nature of Roget's work (and Roget had obviously never heard of Johnson). However, having ascertained Roget's address, Johnson wrote him "to enquire whether he had not seen my plan."

To this indirect charge of plagiarism Roget replied with great dignity in a letter [35] dated February 20, 1854:

> I have just received your letter of the 27th ult.° by which you inform me that you had, many years ago, projected a work somewhat similar in principle to the one I lately published under the title "Thesaurus of English Words & Phrases, classified and arranged so as to facilitate the expression of Ideas, and assist in Literary Composition;" and of which an improved & enlarged edition was published a year ago. This circumstance was quite unknown to me, & I shall feel much interest in perusing

the pamphlet you mention as having been published by you at the time, if I should ever be so fortunate as to meet with it; as also your more recent work on Language [*The Meaning of Words*, 1854?]. I have not yet received the book you announce it to be your intention of sending me, but beg to thank you by anticipation.

He then neatly turns the personal charge of plagiarism on his part into a national charge of plagiarism against American publishers in general:

> I am rather surprised that you have not met with my Thesaurus, for I have learned that a pirated edition of it has been printed & sold in the United States—of course without my consent or participation. To this flagrant national disregard of justice, by which English authors are much injured, I must necessarily submit. I only hope that my buccaneering editor has not introduced into the work any corruption of his own;—a fraud which I understand has been occasionally practised, & against which the aggrieved author is allowed no means of protecting himself.

It is tempting to read into the interchange between Johnson and Roget the suspicion that the chief grievance of each of these two old gentlemen (Johnson, 70; Roget, 75) was the fact that his work was unknown to the other. They could have had much to say to one another. But it was Johnson's great tragedy (and the tragedy of American thinking in so many diverse fields, which this Conference is belatedly atoning for) that he was so isolated (or had so isolated himself) from kindred spirits in other places.

Allen Walker Read has collected no fewer than forty-four plans for English dictionaries projected between the publications of Samuel Johnson's *Dictionary* in 1755 and that of Noah Webster's *American Dictionary* in 1828, but never carried out.[36] Since Johnson's plan, as seems likely, originated at least a couple of years before his announcement of it in 1830, it must join this gloomy list as forty-fifth.

It is, of course, unfortunate that Johnson's "Collated Dictionary" was never completed. The two folio volumes of collations which he had begun and which he lent to Cobb may come to light some day to give us a somewhat clearer notion of how his theories would have worked out in practice. But we have enough knowledge of it to warrant the conclusion that his plan (although not as original in all respects as he thought it was) had great merit, and would have been an invaluable tool in helping readers become better acquainted with "the whole compass" of the English vocabulary.

It is interesting to find a recent writer on lexicography, R. W. Chambers, speaking in terms almost echoing Johnson's of the grievance he has long had against the ordering of words in dictionaries according to the alphabet, "that blindest of guides." [37]

> A vocabulary (unlike, in my view, an index) is necessarily alphabetical. But . . . is it worth considering whether all the words that come from Latin *cedo* . . . might, while retaining their several places, be referred to a central article on *cedo* (*cede, proceed,* etc.)?
>
> And so with other groups, like those that have to do with *sit* (*session, president*), or those that come from *caedo* "I cut" (*concise, homicide,* and *caesura*).
>
> You may agree with me that much space would be saved in etymological and other explanation, and that our dictionaries would be even more edifying, even more entertaining than they are.

Finally, it is ironical to notice that one of the current editions of Roget's *Thesaurus* has adopted an alphabetical order, and that it is advertised in the following terms:

> You get the word you want *instantly* because you use it just as you do a dictionary. All entries are in alphabetical order, synonyms are grouped according to meaning. . . .[38]

The problem, then, of providing a "complete index to the English language," and of reconciling the advantages and disadvantages of alphabetical versus subject arrangement seems still to exist. It might possibly have been solved with the completion of Johnson's "Collated Dictionary."

NOTES

1 From the autobiography. I follow the editorial policy adopted for the publication of these *Proceedings* in omitting page references for quotations from this unpublished work. I have not seen a copy of the 1830 prospectus.

2 *Proceedings of the First Annual Meeting of the New York State Lyceum, Held at Utica, August 10th and 11th, 1831* (Utica: Northway & Porter, 1831). Johnson's lecture occupies pages 3–27. In his autobiography Johnson says mistakenly that the lecture was first presented before the "New York Lyceum" in New York. He was invited to repeat his lecture in New York at a later date, but before the American Lyceum (see footnote 4, below).

3 *A Method of Acquiring a Full Knowledge of the English Language, Propounded at Their Invitation by A. B. Johnson, Utica, August 10, 1831, before the New York State Lyceum* (Utica, Northway & Porter, 1831).

4 The letter of invitation, over the signature of Theodore Dwight, Jr., Corresponding Secretary, is dated January 17, 1834. It states "that the Executive Committee of the American Lyceum . . . have appointed [Johnson] to write an essay for their 4th Annual Meeting, on a 'New Classification of the Language in the Dictionary,'" and announces that the meeting will be held early in May *(Miscellaneous Letters, 1829–1836,* No. 113). References to letters received by Johnson are to the collections of letter-books on deposit in the Hamilton College Library. These letter-books are the property of Alexander Bryan Johnson of Darien and New York. Johnson did not actually present the lecture orally. Disappointed at the size of his audience, he stalked out, leaving a copy of the lecture with the Secretary.

5 "Title and Plan of a New Dictionary," in *A Guide to the Right Understanding of Our American Union, or, Political, Economical and Literary Miscellanies* (New York: Derby and Jackson, 1857), pp. 300–308. Johnson repeats here, in a footnote, the confusion between the New York State Lyceum and the American Lyceum.

6 Johnson is referring to Noah Webster's great dictionary in two quarto volumes, *An American Dictionary of the English Language* (1828).

7 The classic misquotation, "First catch your hare," is usually attributed to Hannah Glasse, *The Art of Cookery* (1747), but the original reads, according to the *Oxford Dictionary of Quotations,* "Take your hare when it is cased [i.e., skinned]."

8 Obviously there is no relation between this "index" and the "system of word-indexing" which Johnson proposed in *The Meaning of Words,* 1854 (pp. 89–92; quoted by Rynin in his paperback edition of the *Treatise on Language,* pp. 60–61). "Orthoepists designate which of [its] sounds the letter A denotes in any given use of it, by plying [sic] over the A some character which conventionally reveals the intended sound. Philosophers might adopt a like contrivance when using any nominal unit that aggregates objects generically different. I, might denote intellection; S, sight; F, feel; T, taste; L, smell; D, sounds; G, internal feelings. For instance, *thickness* is a nominal unit, but sensibly I can feel thickness and I can see thickness; consequently, the intellectually conceived nominal unit thickness names a sensible duality. We, however, possess an entire control over the definition of the word thickness, and can define it to signify the *feel* thickness [that is, thickness (F)], excluding the *sight* thickness [that is, thickness (S)]. This definition is as good as any other when we understand the intended limitation; but we may convert such a limitation into a puzzle when the limit is not avowed." He applies this to the "unconscious quibble" of which Hume is guilty in saying " 'The table (S) which we see, seems to diminish (S) as we recede from it, but the real table (F) suffers no diminution (F).' The whole zest of the proposition consists in the sensible duality of each of the

nominal units table and diminution. That the *sight* diminution and the *feel* undiminution can exist thus together is a physical fact of much interest; but we make a mystery of it only when we play bo-peep with words, by neglecting to discriminate the intellectually conceived oneness of diminution, and its physical duality [which Johnson has made clear by adding S or F where appropriate]."

In fact, apart from the speculation about the impossibility of knowing a condition without knowing what its "not" condition is, the lecture on the dictionary shows little of Johnson's preoccupation with the philosophy of language. His purpose in the dictionary is a practical, pedagogical one—to increase the reader's vocabulary.

9 The bibliography on the history of English dictionaries is vast. The material in this section of my paper is based chiefly on R. W. Chapman, *Lexicography* (London, 1948); Mitford M. Mathews, *A Survey of English Dictionaries* (New York, 1933); Sir James A. H. Murray, *The Evolution of English Lexicography* (Oxford, 1900); James Sledd and Wilma R. Ebbitt, *Dictionaries and that Dictionary* (Chicago, 1962); James H. Sledd and Gwin J. Kolb, *Dr. Johnson's Dictionary* (Chicago, 1955); DeWitt T. Starnes, *Renaissance Dictionaries* (Austin, 1954); DeWitt T. Starnes and Gertrude E. Noyes, *The English Dictionary from Cawdrey to Johnson, 1604–1755* (Chapel Hill, 1946) Ernest Weekley, "On Dictionaries," *Atlantic Monthly*, June 1924, pp. 782–791 (reprinted in Sledd and Ebbitt, pp. 9–21).

10 Sledd and Kolb, *op. cit.*, p. 168.

11 *Ibid.*, p. 210, fn. 74.

12 *Ibid.*, p. 24.

13 *An Address to the Utica Forum, Delivered December 9, 1824* (Utica: William Williams, 1824), pp. 8–9.

14 *Treatise*, ed. Rynin, p. 151.

15 *Miscellaneous Letters, 1829–1836*, No. 62

16 A pamphlet published at Constance in 1784 in defense of Mesmer (*Mesmer justifié*) and attributed to one Jean Jacques Paulet nevertheless quotes (p. 26, footnote) this malicious epitaph which circulated in Paris:

> Ci gît ce pauvre Gebelin [sic],
> Qui parloit grec, hébreu, latin;
> Admirez tous son héroisme;
> Il fut martyr du Magnétisme.

17 *Miscellaneous Letters, 1829–1836*, No. 64.

18 *Ibid.*, No. 61.

19 *The Evil Tendencies of Corporal Punishment as a Means of Moral Discipline* (New York, 1847).

20 *Flagg Papers*, Manuscript Division, New York Public Library.

21 See Harry R. Warfel, *Noah Webster: Schoolmaster to America* (New York, 1936).

22 *Miscellaneous Letters, 1829–1836*, No. 73.

23 *Ibid.*, No. 77.

24 *Ibid.*, No. 98.

25 *Ibid.*, No. 99.

26 *Ibid.*, No. 100.

27 The work did not sell well. On Webster's death in 1843, the remaining unbound sheets and the rights were bought up by George and Charles Merriam of Amherst, Mass. In 1846, Worcester's *Universal and Critical*

Dictionary of the English Language appeared, almost coinciding with the publication in 1847 of the first edition of the "Merriam-Webster," edited by Webster's son-in-law, Professor Chauncey A. Goodrich. Worcester's 1860 revision followed close on the heels of the 1859 Webster. And so "the war of the dictionaries" raged, with the field now reduced to two chief contenders, Webster and Worcester (the latter preferred by some as being more conservative). The supremacy of Webster was finally established with the publication of the first "unabridged" Webster, edited by Dr. Noah Porter, in 1864.

28 *Miscellaneous Letters, 1829–1836*, No. 101.

29 *Ibid.*, No. 106.

30 *Ibid.*, No. 159.

31 *Ibid.*, No. 174.

32 *Misc. Papers, Lyman Cobb*, Manuscript Division, New York Public Library.

33 Simon Potter, *Language in the Modern World* (Baltimore: Penguin Books, 1964), p. 174.

34 J. R. Firth, *The Tongues of Men* (1937), reprinted in paperback in *The Tongues of Men and Speech* (London: Oxford University Press, 1964), p. 66.

35 *Miscellaneous Letters, 1849–1854*, No. 277.

36 Allen Walker Read, "Projected English Dictionaries, 1775–1828," *Journal of English and Germanic Philology*, 1937, pp. 188–205 and 347–366.

37 R. W. Chambers, *Lexicography* (London: W. & R. Chambers, 1948), p. 27.

38 *The New Yorker*, September 9, 1967.

II

ECONOMIST AND BANKER

It is doubtful whether any man in our country better understood the principles which govern all financial affairs than he did, and he was eminently practical in their application.

The Utica Morning Herald, *September 12, 1867*

A PIONEER IN THE THEORY
OF ECONOMIC POLICY

◆ ◆ ◆ ◆ ◆ *JOSEPH DORFMAN*

IN 1842, Governor William H. Seward of New York (later President Lincoln's Secretary of State) asked the Utica banker Alexander Bryan Johnson to aid in the preparation of a report on "the progress and present condition of science and the arts in the state" by providing notes on philology and finance, "two departments which though widely separated, you have labored in with eminent success." [1] That perceptive statesman was, of course, referring to Johnson's work in the fields which today are called semantics (linguistic philosophy) and economics. My function is to discuss his contributions to economic doctrine. Let me say at the outset that he was a worthy representative of an era in the Anglo-American world remarkable for the large number of first-rank thinkers who derived their livelihood from business and finance. He was original and willing to depart from accustomed paths in both his philosophical and economic speculations. We may find a clue to his uninhibited ways of thought in that he was an "outsider," brought here from England at the age of fourteen by his immigrant parents of Jewish ancestry. Johnson himself pointed out, in his delightful essay in *belles lettres* quaintly titled "How to Prosper: or the

◇ ◇ ◇ ◇ ◇ *Professor of Economics, Columbia University. Author,* Thorstein Veblen and His America *(1934);* The Economic Mind in American Civilization *(5 vols. 1946–59); "John Marshall, Political Economist," in* Chief Justice John Marshall: A Reappraisal *(1956), Editor.* Types of Economic Theory: From Mercantilism to Institutionalism *(1967), by Wesley C. Mitchell.*

Fatal Mistake," the high proportion of those who had built large fortunes in this country who were foreign-born; that is, "outsiders" in modern sociological parlance.[2]

By implication, it was the outsider, the man not bound very strongly by the conventional preconceptions of the dominant culture, who saw the magnificent opportunities for economic advance for the community—whether it be a city or a nation—and for himself. But the concept of the outsider has a bearing not only in the realm of economic affairs but also in the realm of intellectual advance. Thus Thorstein Veblen argues that the reason the Jews were preeminent in the advance of knowledge in the Western world was that leaving their native culture and coming into contact with another and different culture they were stripped to a considerable degree of the intellectual preconceptions of either and thereby enabled to analyze, more clearly than the natives, the developing scene.[3]

Johnson's father, Bryan, joined the Episcopal Church in Utica and Johnson himself followed in his father's footsteps to the degree that both father and son became pillars of the church. While in the religious sphere Johnson chose to identify himself with one of the most socially acceptable and orthodox groups, his intellectual contacts were with a wide variety of heterodox and in some cases even radical thinkers. He was not a radical, but was enough of a freethinker to advocate transmission of mail on Sunday by the post office, and for this he drew sharp criticism.

Johnson had little formal education. Early in life, however, he amassed substantial wealth through his investments in manifold enterprises, particularly banks and land dealings. As a result, he had the leisure to pursue his varied intellectual interests. We might speculate that another factor in his intellectual development was his marriage with a granddaughter of President John Adams, through which he became related to what was then one of the most eminent families of the nation. Though seemingly proud of this relationship, he was still sufficiently the maverick to be unwilling to embrace the Federalist political and economic philosophy of the Adams clan.[4]

Johnson displayed openmindedness and broad-gauged curiosity in his readings in economic theory. In 1811–1812, while he was visiting in New York City, a fellow boarder, a Scotsman, lent him a number of books on economics. The list is revealing of the diversity of views of the specific authors he later mentioned with evident approval in his autobiography, namely Adam Smith, Bernard de Mandeville, and the Earl of Lauderdale. He read both of Adam Smith's major works, *The Theory of Moral Sentiments* and *The Wealth of Nations,* and like most economists of his day, considered himself a follower of "Professor Smith" and his system of natural liberty.[5] But his adherence to Adam Smith was not such as to cause him to follow his master in his sharp condemnation of Mandeville's *The Fable of the Bees, or Private Vices, Public Benefits,* which maintained that private vices such as luxurious expenditures were in themselves or "by the dextrous management of a skillful politician" public virtues in the sense of animating and developing the economy. Adam Smith, had he lived to read it, would similarly have condemned Lauderdale's *An Inquiry into the Nature and Origin of Publick Wealth and into the Means and Causes of Its Increase* (1804) which asserted that the redemption of the public debt was the most active means of diminishing the nation's wealth and prosperity.

Johnson's material success which, as we have already noted, made it possible for him to write and engage in the intellectual give-and-take of the day, had still another effect on his economic and social thinking. This was the influence of the manner and type of enterprises through which he gained wealth. He ran a store, dealt extensively in lands, and was quite a real estate developer in Utica. Barely more than a youth, he promoted a glass factory in Geneva, New York, speculated in New York City banks stocks, established or invested heavily in banks throughout western New York, and was active in communications, beginning with the Erie Canal system, and then railroads.

His first occupation, which provided the foundation not only of his fortune but also for the understanding of the economic mechanism, was his participation in the operation of his father's general store in Utica. By the time he and his father retired from this enterprise in 1810, they controlled most of the business of receiving produce and distributing merchandise in the Mohawk Valley.

Johnson's description of his father's aim showed his insight into what some influential students hold is the objective of leading enterprisers—namely, not maximization of profit but an increasing share of the volume of business of the industry. "My father's ambition," he wrote in his autobiography, "was more devoted to the transaction of a large business than to make money therefrom. To attain his objective he sought the reputation of selling goods at lower prices than his village contemporaries and to purchase country produce at higher prices." Interestingly, Johnson thought that his father had overdone this and claimed that in the last few years he convinced the elder Johnson "not to participate in the rivalry so as to disregard the acquisition of money." However, his investments in an ever-increasing number of banks in the region, some of which proved quite troublesome, suggest that he, too, was motivated by the desire to obtain a greater share of business and power in his industry, a motive he may not have cared to admit lest he lose his reputation for having a keen interest in money-making.[6]

Let me now turn to Johnson's systematic economics. At the age of twenty-seven he began to write on the subject and continued to do so for over half a century. His first and most important study was *An Inquiry into the Nature of Value and of Capital, and into the Operation of Government Loans, Banking Institutions and Private Credit* (1813; reprinted 1968 by Augustus M. Kelley, Publishers, with an introduction by Joseph Dorfman). He recalled in the autobiography that at the time of publication during the War of 1812 "the banks had not yet suspended specie payments, and an opinion was prevalent that on such an occurrence bank notes would become worthless." But when the suspension occurred shortly afterwards, then, as he had predicted in his abstruse investigation, it

> impaired not the currency of the notes, a sufficiency of bank debtors existing to whom the notes answered all the purposes of specie and who had to obtain them or obtain specie. The specie suspension of the banks was in truth a specie suspension of only the bank's debtors—for as long as the debtors could pay in specie the banks could pay.[7]

The view that inconvertible paper could serve as money, at least for a time, was one of the greatest heresies in dominant economic theory. But to get a clear view of Johnson's position in this as well as other subjects, we should begin with his theory of value, for he held that policy must be based on a sound theory of value. Actually, Johnson's theory of value was for the most part the standard classical doctrine, emphasizing mainly scarcity and cost of production and devoting very little attention to the place of demand.[8]

The preoccupation of Johnson (like most of his contemporary workers in the field) with value theory was closely tied to his interest in the production and maintenance of the nation's wealth. Where Johnson did depart from the mainstream was in his thesis that both government debt and banking institutions were important and useful tools for increasing the total wealth of the state and the nation as a whole.

Following this line, he contended that public loans increased the nation's capital to the amount of the loans. The holders obtain

> all the advantages that other articles of capital yield. . . . [T]hey are exchangeable in a foreign or domestic market, in the same manner and to the same effect, that so much gold or silver may be exchanged, or indeed any other object or man's desire.[9]

In general, Johnson felt that the economic effect of issuing government bonds was almost the same as if a new gold strike were made within the country. The difference was in the administration and the need for sufficient revenues to meet the interest payments. He implied that the collective (that is, public) use of the money may have been more productive than if the money were left to be expended by the individual citizen.

Commenting on the Revolutionary War debt, which in its original form had not included provision for funding, Johnson said that when funded, it constituted an addition to the nation's wealth. "The new capital was employed in multiplying the objects of man's desire; in stimulating industry, and in rendering its efforts more productive," so that the profit far exceeded the interest charge. This effect was achieved because the negotiable securities "were used as a trading capital and therefore benefited not only the first receivers . . . but every other person who could be influenced by the magnitude of capital in the nation." [10] Any taxes beyond those required for minimum government functions and to service the public debt would tend to reduce activity. Taxes levied for the purpose of reducing public debt are of this destructive type.

Besides his shrewd and incisive analysis of the deflationary tendencies produced by repayment of the public debt, Johnson put forth a strikingly ingenious description of how such repayment affected the individual bondholder. The bondholder upon being repaid would not find himself any richer because the face amount of the bonds he had always calculated as part of his wealth. Indeed, to the extent that he was taxed to help liquidate the debt, his net worth was reduced. An individual, when he calculates his fortune, does not estimate how much of the national debt is his share and deduct it from his estate.

> In owing an individual debt, the debtor is conscious that the principal must be . . . liquidated at some period . . . and that the interest will be chargeable to him until the debt is satisfied. In owing a public debt, however, there is no such necessity for

the payment of it being made by him, and no such positive knowledge that the interest will continue chargeable to him until it is paid.[11]

The only valid reason for liquidating a national debt is that it would eliminate the taxes necessary for meeting the interest; but the same objection holds against bank notes and other "credit capital." Whether a measure is expedient or not depends upon

> the balance of advantages and disadvantages . . . and so long as the use of capital is found more productive than the amount of interest necessary to keep it in existence, so long will its being kept in existence prove advantageous to the nation.[12]

Johnson's unorthodox monetary theories were consistent with his stand on the useful function of a public debt to the growth of a nation's economy: to wit, he argued that unrestricted convertibility of bank notes into specie was not essential and indeed could at times hamper business activity. He pointed to the experience in England in the period 1797–1821 during which time the notes of the central Bank of England were not convertible into gold. Despite the lack of convertibility, such paper was still in good demand. Individuals exchanged their private notes for those of a bank because of the superior and more widely diffused confidence that is placed in bankers. The discount charge is for the use of a banker's name and credit. Even where there is specie redemption, bankers could never redeem all these notes at once for the bank note capital far exceeded the specie capital. Suppose the banks found they could not meet the demand for specie in return for their obligations and suspended redemption of specie payments? Judging by the experience of the Bank of England, the acceptability of bank notes would hardly be impaired. There would still be a profitable use for all the bank notes in circulation, because the banks would have enough notes of individuals to represent their own. Consequently, a bank's debtors would be as anxious as ever to obtain them in order to redeem their obligations, and demand would be kept up. Johnson added the important qualifications: this would be the case only if "the bank . . . has not acted fraudulently, or . . . has not been unfortunate or indiscreet in loaning to individuals who are incapable of refunding the amount borrowed." [13]

Later Johnson conceded that the notes of the Bank of England had depreciated during the suspension of specie payments, but felt that this did not affect the argument. The government's creditors were paid in bank notes though the price of gold in bank notes increased in 1814 by 25 percent. Johnson claimed that the apparent injustice was

130

greater than the real, because the suspension operated on gold like a monopoly. As gold became a scarce article, those needing it for export, manufacture, or for any other use which paper money could not perform had to purchase gold as merchandise, at the price it "had attained by the well-known laws of scarcity." [14]

In *A Treatise on Banking*, Johnson scathingly denounced the rigidities of the hard-money standard which forced a bank to redeem in specie, notes, and deposits on demand. Thus a bank must "subordinate the amount of its currency, and consequently the amount of its . . . loans to the accidental fluctuations . . . in the demand for specie, how disastrously soever the subordination may affect the internal commerce of the kingdom." If a bank could substitute inconvertible notes, specie could be exported or imported according to the requirements of commerce, without any derangement of business. Such a currency would be as expandable as the nation's business needs; "and without losing, intrinsically, its ultimate specie value," since bank debtors would be compelled to get specie to the extent that they could not obtain bank notes.[15]

With all his strong advocacy of "soft money" policies, Johnson nevertheless retained certain doubts as to how an all-out inconvertible standard would function in actual practice. In 1849 he suggested that the natural supply and demand processes of the money market might break down and the central bank might blunder into issuing excessive quantities of paper money, resulting in disastrous inflation. While he did not offer a specific policy of safeguards to prevent such an occurrence, he did warn that it was dangerous to leave the issuance of paper money entirely in the hands of central bank managers.[16]

In the bitter contest between the supporters of the Second Bank of the United States (led by Daniel Webster, Henry Clay, and the bank's president, Nicholas Biddle), and President Jackson over rechartering the Bank, Johnson was an effective writer and speaker in support of the President. The President had followed his successful veto of the recharter bill (1832) by directing the discontinuance in October 1832 of the Bank as the depository of the government funds, and the use instead of selected state banks in order, as Johnson put it, "to diminish the means of the Bank to create a pecuniary distress [by destroying credit and confidence that should admit of no relief but a renewal of the Bank's charter]." [17] The Bank brought such pressure to bear on individual debtors and the state banks, that by the beginning of 1834, the New York banks "were generally in great danger of being compelled to stop payment." In March, Johnson informed two of the most powerful men in the ruling Democratic party of the state of his novel plan to relieve the banks through the use of the state's fiscal powers. To Thomas W. Olcott of the Mechanics' and Farmers' Bank, Albany, Johnson wrote that the commissioners of the Canal Fund had the power to sell state-guaranteed bonds prematurely for the construction of the Chenango canal, between Utica on the Erie Canal and Binghamton on the Susquehanna River. The bonds, he wrote, were as good as gold and silver, for they possessed a ready market in Europe. "I suggested that a sufficient amount should be created and sold and the proceeds deposited in the banks of Albany," which would serve as general redeeming agents for the bank notes of the country banks.[18]

On March 15 G. C. Bronson, the state attorney general and a commissioner of the Canal Fund, informed Johnson that Olcott had presented the plan to him and that he and his fellow commissioners have authorized advertisement of the Chenango Canal Loan of $900,000. It was now up to the Albany banks, Bronson continued, to be the highest bidder (in order to secure the payments from resale and thus be in a position to become the depository for the proceeds until they were actually needed for construction some time in the future). He warned: "Do not give way to alarm; the country is safe. Much has been done to cripple New York, but not a bone of her is yet broken— and will not be, if our bankers and capitalists will not give way to unnecessary panic." [19]

Johnson felt that this relief would not be enough, and meanwhile presented to Olcott the idea that the state issue bonds and lend the proceeds to those who needed assistance. Olcott replied that the suggestion had been favorably received by the state administration but the legislature could be moved only

> if it can be made to appear necessary by public meetings, as suggested by you. . . . You will, therefore, have the goodness to adopt the necessary measures for accomplishing the important object. The crisis is not yet arrived. Our country banks have yet to meet the spring pressure. The comptroller suggests loans to individuals, through the officers of each county in the state as well as through the banks. You will, therefore, open the necessary correspondence for bringing out the greatest amount of public expression in favor of this measure for relief. We may yet bid defiance to the monster.[20]

Johnson arranged for a mass public meeting on March 25. There he exclaimed that the distress was produced by an invasion by a private corporation, from Chestnut Street, Philadelphia. He declared:

I care not now whether the Bank of the United States be constitutional or unconstitutional; a necessary fiscal agent or unnecessary; whether the public deposits were rightfully removed by Government, or wrongfully—these questions are all merged in the greater issue of whether the country shall be coerced to grant the Bank a recharter.

Irrespective of any great services the Bank might render, the question was: should the Government conquer the Bank, or should the Bank conquer the Government? He concluded by urging that people of every state call on their legislatures to remove their pecuniary difficulties; and for New York the best remedy was a bond issue, its "ability to create, at a moment and without cost, an issue of bonds that is equivalent to gold and silver." [21]

On April 19, 1834, the legislature passed An Act Authorizing a Loan for the Benefit of the People of This State. The state could issue $6 million of bonds; of these $4 million would be lent to New York city banks, and the proceeds of the remainder would be lent to individual citizens by the Commissioners for Loaning Money in each county "as provided by the Act of April 11, 1808." This action Johnson shortly afterward eloquently described as "the majestic efforts of the state itself, which nobly opened its veins to our exhausted mouths, and revived credit at its expiring gasp." [22]

The controversy over the Second Bank stimulated interest in the entire area of monetary and banking affairs both at the federal and state levels. Numerous reform proposals were put forth. Toward most of these Johnson was at least skeptical and in several instances actively opposed. Generally, in his thinking, any proposal for reform had to meet one test: what effect would the measure have on the supply and utilization of specie? This concern carried until the California gold rush of 1849 which resulted in the nation's having for the first time in its history a large addition to the supply of specie.

Typical of this position was his criticism of the recommendation of his fellow Democrat, Governor Marcy, in 1838, that banks be compelled to maintain a specie reserve of 15 percent of their capital or 20 percent of their bank notes and deposits. "Our banking difficulties," Johnson contended, "spring from the fact that there is a scarcity of specie and enough of it does not exist in the world for the present extended use of commerce and credit."

The governor's remedy would create "a new use" for $6 million in specie for the reserves that would be idle and useless at the very time that the government should be reducing as much as possible the use of specie, as do small notes.

Johnson successfully fought the demand of the extreme hard-money Jacksonian leadership in the legislature to end corporate banking with its privilege of limited liability and to replace it with a system of private banking with unlimited liability and bank notes backed practically by 100 percent specie or equivalent. Along the same line, following the demise of the Second Bank of the United States, he strongly opposed the policy of Jackson's heir, President Martin Van Buren, by which the government held all its specie in its own treasury (and subtreasuries) rather than in selected state banks. The system, he complained, was "locking up and subtracting specie from the business wants of the country." [23] So strongly did he attack the policy of "divorcing the federal government from the banks" as it was called, that he temporarily forsook the Democratic Party in the presidential campaign of 1840 and, as a member of the Conservative Democratic faction, supported the successful Whig candidate, General William Henry Harrison.

Toward the end of his life, Johnson acquiesced in the subtreasury system on the ground that "after a time business became shaped to the new measure, and derangement therefrom ceased." [24]

In upholding usury laws Johnson took a most unusual position for a banker. However, in this instance his unorthodoxy may have sprung in part from the fact that he was engaged in a number of other enterprises besides banking in which his role was often that of a borrower.

His attitude toward government aid for internal improvements or, as they are called today, public works, was similarly influenced by his participation in the financing of the construction of the Erie Canal. He did have certain reservations concerning the role of the federal government in public works, primarily the fact that the largeness of the national government created a tendency for despotism, more waste, and corruption. He put forth the usual arguments for internal improvements, such as that they facilitated commerce and thus added to the nation's wealth. But he went beyond thinkers of the day in questioning that financial self-sufficiency was a necessary criterion for judging the desirability of a project. He held that

> so far as income is a test of the amount of business which a canal facilitates, it is important, but whether any such income shall be collected or not, is a question of national policy, the benefits of abandoning an income being, in some cases, greater

than the income. The debt, also, which our State has contracted in the construction of its canals will not surprise posterity should we not pay it, provided we transmit the canals with the debt . . . [for the] canals . . . promise to increase in lucrativeness as our country increases in population and productiveness. The true question, therefore . . . in relation to completing our canals is, Whether the additional debt . . . will yield a permanent equivalent for the interest of the debt? [25]

This position was bound up and consistent with his stand on the usefulness of maintaining public debt as a revolving source of capital.

Johnson consciously recognized a need for government aid to internal improvements, usury laws, and certain limited bank regulations but, at the same time, expressed in other areas the most extreme laissez-faire views, calling for the discontinuance of almost every form of public inspection and licensing. He criticized even the licensing of physicians, feeling that the best protection lay in the traditional doctrine of buyer beware. In this he went beyond the stand of his mentor, Adam Smith. His laissez-faire views carried over into his advocacy of unrestricted entry into all fields of business enterprise. He maintained that the right to incorporate should be open to all on the same terms.

Let us turn now to Johnson's ideas on the corporate form of industrial organization. He was among the pioneers in stressing the great importance of the corporation as a device for furthering the economic and social progress of the nation. The corporation with its privileges of limited liability and continuity made possible the combining of the relatively small resources and efforts of many persons; that is, it extended "the sphere of personal efficiency—the great reservoir of all efficiency." Since there were few massive private fortunes, the state in the absence of corporate associations would have had too few large manufacturing establishments and would have accomplished little in banking, insurance, and railroads. Further, since the ownership was in a multitude of persons rather than in great monopolistic capitalists, the corporations yielded the advantage of large capital without the supposed disadvantages of great private fortunes. Corporations therefore were "artificial pecuniary giants, without the dangers that might be consequent to the existence of natural giants."

Unfortunately the politicians insisted that the protection of the interests of the community required that corporations be created sparingly, and thus grew up the system of monopolies through the grant of special acts or charters of incorporation. It was argued that capitalists would not invest in corporate enterprises, notably banks, unless they had a monopoly right, for they feared that corporations could not survive under "unrestricted competition." The result was bribery and corruption of the legislature for charters. The remedy lay, Johnson wrote in 1845, not in suppressing corporations but in allowing them under general acts which specify the conditions and regulations under which any group of people could secure the privileges of incorporation. In other words, the monopoly feature would be eliminated by making

> all privileges granted by law to any one association of men . . . common to every other set of men who choose to associate and possess them. . . . If a railroad route shall then be deemed capable of sustaining two establishments, an opposition will be produced, and the community will enjoy the benefit of competition . . . at half the present charges, and perhaps twice the speed.[26]

Specifically he urged, for example, that the state allow a competing railroad from Utica to Schenectady. Johnson contended that thereby Utica would enjoy not only cheaper and faster travel but also better mail service. He said, "We now receive no night mail from Albany, though since the meeting of the legislature, we have been favored with a night train." If there were two lines, "we should doubtless enjoy a night mail, but the absence of competition places the post office department so much at the mercy of railroads, that . . . [its] utility . . . is almost destroyed." He added that "even our cheap postage system is endangered by the blind avarice of our existing railroads," and nothing would contribute more to the continuance of the present letter rates than competing roads.[27]

This fight for a general incorporation act in which Johnson was a prominent leader was crowned with success. In 1846 New York pioneered by providing in its new constitution for a broad general incorporation act, a provision that Johnson saluted as "the greatest triumph that our American experiment of equal rights" ever achieved in practical results. [28]

One of the most appealing aspects of Johnson's character was his ability to be a strong advocate of a given program or doctrine while at the same time recognizing the possible weaknesses or limitations of such. Thus he believed that the advantages of corporations far outweighed their disadvantages, but this did not mean that the latter should be ignored.

There is a tendency in our own day to assume that the divorce of ownership and control in large corporations is a problem of the twentieth century. But over a hundred years ago Johnson wrote that "the most inveterate danger that attends corporations" was the "natural antagonism between the interest of a corporation and the interest of its managers." In equally modern tones he pointed out the ineffectiveness of existing laws enacted in the name of corporate democracy. Thus "the power to vote by proxy enures . . . more to the perpetuation of an existing board of directors than to its insecurity." He proposed what in effect was a system of cumulative voting for directors. The owners of a substantial amount of stock, say one-twelfth of the capital, could choose a director, and several stockholders who together owned an equal share could also choose a director.[29]

Another area in which Johnson pioneered was in the use of census statistics to describe empirically the course of population growth. In this field he was thoroughly the man of the new world. The pessimistic predictions of Malthus were not for him. From his empirical studies, he believed that he had "discovered a relation between the increase of any given set of men in society, and the space which they occupied on the earth's surface; those who occupied the largest space, increasing most in population while those who occupied the smallest space, increasing least." [30] In reaching this conclusion, he postulated a natural maximum to population density. If this ratio were surpassed, the number of deaths would exceed the number of births or immigrants, and population would decline to its natural maximum level.

Interestingly, while denying the ratios of Malthus—that population increases geometrically but food supply arithmetically—he offered no hypothesis as to the causal factors that made fecundity increase inversely to density of population. It is difficult to believe that a mind of such originality and intellectual curiosity did not speculate on why this relationship between space and fecundity existed. If he did indeed engage in such speculation, then perhaps the clue to his unwillingness to put his ideas on paper lies in his view that Malthus would find such ideas expressing a belief in "the agency of miracles rather than sound scientific reasoning." [31]

Johnson's demographic work is typical of the strong preference for empirical methods in all areas of economic inquiry. On the other side of this coin we find a recurring distrust of armchair speculation. As he strikingly put it, there was a need to differentiate "the tinsel of indolent conjecture from the gold of laborious observation." The relative importance of accurate premises he illustrated as follows:

> When a tradesman brings me an account which asserts that I am his debtor, say a hundred dollars, I may be sure that the aggregate is fairly stated, for few men are careless enough to

commit an error in addition. The items of the bill may require examination. So, when a logician tells me the conclusion to which he is arrived by any process of argumentation, I seldom care to investigate his arguments. I assume that he will not make a false deduction, any more than the tradesman will make a false addition. The part which requires examination is the logician's premises;—those are like the tradesman's items. Most people, however, waste all their attention on a logician's arguments, and let him assume what premises he pleases. This is analogous to permitting a tradesman to charge you without restraint, provided he will be honest in his addition of the items.[32]

In dealing with the thinking of a man of such varied and wide-ranging interests as Johnson, a summation is desirable in order to obtain a coherent view of his ideas. Let us refer again to his roots outside the Anglo-American dominant culture. Certainly this contributed greatly to his sensitivity to changing events, to his avid intellectual curiosity, and to his objectivity when writing of conditions and proposals current in the America of his day. To his credit was his independence in stands on monetary, banking, and fiscal policy matters. In a number of instances these positions were sharply opposed initially to those of most of the members of the financial community. Yet he stubbornly persisted and was able on occasion to see his heretofore heretical views become the basis for legislation and policy.

A few of his most advanced ideas were not appreciated until after the first quarter of the twentieth century, especially those which today are popularly called Keynesian. Wesley C. Mitchell, the pioneer in business-cycle theory, in discussing Civil War monetary phenomena, characterized Johnson as the earliest of the very small group of writers "who studied the situation with care" and "did not allow their conclusions to be controlled by preconceived theories." [33] Certainly much the same could be said of Johnson's insights into the nature and problem of control of the giant corporations, his demographic studies, and his ideas of the role of government in economic development.

Although an outsider by background, Johnson completely embraced the lusty optimistic view which dominated all stratas of society in his adopted land. Throughout his writing appears the note that the opportunity for unlimited progress is at hand if only the people have the sense to seize it. Missing is the notion that parsimony is to be praised and hedonistic consumption is to be frowned upon. But here again he seemed more the man of the twentieth century, in declaring

138

that consumption, rather than tending to impoverish a nation, in fact tends to enrich it with additional production.[34]

In a tribute to Johnson, Henry Schoolcraft, the pioneer ethnologist and a contemporary, described him as "a gentleman of wealth, intelligence, and enterprise."[35] To this we may add that he was a spirit untrammeled, yet practical; conservative in the sense that he celebrated the accomplishments of the society which had been built in this new land, but too clear-headed not to see also its failings; and finally the possessor of that rare gift which most gains any thinker a place in history, an original imagination with the strength and character to advocate and defend his insights for the benefit of mankind.

NOTES

1 Seward to Johnson, June 11, 1842, in Johnson's autobiography, Chap. 12.

2 *The Knickerbocker* or *New York Monthly Magazine*, February 1850, p. 95.

3 "The Intellectual Preeminence of Jews in Modern Europe," 1908; reprinted in *Essays in Our Changing Order*, ed. Leon Ardzrooni, with the addition of a recently discovered memorandum, "Wire Barrage," supplied by Joseph Dorfman (1934; 2nd ed., New York: Kelley, 1964), pp. 219–231.

4 On the creed of John Adams, see Joseph Dorfman, "The Regal Republic of John Adams," 1944; reprinted in John P. Roche (ed.), *Origins of Political Thought* (New York: Harper & Row, 1967), pp. 115–138.

5 *An Inquiry into the Nature of Value and Capital, and into the Operation of Government Loans, Banking Institutions and Private Credit* (New York: privately printed, 1813), p. 3. Hereafter referred to as *Value and Capital*.

6 Johnson recorded in his autobiography that when he was courting his first wife, her mother consulted a friend as to Johnson's character. The friend said he "possessed only one fault . . . and that was too much fondness for money and that Mrs. Adams deemed in my favor as she had seen in her own family the bad consequences of an opposite character."

7 *Ibid.,* Chap. 3.

8 A decade or so later, complaints were made that economists were concerning themselves almost exclusively with a theory of value. The following amusing sketch is from "Political Economy," in the *Belles Lettres Repository* (December 1820), a journal for which Johnson wrote. "Mr. Editor: Stopping at Lang's last Sunday, after church, as is usual with us men of business, to hear the news, and learn the prices of stock, etc., my attention was arrested by a debate between two gentlemen that seemed to wax a little warm. . . . [T]he subject in dispute was the new tariff of duties as it is called but whether the disputants were merchants or manufacturers I was not able to ascertain; perhaps you, or your readers may. 'You,' said Mr. A., 'talk a great deal about the science of political economy. Do you know what it is?

B. I will give you my definition of it.

A. What is it?

B. The knowledge of the relative value of a thing.

A. Is that the extent of the important science you speak of?

B. That is only my first head.

A. And pray, what is the second head?

B. Why, a knowledge of the relative value of everything.

A. Then it is *any*thing, and *every*thing.

B. Yes, relatively considered.

A. I can't understand your definition. Good bye, sir.'

I reflected upon this, but with little satisfaction. Will you, Mr. Editor, a man of your estimable competence, be kind enough to explain what the science of political economy is? The argument I heard set me thinking on the subject, and my mind has ever since been afloat on the ocean of uncertainty.

Yours
Interrogator"

9   *Value and Capital*, p. 68.

10   *Ibid.*, pp. 85–87.

11   *Ibid.*, p. 89.

12   *Ibid.*, p. 90.

13   *Ibid.*, p. 23.

14   "The Present and Prospective Value of Gold," 1851; reprinted in *A Guide to the Right Understanding of Our American Union* (New York: Derby and Jackson, 1857), p. 288. Hereafter referred to as *A Guide*.

15   "A Treatise on Banking," in *The Bankers' Magazine*, June 1849, p. 745. At least as early as 1834 Johnson pointed out that the circulating medium was bank checks rather than bank notes.

16   "Possibly, therefore, the power to create such a currency cannot be safely committed to any institution and evils less radical, result from the existing system of paper money, notwithstanding its sudden contractions on a foreign demand for specie, than would result from any different system." *Ibid.*, p. 746.

17   Autobiography, Chap. 7.

18   *Ibid.*, "[In 1834] some of the banks of Albany undertook the purchase of country bank notes at a moderate discount, and sent them home for redemption by a messenger." [D. R. Dewey, *State Banking Before the Civil War* (Washington, D.C.: Government Printing Office, 1910), p. 96.]

19   Bronson to Johnson, March 15, 1834, in autobiography, Chap. 7.

The Annual Report of the Commissioners of the Canal Fund for 1835 states that Olcott and Richard Yates in behalf of the New York State Bank, Albany, and the Mechanics' and Farmers' Bank made the best offer. They offered "to loan the whole sum of $900,000 and to pay a premium of 6½ per cent for a five per cent stock, redeemable after 1845. . . . The stock to be issued at once, and the money deposited equally in the banks making the loan, to the credit of the Commissioners, and not to be drawn from faster than required for actual disbursements in constructing the canal. The funds now on hand to be first used. The interest on the deposit not to exceed the interest now allowed the Commissioners of the Canal Fund.

"The two banks . . . are the general depositing banks of the Canal Fund, for which deposits, as they are drawn upon from day to day for the current expenses of the canal, they pay an interest of only 3½ per cent. As the Commissioners had, during the preceding year, made numerous loans at 5 per cent, and had in their files several offers at the same rate, the persons making the offer were informed that if the deposit were given to the two banks in question, an interest of five per cent, payable quarterly, would be exacted, and with that understanding the proposition of the two banks was accepted."

20 Olcott to Johnson, March 18, 1834, in autobiography, Chap. 7. The Comptroller, Azariah C. Flagg, was a powerful Democratic leader.

21 "Speech Before a Meeting of the Democratic Citizens of Utica on the Subject of the United States Bank," 1834; reprinted in *A Guide,* pp. 132, 136. In the original version, in consistency with his views on public debt, he argued that the principal need not ever be repaid.

22 "Letter of A. B. Johnson, Esq.," 1834; reprinted as a pamphlet with a "Prefatory Note" by Jacob Zeitlin (Pasadena, California: privately printed, 1948), pp. 7–8. The original copy was supplied by Stillman Drake. Governor Marcy declared in his annual message to the legislature on January 6, 1835, that the mere announcement of the Loan Law had played a large part in bringing about a return to prosperity, and as a consequence it had not been necessary to pledge the credit of the state; that is, no positive action had to be taken.

23 Johnson to F. C. White, January 3, 1838, in autobiography, Chap. 9.

24 Autobiography, Chap. 11.

25 "The Alternative of Continuing Our State Debt or Liquidating It by Taxation," consolidated from two articles published in 1834 and 1842 and reprinted in *A Guide,* pp. 253–254.

26 "Reasons for Calling a Convention to Revise the Existing Constitution," 1845; "The Delegates Which Should be Selected to Form a State Constitution," 1845; "Advantages and Disadvantages of Private Corporations," 1850; reprinted in *A Guide,* pp. 163–164, 169, 210, 216.

27 Johnson to J. A. Spencer, January 17, April 6, 1846, in Historical Society of Pennsylvania.

28 "Legislative History of Corporations in the State of New York: Or, The Progress of Liberal Sentiments," 1851; reprinted in *A Guide,* p. 208.

29 "Advantages and Disadvantages of Private Corporations," 1850; reprinted in *A Guide,* pp. 216–217.

30 Autobiography, Chap. 4.

31 "Thoughts on Population," *The New York Literary Journal and Belles Lettres Repository,* September 1820, pp. 355–359.

32 *A Treatise on Language,* edited with a critical essay on his philosophy on language, by David Rynin (Berkeley and Los Angeles: University of California Press, 1947), pp. 111, 190.

33 *History of the Greenbacks with Special Reference to the Economic Consequences of Their Issue: 1862–65* (Chicago: University of Chicago Press, 1903), p. 189. Mitchell was particularly referring to Johnson's *The Advanced Value of Gold, Suspended Specie Payment, Legal-Tender Notes, Taxation and National Debts, Investigated Impartially,* 1862.

34 Commenting on the destruction of Moscow by the retreating Russians during the Napoleonic invasion, he daringly argued that while it is true that the action "consumed an almost incalculable quantity of capital, yet from what we know man can perform when greatly induced . . . even this unparalleled waste of desired articles may give rise to such increased exertions as to make it a means of increasing eventually the wealth of that empire." (*Value and Capital,* p. 7.)

35 *Personal Memoirs of a Residence of Thirty Years with the Indian Tribes on the American Frontiers* (Philadelphia: Lippincott, 1851), p. 18. Schoolcraft dedicated the book to Johnson.

ALEXANDER BRYAN JOHNSON: BUSINESSMAN, BANKER, AND AUTHOR OF "A TREATISE ON BANKING"

♦ ♦ ♦ ♦ ♦ *SIDNEY WERTIMER, JR.*

THE PURPOSE of this paper is to give a brief review of the business and banking life of Alexander Bryan Johnson, together with some reference background regarding the period during which he lived. Inasmuch as the "Treatise on Banking" will subsequently be re-published, only a sketchy description of its contents is included here. There is, in conclusion, some comment about Johnson as a banker, and there is an attempt at an evaluation of his banking writings from a modern point of view. Johnson, it will appear, was a nervous man with a stomach full of pecuniary butterflies whenever money was at risk, particularly if it were his own.

Johnson's Business Life

A. B. JOHNSON, as we know, was born on May 27, 1786, in Gosport, England. He took thirty days to cross the ocean, arriving in New York in April 1801, "two months short of fifteen, small of his age, but intellectually premature." [1] At the age of twenty-four he was a director of a glass factory in Vernon, New York. The glass business was a good one, and there was another factory also in Marcy, New

◊ ◊ ◊ ◊ ◊ *Chairman, Department of Economics, Hamilton College.* Studies in Nineteenth Century British Bank Amalgamations *(in preparation);* coauthor *(with John S. Gambs),* Economics and Man *(1957).*

York. Anxious to establish his own factory, but wary of the legislature which he did not think would approve a third glass factory in the county of Oneida, he organized one in Ontario county. It is not at all clear that he was successful in this venture, and in 1811 we find him in New York City investing his own and his father's money in bank stocks. At the beginning of the War of 1812, fearing bombardment of New York City, he sold these stocks at a sacrifice, returned to Utica, and invested his money in the Bank of Utica, which was then organizing. He became one of its state directors.

In 1812–13 he wrote *Value and Capital*. "The book found a few approving readers and brought him into notice as a thoughtful speculator on the subject of finance." [2] According to Johnson himself, "the best criticism I ever heard on the work was from a lady who said it seemed to her full of self-evident propositions." [3] He sold his bank stocks in New York City at a small sacrifice, "but [it] left me with no pecuniary remuneration for all my trouble and exertions . . . but the anxiety and labor I had undergone told severely on my sensitive organization." [4]

To avoid the opposition of lawmakers in Albany and the hostility of bankers already in existence, Johnson next drew up a charter of the Utica Insurance Company, "which was so cunningly worded that while it seemed to convey only permission to insure property, it granted, as was manifest to the reader aware of its intent, the privilege of banking also." [5] The charter was maneuvered through the legislature, "eluding even the vigilance of that astute lawyer and politician Martin Van Buren who was chairman of the committee in the Senate that reported the bill." [6] The bank was opened and operated with considerable success for its customers, but it generated hostility in the legislature and among its competitors, who collected and presented its notes as quickly as possible. After a change in the law, Johnson wound up the affairs of the Utica Insurance Company with "a trifling loss," on July 6, 1819. No other act in his life, according to Bagg, gave him so much pain in the recollection.

By 1819 Johnson was thirty-three, married, the father of two, and the owner of $55,000 in property. He studied law and was admitted to the bar. In June 1819 he became a director of the Ontario Branch Bank in Utica and in September became its president. The main office of this bank was in Canandaigua, New York. (The Bank of Utica, incidentally, had a branch in Canandaigua. The competition seemed to be mutually satisfactory.) When Johnson took over the branch, it was in low estate, its notes selling in New York City at a 12½ percent discount.

In 1852 Johnson went abroad following the death of his second wife. The charter of the Ontario Branch Bank expired in 1855, and a new bank, the Ontario Bank, was formed. Within eighteen months it was declared insolvent. "Elaborate means were used to conceal the progress of the ruin from the president," but Johnson paid off all the billholders and creditors in full and returned a trifle to the stockholders. About this unfortunate incident, we will have more to say later.

Alexander Bryan Johnson died in 1867, having written much on many subjects in his lifetime. In *Pioneers of Utica,* Bagg says, "He wrote treatises upon the subject of banking and finance which received high commendation from those who were best qualified to judge their merits; few men in our country understood better than he the principals which should govern all financial affairs, or were more practical in applying them."

Banking and Monetary Arrangements in the United States During Johnson's Lifetime

IN ORDER TO understand the writings of Johnson it is important also to know something of the monetary structure that existed in the United States during his time.

The first commercial bank on this continent was the Bank of North America chartered in 1781 by the Continental Congress. It later became a state bank in Pennsylvania, subsequently joined the National Banking System after 1864, and exists now as the First Pennsylvania Banking and Trust Company, Philadelphia.

At the urging of Alexander Hamilton, the First Bank of the United States was chartered for twenty years in 1791. It lasted through the administrations of Presidents Washington, John Adams, Jefferson, and Madison. The charter expired under Madison's first administration, and for five years (from 1811 to 1816), the nation enjoyed "free" banking. It was during this time that the Ontario Bank in Canandaigua was chartered by the legislature of the state of New York. During Madison's second administration, the Second Bank of the United States was chartered for another twenty years. Its capital was $35 million; its branches numbered twenty-five. Any money and banking textbook recounts the problems of the Second Bank of the United States. An excellent description is contained in Walter Blaines', *Money, Prices, and Policy,* as follows:

> The career of the Second Bank was not as uniformly successful as that of its predecessor. It experienced considerable difficulty in its first three years as a result of serious mismanagement and outright fraud on the part of several of its officers. Loans were seriously overextended, specie tended to flow out of the bank, stockholders failed to pay installments due on their stock, and the president and cashier of the Baltimore branch embezzled more than $1 million.
>
> Langdon Cheves accepted the task of cleaning up this mess in 1819, and by the time Nicholas Biddle began his brilliant but erratic administration as president in 1823, the bank had overcome its earlier difficulties and had reestablished the sound banking structure that was characteristic of the First Bank. In the process, however, it had gained the enmity of many state banks by its attempts to force them to redeem their notes in specie.
>
> This precipitated the "bank war," in which the Second Bank, Biddle, and the National Republicans were pitted against the state banks, Jackson, and the Democrats. Jackson in particular —representing the debtor class and the West—objected to the monetary aristocracy of the Bank as well as its conservative lending policies. He felt that the monopoly exercised by the Bank was undemocratic and should be abolished; and he felt that the expansion of currency circulation based on a continually increasing issue of paper money would benefit the country.[8]

President Jackson was a man of the people, an antimonopolist, and vigorously opposed the Second Bank of the United States. Henry Clay and Daniel Webster urged the Bank to apply for a renewal of its charter in order to embarrass Jackson in the campaign of 1832. Jackson was aroused to the point of vetoing the measure, and he construed his election over Clay as popular approval of that action. Resolving to crush the Bank, in 1833 Jackson began to remove government deposits to certain state banks known as "pet" banks. When the charter of the Second Bank of the United States expired in 1836, the Bank obtained a charter from the state of Pennsylvania and continued until 1841, at which point its unsound policies caused it to crash ignominiously in a cloud of broken fortunes.

> The Bank's final excesses had two rather interesting side consequences. They made the country extremely skeptical of the

benefits of the nation-wide bank, so that even today we have not returned to a single central bank. Second, they discredited Philadelphia, the seat of the Bank, as a money center and aided tremendously in the growth of New York banks, which had stuck to conservative banking practices throughout the period of the Second Bank's inflationary zeal and were thus able to survive the storm of its collapse in much the same way as the Bank of England rode out the South Sea Bubble. Except for Nicholas Biddle, Philadelphia might still be the monetary heart of the United States.[9]

One of the themes which will be picked up was Johnson's opposition to the Bank of the United States. It is quite clear that he was bitterly against any form of central bank. At a public meeting in March 1834,[10] Johnson recalled that twenty years before, when the British sacked Washington, he was secretary of a meeting at which he urged his listeners ("in the contest of whether the country shall be coerced to grant the Bank a charter," [11]) to keep separate the bank seeking a new charter, and politicians seeking power. Back in 1811 Clinton had "pronounced the death of the former bank—an event which demonstrates that we, at least, date our hostility to such institutions beyond the commencement of General Jackson's era." [12] Providence gave us, he says, Washington to fight the British and Jackson to defeat the Bank. Jackson is able to "sustain not only himself in this trying moment, but to sustain his friends, and to hold back even a nation, should it be inclined to bow its crest at the bidding of a creature of its own bounty." [13] (Johnson's writing style when it comes to banking is often long-winded, convoluted, and full of what grammarians call "comma splices." This style, evidently, is not true of his other writings.)

Later on Johnson remarks that "every petition is a new monument of power of the bank and an additional argument against its continuance." He wants to leave each man free and independent; he wants no government interference which would inevitably invite a concentration of political power and which he sees as the most abhorrent by-product of the Second Bank of the United States. The Bank was "down" in 1832 with Jackson's veto of the renewal, and "out" in 1836 with the expiration of the charter.

From 1836 to 1863 the nation experienced a period known as "free banking." Prior to the "free banking laws" passed in Michigan in 1837 and in New York in 1838, no bank could obtain a corporate charter except through specific act of the state legislature. This proce-

146   LANGUAGE AND VALUE

dure gave rise to many opportunities for favoritism and other abuses. One is recorded as follows:

> The bank of New York, for instance was owned by Federalists, who, because they controlled the State Assembly, were in a position to prevent any other group from obtaining a charter. In 1789, Aaron Burr managed to get a charter for a water company with an obscure clause permitting it to use any capital not needed for the water works "in the purchase of public or other stocks, or in any other money transaction for operations not inconsistent with laws and constitution of the state of New York." While the Manhattan Company, so chartered, did actually supply some water until 1842, its real purpose was achieved through the Bank of the Manhattan Company, which was thus enabled to compete with the Bank of New York, but only by such a ruse.[14]

In 1955 the Bank of Manhattan, which still operated under that original charter, merged with the Chase National Bank to form what we now know as Chase Manhattan Bank. For a parallel of Burr's astonishing procedure (depending upon one's point of view), I have already intimated that Johnson emulated it with the Utica Insurance Company.

Banks under the "free banking system" came and went as if by magic. In 1829 New York established a Safety Fund System. Under it each bank in the state paid a yearly assessment of one half of one percent of its capital into a common pool for six years. The fund was used to pay the creditors—both depositors and noteholders—of failed banks when they could not otherwise collect their claims. When the fund was depleted, further contributions were to be levied. Johnson, as we shall see, comments on the desirability of such a system in his "Treatise." Although this scheme has since been looked at as a precursor to the Federal Deposit Insurance Corporation, it was not strong enough to withstand the tide of failures which engulfed it. Like most bank-deposit insurance schemes, if it proves effective and fully sufficient it is not necessary; if it is insufficient and ineffective, then it is necessary; but all it creates is a false security which leads to overexpansion and abuse.

Let me conclude this section with a few observations about other banking facts of the period from 1836 to 1863.

1. There was a panic in 1837 which resulted from a wave of speculation and reckless expansion beginning as far back as 1833. There were crop failures in 1835 and 1837, and President Jackson, in

his last year of office, required that public lands be paid for in specie (gold or silver coin). The government also decreed that all taxes should be paid in specie, and in turn made its payments also in coin.

2. From 1837 to 1840 there was a struggle between Van Buren and the Whigs over "the independent treasury" proposed by Van Buren, for the deposit of government funds. The Whigs, at this time, favored the establishment of a Third Bank of the United States.

3. The Independent Treasury plan was adopted in 1840, but with the election of President Harrison, this was repealed in 1841.

4. Under President Polk (1845–49), the Independent Treasury plan was reenacted, and turmoil of "on again, off again," continued for a number of years.

All in all, the period 1836–63 was one of great confusion and difficulty. The quantity of money, as issued by first an increasing and then a decreasing number of banks, grew and declined without any control. The changing quantity of money had an enormous economic impact on the nation. We grew in spite of our monetary system, not because of it; we lurched from one expansive economic excess to a collapse, and then to an expansion and economic excess to another collapse.

"A Treatise on Banking"

THE FULL TITLE of this work is as follows: "A Treatise on Banking, the Duties of a Banker and His Personal Requisites Therefore. By Alexander Bryan Johnson, Esquire, President of the Ontario Branch Bank, Utica."

The "Treatise" appeared in at least four different places. Its first appearance was in the *Bankers' Magazine* for June 1849. Its second appearance took the form of a pamphlet issued in October 1850 by Seward & Thurber of Utica, New York. The third appearance of the Treatise is in the *Banker's Common-Place Book,* published in Boston in 1851 by Phillips, Samson, and Company. J. Smith Homans was the publisher, and it is instructive to note that he was also editor of the *Bankers' Magazine* in which the "Treatise" first appeared originally. Finally, the Treatise appears as one section of Johnson's *Guide to the Right Understanding of Our American Union,* which was published in New York City by Darby and Jackson in 1857. Basically, the "Treatise" did not undergo any extensive revision, and the changes from one appearance to the next are essentially minor.

The original "Treatise" is dedicated to the Honorable Charles Stebbins of Cazenovia, who was the Commissioner of Banks for the State of New York. In the dedication, Johnson (casting himself in the third person) states that the

> incessant responsibilities and urgent cares of banking are little suited to the anxiousness of his disposition, and that he has long born himself onward with a determination, indefinite as to the period of its execution, to transfer his position [as President of the Bank] to some person better organized for its duties.

With this design, we are informed, the "Treatise on Banking" was commenced, thus passing to his eventual successor the aid of his valuable experience.

Johnson, in his autobiography, writes of publishing the "Treatise" in 1849 in the *Bankers' Magazine* of Boston, which magazine was in a "very desponding condition." Only 750 copies of the magazine were printed. Not a man to lack confidence, however, Johnson sent a copy to J. W. Gilbart of the London and Westminster Bank, whose letter of praise about the "Treatise" is reproduced in full in the autobiography. Gilbart said (in a letter dated December 12, 1849) that he would send Johnson a copy of the review of his "Treatise" which would appear in the London *Bankers' Magazine* in January. Gilbart evidently sent to Johnson in return his own "Ten-Minute's Advice on Keeping a Banker," which is the second item in the *Banker's Common-Place Book*. Johnson's "Treatise" and Gilbart's article make up the first part of the *Common-Place Book*. The second part of the *Common-Place Book* reproduces articles by Byles on the law of bills of exchange. "Remarks on Bills of Exchange" by John Ramsey McCullough, the famous British economist and follower of Ricardo, and other miscellaneous material on bills of exchange.

One can speculate that Homans was grateful to Johnson for the "Treatise" which appears to have created quite a stir in banking circles. The *Bankers' Magazine* got a new lease on life, and Homans praises Johnson greatly, as can be seen from the Preface, which I quote in full:

> The following "Treatise on Banking" written by, perhaps, the oldest practical banker in America, was published originally in the June number of the *Bankers' Magazine* for 1849. It was extensively noticed by the daily press in many parts of our union, and its information on the subject of banking was deemed so useful for every class of persons, that several of the papers in

the state of New York recommended a copy of the "Treatise" should be placed in every school district library in the state. No doubt the procurement of bank loans would be facilitated by a knowledge that bank loans are not properly accorded as personal favors, or distributed by the caprice of bankers, (though such erroneous opinions are not uncommon) but depend upon principles that the "Treatise" discloses, and which can be conformed to by persons who desire to become borrowers.

The *Bankers' Magazine* of London, quoted largely from the work, and with much commendation; and bankers everywhere who have seen it seem to unite in its praise. The first edition is now out of print, except as it exists in the third volume of the *Bankers' Magazine*, bound up with the other matter of the volume, and some copies of which are still for sale by the editor and at several of his agencies in different cities. But as inquiries for the "Treatise" are numerous, from different places, and an order for a copy of the work has just been received from Paris, the editor has republished it, carefully revised by the author, and accompanied it with several other articles from other sources; but making, in the whole, a volume that cannot fail of being useful to bankers, and to readers of every kind who desire a knowledge of what has heretofore been deemed the occult science of banking.

The ecclesiastical doom and gloom with which Johnson treats the topic of banking finds expression on the title page, which Homans quotes from the very last chapter of the "Treatise." This reads as follows: "While a banker adheres with regularity to known forms of business and settled principles, Providence is a guarantee for his success; but when he deviates from these, Providence is almost equally a guarantee of disaster, both personal and official."

The "Treatise" is divided into three parts. The first part has to do with "the Bank" and deals with the business and legal structure of money and banking as it existed at the time of writing, 1849. This is, I suggest, good as far as description goes, but heavily larded with Johnson's own predilections about what ought to be as well as what is. The second section has to do with "the Banker," and is piously full of hellfire and damnation in the best sense of the Protestant ethic. It is full of dire warnings about how to avoid disaster, quotations from the Scripture, and exhortations on how to make money. Some of this advice, Johnson, alas, did not take himself. The third section has to do with "the Man," is also cautionary, and probably need not have been separated from section two. Let us look at each section in a little greater detail, quoting here and there to try to capture the flavor.

"Part I: The Bank"

The "Treatise" opens with definitions of discount and interest. Seven percent interest is not usurious; seven percent discount is. Johnson describes the "Safety Fund Banks," which had to make contributions to the insurance scheme and contrasts them with "free banks," which, while they do not make insurance company contributions, may not issue notes in excess of their reserves in the form Federal and state bonds. We must remember, incidentally, that it was the function of the banks to issue their own bank notes at this time, a privilege which was circumscribed with the passage of the National Banking Act of 1863, and which finally expired only in 1933.

The profit of a bank, Johnson observes, does not come from investing its own capital, but rather on the loans it makes in the form of notes based on deposits received. He is quaint but clear. "The effect is alike, therefore; of circulation [i.e., bank notes] and deposits; the nature of them is similar; circulation is deposits inside out, while deposits are circulation outside in." [15]

Bank notes, he points out, are useful to the public as well as to the banks as loans, "deemed favors by borrowers," and when these notes are spent, they become income to people, "for whoever receives money receives it in exchange for his labor or property that he values *less* than the money for which he exchanges it." [16] The use of money "is too costly to permit any person to retain it long in inactivity," and this accounts for the fact that there cannot for very long exist too great a supply of currency. " 'Dust thou art and unto dust thou shall return,' is not more appliable to the human body with reference to the earth, than to bank currency with reference to bank loans." [17]

Johnson seems a trifle biased, if not misleading, when he comments on the loss to the public from insolvent bank notes. He said that the loss is greater to a rich man than to the laboring poor, whose loss arises from the casual possession of an insolvent bank note which he can correct by an hour's labor. The rich man, however, loses the whole value of bank stock, which may take years to replace (!).

He inveighs against the Safety Fund, one of those damnable creations of the legislature. It punishes, he says, honest bankers for the frauds of the dishonest. "It is, also, vicious in its tendency, for it promises indemnity against a bank insolvency, and thereby prevents the scrutiny of the public in the conduct of bankers; permitting extravagance, improvidence, and dishonesty to unmolestedly effect their ravages." [18] This was perhaps all very well for his time, when most customers knew their bankers not only as businessmen but socially also. This is even true of those of us who dwell in small towns, although our bankers do not readily permit us very much "scrutiny" into their business conduct. Certainly it would not apply to any large New York bank, much less to Chase Manhattan, and we may take this occasion to remind ourselves again how, in spite of Johnson's vaunted public scrutiny, that bank made its unique beginning under Aaron Burr.

Johnson concludes that Safety Fund banks (outside of New York City) are more profitable, while in New York City, free banks are more profitable, since they have fewer bank notes and do more business through deposits. Free banks, also, may charge 7 percent on loans, whereas Safety Fund banks are limited to 6 percent. More loans take the form of bank notes in the country, whereas loans in the city take the form of created deposits. He speaks of the greater use of checks in cities.

A section of some interest to economists was dropped from the edition of the "Treatise" which appeared in the *Guide*. In this section, Johnson points out that some magnitudes of capital seemed to be more lucrative in a place than other magnitudes there. This is a question of the scale of banking, the implication being that a large bank and a small bank would tend not to locate in the same place. "To investigate the source of the above differences . . . would involve us more deeply in the philosophy of banking than is necessary to our present designs; and we have introduced the subject only to excite attention to it, should any person wish to investigate it further." [19] In other words, one would expect to find banks of about the same size in a given city, and these would be of different sizes as compared to banks existing in other sized cities. Banks of five different sizes, he thinks, would not locate in the same city.

Johnson makes an eloquent defense for what we call the "Goldsmiths' Principle." This familiar principle amounts to saying that banks may safely promise to pay total sums considerably in excess of the cash actually on hand for meeting such promises. He begins to develop a real theory of money as a causative factor in business and economic activity when he says, "Business is more usually contracted from inability to obtain currency than currency is contracted from a diminution of business, a proof of this is the expansion, apparently illimitable, that gradually occurs in business whenever banks become able to expand the currency." [20] The business which goes on in the state guarantees to banks that all their bank notes will not be demanded for

152

payment, or all deposits withdrawn from the banks. Here, again, he makes the point that a surplus of currency can never long exist, pointing out that the extinguishing of bank notes and deposits on the one hand and loans to the public on the other "preserve a pretty uniform equality." [21]

When it came to the concept of legal tender, Johnson was suspicious in the extreme. "No law . . . can confer a value on insolvent paper except as the law may act on preexisting contracts. The law may, indeed, forbid you from refusing to receive the money on new contracts, but you will enter into none." [22] This is of course exactly what happened under the Legal Tender Act of 1862, which required a creditor to accept greenbacks in payment of old debts. It could not, however, force a seller to accept greenbacks for goods since his alternative was to refuse to make the sale. He would accept greenbacks only at a depreciated value in terms of specie. Thus gold and silver represented the monetary unit of the country, while paper currency was the predominate medium of exchange. During the most dismal days of the Civil War, greenbacks sank to a value of 36 cents in terms of specie. That is, an article that could be purchased for one dollar required $2.85 in greenbacks.[23] We must not give Johnson too much credit for being prescient, however, for this is exactly the same sort of thing that happened with the Continental Currency from which experience we derived the expression "not worth a Continental."

When it comes to a national currency, Johnson comments on the Bank of England's ability to issue bank notes, but he expresses his usual fear of the possibility of an overissue, so "the power to create such a currency cannot be safely committed to any institution." [24] In a footnote on the same page, he says that Safety Fund banks, on which there is no statutory limit to an increase in the issuance of bank notes, are better than free banks, which have to limit their bank notes to the amount of specie or state bonds available. He gives as a reason for this statement the fact that "The unexpansibility [of the free banks, ability to issue bank notes] would constitute a great practical check on competition and on enterprise generally." He then goes on to contradict his earlier "theory of money statement" by saying that high prices require a large money supply and "proceed from a large demand."

Johnson writes that the expansion of deposits is more apt to occur in cities, whereas expansion of bank notes is apt to occur in the country. Banks readily encourage this, he says boldly, "because bank profits are thereby augmented." [25] When it comes to the contraction phase, "each bank is a sort of independent sovereignty, each guards vigilantly its own interest." And further: "Every bank is a heart from which flows its notes through all the business ramifications of the state; while every other bank is a vein [that absorbs the notes and returns them]." There are, however, he laments, periodic contractions. "Banks are, as well as men, subject to an occasional rush of blood to the head," and if specie is demanded in a pressure contraction, each bank tries to strengthen its own position at the expense of the other, and we get mutual impoverishment. The section describing panic where money becomes scarce, prices languish and fall, is vividly done. Finally, he says, prices fall so low that the nation becomes a good place from which to export, the outlook finally turns sanguine, and we reach what later economists have described as the "lower turning point" of the business cycle.

In the last sections of this part of the "Treatise," he describes the bill of exchange and mechanisms for collection within and without the state. These sections complete his discussion of banking operations, and in all, it would appear to be a tolerable description of the banking mechanism of the period which he knew.

"Part II: The Banker"

Johnson is forthright. "The object of banking," he says unequivocally, "is making pecuniary gains for stockholders by legal operations." [26] Acting altruistically, bringing benefit to the community, or doing any of the things the Bank of the United States did, adds up to nonsense. Here we have the nineteenth-century liberal doctrine at its articulate best. The prosperity of his bank should constitute the primary object of the banker. Then follows a diatribe against the suspension of specie payment of which there were three during his life in New York—in 1813, in 1819, and again and most notably in 1837. Specie suspension is never necessary if attention is paid to the quality of the loan and the vigor of its collection.

> A violation of this principle produced, in the year 1837, a suspension of specie payments, which was visited on bank stockholders by a legislative prohibition of dividends, and visited on banks and bankers by a general obloquy. The banks suspended that the debtors of the bank might not suspend; or worse, the banks suspended that the debtors might be spared the pecuniary loss that would have resulted from paying their debts. A conduct so suicidal was probably fostered by the pernicious union, in one person, of bank director and bank debtor;

a union from which our banks are never wholly exempted; nor are they always exempted from the same union still more pernicious, in bank president and cashiers.[27]

Had banks refused to suspend, business, it was true, would suffer, but this is a problem of the legislature, not of banks. The bank should obey the laws; it should not "do-good" for business. "The owner of a steam-engine regulates its business by the capacity of its engine, but should he regulate it by the necessities of its customers, he would probably burst his boiler." [28]

That loans should be made only for "productive purposes," a doctrine which was solemnized in the "automatic short-term, self-liquidating principle of lending," is expressed by Johnson where he talks about information to be found in the application of the loan. When money is to be invested into goods, the investment yields to the borrower a means of repayment; if the loan is to pay a preexisting debt, "you are merely taking a thorn out of another person's side to place it in your own." [29]

Hereafter follow a number of sections cautioning bankers to be fully lent yet moderate, how to select loans, and what paper is preferable. Competition for profitable customers is great, "hence liberality to customers by a banker is as much a dictate of interest as of justice." [30] He goes on to talk about loans as regards their place of repayment, the sale of exchange, commissions for collection, the amount of time the loan is to last, and timing with regard to panics and pressures. I respectfully submit that he does not miss a penny on the points of how to earn interest.

City banks can make very short-term loans or even demand loans, remain fully lent, and yet have funds quickly available to meet demands for payment. Country banks cannot, however, like those city banks, have their cake and eat it too. Their loans must of necessity run for longer periods of time so that keeping fully lent means there is less available to meet runs in the event of panic or emergency. Country banks are sometimes required to keep their spare funds in Albany or New York, and while they can get 4 or 5 percent on these deposits, Johnson is thoroughly against the idea of keeping a redemption fund for country banks. Evidently a bank had failed in New York or Albany sometime in the recent past, and the banks which had used it as depository suffered. The legislature looked solely to the convenience of the public, "and possibly estimated too lightly or disregarded the hazards to the banks." [31]

Johnson says that the banker should know the pecuniary circumstances of his dealers. He speaks of nonreliance on the board of directors, since what is everyone's business is nobody's. There must be a heavy reliance on the banker who is omniscient. People will tell a banker when one of his debtors becomes insolvent, but this merely serves to shut the stable door after the horse is gone. "The information which is useful must be made while the person in question retains a reputation for solvency; and the information will be valuable in proportion as 'it scents any coming mischief in the far off gale.' " [32] He suggests that bankers should keep an information book on everyone and never be in a position to refuse a loan to an unknown person; rather he should acquire the knowledge. "Every note, therefore, that he rejects for want of knowledge, is ostensibly a slight reproach on him . . . while every note he rejects or accepts by means of his knowledge of the parties is a tribute to his industry and vigilance." [33]

Johnson makes another practical suggestion. A banker, he says, should know signatures to prevent forgeries. People in the country often write poorly, write differently at different times, and with different inks and pens. This makes things difficult indeed. He suggests keeping a book with signatures in it alphabetically. Also, when notes are paid, the names of the endorsers, with their permission, should be cut from the note and pasted into the book. "Some names on notes may not be deserving of preservation; and in this particular, as in all others, the banker must exercise his judgment," [34] he concludes darkly.

And so he goes on with other suggestions. A banker should know the residence of his endorsers, the pecuniary position of his bank, and the vagaries in demand for loans and funds; "practically, however, if a banker has funds enough, day-by-day, to meet the requirements of the day, he has funds enough. 'Sufficient for the day is the evil thereof,' is a proverb peculiarly applicable to banking." [35] A banker "should never promise prospective loans," and thus, "be placed in the wholesome dilemma of injuring his personal character or of preventing the injury only by a sacrifice of the interest of his bank." [36]

A banker must be vigilant against robberies, and has to employ trusted officers. "No man plunders to accumulate property that is not to be used . . . nearly every plunderer is a prodigal and may thereby be detected. . . . The sentinel whose post happens to be surprised by the enemy may escape punishment as a criminal, but he can rarely gain commendation for vigilance, or escape censure for carelessness." [37]

As to overdrafts, he observes that to permit this practice is

156

to make loans without endorsers or without payment of interest. It is a practice to be avoided. Alert tellers and bookkeepers can help: " 'The eye of the master maketh diligent,' say the Scriptures." Be prompt in collecting debts, but if a banker can get added security by extending the loan, then this is "less [of a] banking evil than insecurity; just as the protraction of disease that results in health is a less physical evil than death." [38]

Adhere to sound principles. Stick to the rules. Here follows the dictum which appeared on the title page of the *Common-Place Book:* the homily about Providence being a guarantee for success. Johnson sometimes makes the bank sound like a church, ringing with ecclesiastical phrases and preaching sermons of rectitude and financial virtue. As the high priest, he is, of course, against monetary sin. His altar boys, the cashiers, had to be also.

Beware of persuasion and "undue pertinacity" in applications for loans as evidence of some latent defect in the applicant's pecuniary position. Beware of speculators: they are ruinous. Bankers should keep independent of their debtors. "When a debtor arrives at a certain magnitude of indebtedness, he becomes the master of his creditor, who is somewhat in the position of Jonah when swallowed by the whale." [39] Johnson's advice is not to get into Jonah's position. If you do, don't lend any more; in other words, don't let the whale get any bigger.

Concluding this section, Johnson cautions against unnecessary expenditure and preaches a doctrine of economy. He says that banks frequently spend too much on architecture "to ornament the city of their location, or to rival some neighboring institution whose extravagance ought to be shunned not followed. No person has yet shown why the banks should be built like palaces. . . ." [40] Don't confuse great capital with great wealth. But if two or three should gather together and unite their small capitals, they may need a bigger building, "but that the association can afford an organization increased in splendor as much as in magnitude, is a fallacy, somewhat analogous to the blunder of the Irishman who, hearing that his friend intended to walk forty miles during a day, said that he would walk with him, and they could then walk eighty miles." [41]

"Part III: The Man"

Why this should be a separate section is not quite clear, but nevertheless it is. Johnson proceeds to urge more caution. The banker should be wary of recommendations. The man who recommends a loan "acts under circumstances that are much less favorable to caution than the man who is to lend . . . to speculatively believe that we will suffer the extraction of the tooth, is a wholly different matter from sitting down and submitting to the operation." [42]

The second part of this short section urges the man to be governed by his own judgment. By acting on his own, he strengthens his judgment as he proceeds; by subordinating his judgment, he debilitates himself. "Let the council of your own heart stand, says the Bible; and, by way of encouragement, it adds, that a man can see more of what concerns himself, than seven watchmen on the high tower." [43] The third section of the last part is entitled "Finally." Finally, avoid "engagements that may make him needy. If he wants to be *more* than a banker, he should cease from being a banker."

He speaks on the one hand about the irritability which proceeds from refusing loans as against the popularity which follows upon granting them, and recalls the occasion upon which a public dinner was given for a banker who had ruined his bank but had done favors for the community. And he closes, inevitably, with a diatribe against the Second Bank of the United States.

> The service of a massive plate that was given to a president of the late U.S. Bank was in reward for compliances which soon after involved in disaster every commercial interest in our country. The moroseness which we abhor proceeds often from a sensitiveness that is annoyed at being unable to oblige; the amiability that is applauded proceeds from an imbecility that knows not how to refuse.[44]

The Failure of the Ontario Bank

WE NOW RETURN to "real life," as of January 1, 1856, the date on which the charter of the Ontario Branch Bank expired. It was suggested that the old bank be replaced by two new ones, one in Canandaigua and one in Utica. The stockholders responded with alacrity to the offer. Johnson took $40,000 in stock and said that he would have taken more had he not "had regard for the wants of others." [45] A new private bank was opened in Canandaigua, and Johnson became president of the new bank in Utica at a salary of $1,500 giving his cashier $2,500, "as my services in the new institution were to be more supervisory than active."

This is the bank which as we know failed within eighteen months of its inception. Johnson, probably preoccupied with his writings, failed to observe the many dicta which he laid down from time to time on the proper operation of a bank, and which had been noted in the section just above. In particular, he has an article in the *Guide* on "The Duties, Omissions, and Mis-doings of Bank Directors," which devotes a good deal of attention to bank supervision. "The counting of money is not pernicious if the Board choose to amuse their vigilance therewith . . . the ingenuity of concealment being naturally as great as the ingenuity of detection." The best detection, he says, is to keep a keen eye on the "general conduct, habits, and expenses of the management." [46]

All of Chapter 16 of the Johnson autobiography is missing, and we do not have Johnson's own account of what occurred. Professor Stillman Drake, however, with a keen historical eye, found an article in the October issue of the *Bankers' Magazine*, 1858, under the caption "Illegal Bank Drafts," which is herewith quoted in part:

> This is the end of the Ontario Bank. Its powers as a bank have ceased. All paper becoming due there must be paid without renewal of favor. The receiver will collect the assets and pay the various creditors, and provide for the redemption of the bills. No doubt is entertained that all the claims against the bank will be paid, though the loss to the stockholders is variously estimated. . . .
>
> More than a year has passed since the Ontario Bank at Utica was compelled to go into liquidation in consequence of the fraudulent abstraction of about one-half of its capital by the then cashier, and its appropriation to speculative purposes. This misapplication of funds was fortunately discovered in time to prevent the exhaustion of the whole capital. Had this discovery not been made at the time it was, the whole capital would have been gone in less than two weeks. One scheme for raising money to bolster up the cash account was by means of illegal or post-dated drafts on the New York correspondent, and negotiations by special agents outside the bank. The cashier overdrew the bank account with its New York, Albany, Buffalo and other correspondents, and the letters from these parties remonstrating against such a course, addressed both officially and privately to the president, were purloined by the cashier so as not to reach their destination.
>
> Another plan was to hypothecate the bank's issues with outside parties paying enormous rates of interest, in order to cover the delinquency. The illegal drafts have been placed in suit, and the Supreme Court has decided against them. The Utica Ob-

server publishes a part of the written opinion of the Supreme Court of that district in the case of the Oneida Bank against the Ontario Bank, argued at the last general term of the court. The suit was brought to recover the amount of $14,000 due on four drafts drawn by James S. Lynch, cashier of the Ontario Bank, on Duncan, Sherman, and Company, which were discounted by the Oneida Bank before the days of their respective dates, and the payment which was refused at maturity by the drawees.

Johnson's immediate labors were devoted to paying off depositors and noteholders as they came in. The assets diminished accordingly, leaving, we infer, pracially nothing for the stockholders. There is only one reference to the "disruption" in Chapter 17 of the autobiography. Judge Daniel Appleton White of Salem, Massachusetts, had been a stockholder in the old Branch Bank, and he eventually became one in the new bank to the extent of $10,000 ". . . and of course it was lost in the general ruin." Johnson says he felt very bad about the old judge who had retired on the earnings of his investments, but the judge felt sorry for Johnson too: ". . . on the whole, the sentiment of the community was commiserative of my unfortunate position, and that I sustained myself under it was a marvel to many as well as myself." [47]

Conclusions

WHAT CAN WE SAY about Alexander Bryan Johnson by way of evaluation, about him as a banker, and as a writer on banking subjects? He wrote, as we have seen, on broader economic topics and about banking in other places besides in the "Treatise."

As a banker or investor in banks, his record is spotty. As an investor, evidently, if we may believe the autobiography, he did well, very well, or superbly. As a businessman, he was competent in Utica as a director of the Bank of Utica, less so in the glassworks enterprises—and if the Corning Research is valid, Johnson flunked. (See Jasena Rappleye Foley, "The Ontario Glass Manufacturing Company," *Journal of Glass Studies,* Corning, New York, Vol. VI, 1964.) He would get a "B minus" from his teachers as a grade in the Utica Insurance Company, but no credit for originality regarding its charter. As president of the Ontario Branch Bank in Utica, Johnson appears to have been truly great; a leader, weathering the storms of 1837 with flying colors. As president of the Ontario Bank in Utica, in 1856, he spent entirely too much time writing, "devoting," as he says, "much time to

160

the *ignis fatuus* of literary speculation." He ignored, alas, some of his own good advice.

With regard to his writings, first, one observes that they are more of a practical than a theoretical nature. In the practical sense, he could tell us little to illuminate *how* to run a bank today (save his observations on human nature and how they apply to banks). His remarks in a historical context are, however, very useful to the banking historian, for they tell us much about the banking system and structure of the period. His value judgments are also of great interest, but we are faced with a paradox which needs resolution.

Although professing the ideals of a Jacksonian Democrat, A. B. Johnson would be far from that, were he alive today; rather the reverse. He would, indeed, be an ultraconservative. Johnson is not a Jacksonian Democrat because he is *"of* the people"; rather he is a Jacksonian Democrat because he is antigovernment, antipolitics, and antibigness. The Second Bank of the United States might be desirable in itself, but its power attracts politicians and this is wrong, dangerous, and will be the object of their manipulation. Many small banks are all right in a laissez-faire economy based on perfect competition. This is an example of Mandeville's *Fable of the Bees,* but in the nineteenth century.

The paradox of Alexander Bryan Johnson as a Jacksonian Democrat may be seen also, I think, by a reverse illustration. A number of years ago Broadus Mitchell of Rutgers University published a two-volume biography on the life of the first Secretary of the Treasury, Alexander Hamilton. Mitchell made the point at a lecture that Hamilton might be regarded as the first Democrat. "The people, sir," Hamilton is sometimes reputed to have remarked, "are a great beast." This is hardly a pre-Jacksonian pronouncement. Hamilton was in favor of an influential central government, a powerful Treasury, and was unafraid of Federal debt. The man we identify with early staunch Republicanism was really a twentieth-century Democrat, and a precursor of Franklin D. Roosevelt. Alexander Bryan Johnson, on the other hand, identified with Jacksonian democracy, would hardly have voted for his namesake in 1964.

In a different sense, Alexander Bryan Johnson danced on the periphery of economic theory. We have seen above that he was speculating on the real cause-effect relation with regard to the influence of money on economic activity. He teetered on the brink of what later developed into a quantity theory of money. He was not in this respect, however, clear or really mature, and in later sections even somewhat contradictory. Perhaps his preoccupation with the individual bank made him miss the forest for the trees.

He did, however, describe with precision and clarity what Hawtrey in England at the turn of the century was to call the "inherent instability of credit." Johnson had thought through and described what we now know as "imputed interest." Professor Dorfman has quoted Johnson's speculations on changes in the gold supply and its influence on prices.

Johnson's essays on the nature of public finance, public improvements, alternatives as between debt and taxation, suspending improvements or increasing debt, are all astonishing for a man of his time. "If we pass debt to posterity," this will be all right if "we pass the canals to posterity too." A careful reading of his essays here, indicates a narrower application for government expenditure than one which, however, would suit a modern Keynesian. Johnson prefers government expenditures in aid of canals and railroads that will expand the economic activity of an area, preferably one in which Johnson has a monetary interest. There is, in short, no great power of economic generalization here as in Adam Smith, Thornton's famous work on **Paper Credit**, or Ricardo and the Bullion Report.

One is surprised that John Stuart Mill, with whom Alexander Bryan Johnson could be easily identified (at least economically), is not mentioned by Johnson. On the other hand, so far as I can discover, Johnson rarely identifies ideas which he has picked up from others—he is, in other words, a poor footnoter. His remark that he read Smith, Lauderdale, etc., is unique where it appears. The only cross-current is with Gilbart—again, a practical banker, not a theoretician.

Johnson is, of course, a precursor of Bagehot, but the latter dealt with a central bank, the Bank of England, established in 1698. A central bank in the United States was anathema to Johnson. He wanted for the United States no "lender of last resort." He wanted for the United States the independence of competition among banks which would aid our economic burgeoning. We burgeoned, it is true—but more in spite of banks and money than because of them. Banking control, to which we are now accustomed, is proper now. Was not Alexander Bryan Johnson right, given his time? Boston, Philadelphia, and New York were the big financial centers, and Alexander Bryan Johnson "went West." In the best of the American expansionist tradition, he built; his area, together with the nation, grew. We owe much to that type of mind and to that type of independent genius.

NOTES

1 M. M. Bagg, *Pioneers of Utica* (Utica: Curtiss & Childs, 1877), p. 321.
2 *Ibid.*, p. 322.
3 Autobiography, Chap. 3.
4 *Ibid.*
5 Bagg, *op. cit.*, p. 323.
6 *Ibid.*, pp. 323–324.
7 *Ibid.*, p. 325.
8 Walter W. Haines, *Money, Prices and Policy,* 2nd ed. (New York: Mc-Graw-Hill, 1966), p. 81.
9 *Ibid.*, p. 82.
10 A. B. Johnson, *A Guide to the Right Understanding of Our American Union,* Part I, Chap. 5.
11 *Ibid.*, p. 132.
12 *Ibid.*, p. 134.
13 *Ibid.*, p. 135.
14 Haines, *op. cit.*, pp. 85–86.
15 A. B. Johnson, "A Treatise on Banking," in J. Smith Homans (ed.), *The Banker's Common-Place Book* (Boston: Phillips, Sampson & Co., 1851), p. 81.
16 *Ibid.*, p. 10.
17 *Ibid.*, p. 17.
18 *Ibid.*, p. 12.
19 *Ibid.*, pp. 15–16.
20 *Ibid.*, p. 17.
21 *Ibid.*, p. 18.
22 *Ibid.*, p. 20.
23 Haines, *op. cit.*, p. 92.
24 Johnson, "A Treatise on Banking," *op. cit.*, p. 21.
25 *Ibid.*, p. 22.
26 *Ibid.*, p. 28.
27 *Ibid.*, p. 29.
28 *Ibid.*, p. 30.
29 *Ibid.*, p. 32.
30 *Ibid.*, p. 36.
31 *Ibid.*, p. 39.
32 *Ibid.*
33 *Ibid.*, p. 40.
34 *Ibid.*, p. 41.
35 *Ibid.*, p. 42.
36 *Ibid.*, p. 43.
37 *Ibid.*
38 *Ibid.*, p. 44.
39 *Ibid.*, p. 45.
40 *Ibid.*
41 *Ibid.*, p. 46.
42 *Ibid.*, p. 47.
43 *Ibid.*, p. 48.
44 *Ibid.*
45 Autobiography, Chap. 15.
46 *Guide*, p. 237.
47 Autobiography, Chap. 17.

III

UTICA'S "FIRST CITIZEN" AND AMERICA'S "FIRST FAMILY"

If my prognostics are of any avail, the name of A. B. Johnson will do honor to our country.

Letter from Francis Adrian Van Der Kemp to A. B. Johnson, July 24, 1824

Tell my lovely hussy Abby—what! says Abby, does my grandpa descend from his dignity to apply such a vulgar word to me? Hussy, tell her, means housewife. And I hope she will know how a pot should be boiled, and a spit turned, as well as to know how cakes and puddings, and pies and tarts should be made.

John Adams to A. B. Johnson, November 28, 1814

ALEXANDER BRYAN JOHNSON: REFORM AND RELIGION

♦ ♦ ♦ ♦ ♦ *DAVID M. ELLIS*

AS CARL CARMER has pointed out in his essay "Upstate is a Country" the rural inhabitants of the Empire State have often surrendered "to mystic influences which never cease to hover in the otherwise salubrious upstate air." [1] Between 1820 and 1840, in addition to their mysticism, upstaters, particularly the early settlers of Oneida County, also seem to have succumbed to numerous waves of religious enthusiasm, Sabbatarianism, temperance movements, educational reform, and abolitionist fervor.

How did Alexander Bryan Johnson, the well-bred, well-traveled son of a wealthy Utica merchant, react to all this? Did the rhetoric of the reformers have any effect on this urbane banker and scholarly pioneer of linguistic analysis? Did the hell-fire preaching of Charles G. Finney, for example, disturb this tough-minded pragmatist whom some contemporary theologians felt was well on his way to exorcising the words "truth" and "spirit" from the English language? In attempting to answer these questions one runs squarely into the enigma that was A. B. Johnson.

The Oneida country, or the region of the upper Mohawk Valley, developed spectacularly after the Revolutionary War. In 1784

◊ ◊ ◊ ◊ ◊ *Professor of History, Hamilton College. Author,* Landlords and Farmers in the Hudson Mohawk Region, 1790-1850. *Coauthor,* A Short History of New York State *(1957);* New York, The Empire State *(1961);* A History of New York State *(1967).*

Hugh White of Middletown, Connecticut, led the procession of Yankee pioneers beyond the German settlements around Herkimer. Cheap land, fertile soil, and good transportation attracted hundreds of settlers each year. Some spread west and south to New Hartford, Paris Hill, and Clinton, while others headed north to the lands of Baron von Steuben, William Floyd, and the Holland Land Company, which had two patents in the county.[2] Timothy Dwight, President of Yale College, who often condemned the uncouth manners of frontiersmen, rejoiced in the "sprightliness, thrift and beauty" of the transplanted communities of New Hartford and Whitestown.[3]

Near Old Fort Schuyler (Utica) a safe ford and easy landing led many boatmen to discharge their goods and passengers.[4] A tiny hamlet sprang up despite the baleful policy of the Bleecker family of leasing their lands in the old Cosby Manor. In 1797, the construction of the "Genesee Road," scarcely more than a trace through the trees, opened pack-animal travel to the west. Utica's commercial leadership over Rome was guaranteed when the Seneca Turnpike Company built its first mile of road westward in 1800.

Utica was a village of about 500 people in 1801 when fifteen-year-old Alexander Bryan Johnson and his mother arrived from England to join Bryan Johnson. The elder Johnson had already become a leading merchant whose policy of paying cash for wheat and potash attracted the goods of frontier farmers.

The Reverend John Taylor in 1802 observed that Utica was

> . . . a mixed mass of discordant materials. Here may be found people of ten or twelve different nations and of almost all religions and sects, but the great part are of no religion. The world is the great object with the body of people.[5]

Johnson's autobiography, a storehouse of information and shrewd comment, confirms Taylor's remarks. Utica was indeed a "Babel," but the Yankees far outnumbered the stray persons from England, Scotland, Holland, France, and the German states. Welsh immigrants who had settled the Steuben area north of the Mohawk Valley after 1795 were numerous enough to organize Utica's first religious society in 1802 and to erect the first church building.

Alexander Bryan Johnson described his religious background as follows:

> I had been brought up in the Episcopal Church, but on my marriage, I united with the Presbyterian in compliance with a preference of my wife who had been for some time a communicant of that church.[6]

Utica's First Presbyterian Church in 1813 had detached itself from the United Church of Whitestown and called its own minister to serve its fifty-seven members. The next year a stirring revival brought in almost one hundred new members.[7] Admission meant a searching examination by the Session, which expected some evidence of religious experience. Nevertheless, the revival brought into the church approximately one in ten of all inhabitants over the age of fifteen, since the population of Utica numbered about seventeen hundred, of whom one-half were under sixteen.

Presbyterianism played a leading role in Utica, Whitesboro, New Hartford, and the surrounding areas. It enrolled most of the leaders of trade and professional life. To be sure, Trinity Church had Colonel Benjamin Walker, the former aide to Baron von Steuben and George Washington, and St. John's Roman Catholic Church enlisted Nicholas Devereux, a merchant of wealth and distinction. But Johnson, who was keenly aware of the advantages of social rank whether in a wife or a church, put the matter succinctly in 1823:

> To become a Presbyterian in this region, is like a formal notice to the world, that your conduct and conversation are to be more rigidly correct than that of the ordinary man; that slander, irascibility, misanthropy, uncharitableness, revenge, dissipation, covetousness, etc. are not to be indulged in or secretly practiced in any instance. I admit there is something pharisaical in all this, but it has, with me at least, much practical effect; and I frequently restrain some ill natured speech or feeling by a reflection that it will disgrace me as being out of character etc.[8]

Johnson was a conventional but liberal Christian who lacked evangelical fervor and hated fanaticism. He confided to John Quincy Adams in 1823 that he was void of prejudice. He wanted to see the "mosque and synagogue, the pagoda and the church . . . harmoniously located alongside of each other." He also stated he would "contribute this moment to the erection of any one of them." [9] Furthermore, Johnson chafed under church discipline. When the Session of First Presbyterian refused his contribution of $150 for a new building as inadequate, Johnson withdrew his donation until they relented. He also resented their inquiries about his traveling on the Sabbath.[10]

One of the more outstanding revivals of the nineteenth century began in the little town of Western to the northeast of Rome, N.Y. There the Reverend George Washington Gale lived in retirement after his health broke down. Gale had served several charges in the sparsely settled Black River country where he had converted Charles G. Finney, the handsome young lawyer and choir director.[11] Finney came to visit his former teacher late in 1825 and the visit lasted three months. The two men naturally attended the local Presbyterian Church where the "spirit" touched the expectant congregation. Finney carried the message to Rome where he caused an "explosion," and the excitement spread to other communities. One observer declared that Oneida County was "overthrown by the Holy Ghost" and that the theater "had been deserted, the tavern sanctified." [12]

Undoubtedly the level of conduct in Utica needed improvement. For one thing, the grog houses along the canal did a thriving business. Johnson's autobiography presents abundant evidence that frivolity and intemperance had many devotees among high society. From another high-placed source we have added testimony about high life in Utica. Samuel Dakin, landowner, publisher, and a minor literary figure, wrote to Mary Mumford on January 1, 1826,

> Here we have nothing but parties—invitations follow invitations in such rapid succession as to spread confusion and dismay in my wardrobe and also disturb my inward gear as well as my outward.[13]

Although Finney was not an original thinker, he reflected changes taking place in orthodox Calvinism. He declared that "genuine faith always results in good works and is itself a good work." Moreover the regeneration of the individual would lead to the reformation of society. In fact, the revival spawned a large number of benevolent associations concerned with Sunday School improvement, adult education, and, later, the abolition of slavery.

Johnson's autobiography, written in 1863, apparently underplayed his involvement in the revival and the reform movements. His activities, however, indicated a greater interest than his reminiscences admit. He wrote in his autobiography:

> Finney's imagination being exceedingly active and his language very descriptive of what imagination conceived, I several times went to hear him, and this probably induced the instigators of the society [Oneida Evangelical] to elect me its President.[14]

Two years later he followed Judge Jonas Platt as President of the Tract Society.[15] He also served as the First President of the Utica Temperance Society.[16] It is doubtful that these earnest Christians would have placed Johnson at the head of these organizations if they suspected he was not truly saved and deeply concerned.

Johnson's autobiography is peppered with references to the damage wrought by spiritous liquors. In his address to the Utica Temperance Society on July 29, 1829, Johnson painted a lurid but probably accurate picture.

> Even now, in this orderly town, I have heard the cry of infant distress issue from the abodes of intemperance; and seen, more than once, some pitiable youth fleeing from his miserable home, and the ferocious father stumbling after him with maniacal fury.[17]

But Johnson was a temperate foe of intemperance, for in the same address he vigorously opposed legal coercion. He declared:

> I love temperance but I love freedom more; I abhor intemperance, but I dislike intolerance more. The liberty which I possess of refraining from drink, I would yield equally to those who wish to drink.

And in one of his choicer reflections on the subject, he writes:

> Even Adam was permitted the liberty of eating the forbidden fruit, for barren indeed would have been his total abstinence had it depended on coercion.

During the 1830's Johnson parted company with the leaders of the temperance crusade who insisted on teetotalism and moved toward legal prohibition. Johnson wrote to Edward Delevan of Albany, the famous temperance leader, that he opposed the trend to include beer and wine as targets.[18] In the 1850's Johnson attacked the movement toward prohibition which won a temporary victory.[19]

Johnson, however, was enormously proud of his abstemious habits. In one instance he wrote, ". . . the only circumstances remarkable about me . . . is that all the distilled liquors I ever drunk, either mixed with water or pure, would not fill a wine glass." [20] That was undoubtedly a remarkable achievement for a person who grew up in the brawling canal town on the Oneida frontier.

Johnson's attitude toward slavery and abolitionism deserves attention. His father had slaves and assigned one to Alexander as a servant to accompany him on his travels to Saratoga and New York City. Meanwhile many upper-class New Yorkers, especially those of Federalist opinion, had already taken a strong position against slavery. Back in the 1790's Alexander Hamilton, John Jay, and Gouverneur Morris had urged people to free their slaves and had advocated a state law restricting and ending slavery.[21] Their main opposition came from the laborers in the city who feared the competition of free Negroes. Furthermore, the Democrat-Republicans opposed equal rights for the Negroes since practically all free Negroes voted for the Federalists who had befriended them. In the Constitutional Convention of 1821 Martin Van Buren and his followers reflected this feeling of hostility against the free Negroes by imposing higher property qualifications for black voters while at the same time permitting practically all adult white males to vote.

Johnson proudly relates that in 1824 he attacked slavery in his Fourth of July address in the Presbyterian Church in Utica. His most impressive public pronouncement on the subject, however, took place on the night of January 14, 1834, in a debate before a newly formed Utica Auxiliary of the American Colonization Society.[22] Johnson was allowed thirty minutes (a restriction, he said, which caused him to be more "pungent" than usual) to present the negative side to a proposition calling for an endorsement of the Society's plan for sending the Negroes back to Africa as "best calculated to ameliorate the condition of the free Negro and secure the ultimate emancipation of the slave." Here again, as Gilbert Barnes has pointed out in his *The Anti-Slavery Impulse, 1830–1834,*[23] we must go back to Finney and the Oneida revivals for the origins of this and other important discussions on the turmoil over abolition.

In 1840 William Lloyd Garrison noted the leadership of Boston and New York City in the abolitionist movement and added:

> Remark, also, Utica, the seat of the New York State Society, and home of Goodell and his *Friend of Man;* home, likewise, of Alvan Stewart, whose nearly successful effort to commit the American Society to the doctrine of Federal control over slavery in the States was recorded in the last chapter. Not far to West at Peterboro, lives Gerrit Smith, anxious, as we have seen, to convert the moral basis of anti-slavery into a political one.[24]

Spurred on by the revivalists, George Washington Gale founded Oneida Institute, a manual-labor school which became a model for others and a focal point for student activism.[25] Theodore Weld, who attended Oneida and raised money for it, later helped to transform Oberlin into a manual-labor college. Gale also founded Knox College in Illinois, which in turn hired Hiram Huntington of Oneida County as president. The school secured most of its funds from Utica, but followers of Finney in other parts of the state also gave their assistance. In his autobiography Johnson says he disapproved of the school but gave $40 to help it along. It is also interesting to note that Johnson turned down an honorary degree from nearby Hamilton College, where President Henry Davis held the fort against the revivalists.

In 1833 the Oneida Institute hired Beriah Green, an advanced abolitionist who became first President of the American Anti-Slavery Society, but even before Green arrived the students had formed an abolitionist society, the first in the state. Tradition tells us that it grew out of the so-called "gravel debates." [26] Since the students were poor, they had to shovel gravel in order to pay the road tax. During rest periods, they organized a debate on emancipation versus colonization. One of the student debaters referred his listeners to Garrison's *Liberator,* which was denouncing colonization as a cruel hoax. As a result, an abolitionist society was formed.

Green himself was a dogmatic man who brooked no disagreement. Certain that God was on his side he soon clashed with the Presbyterian Church. Because it failed to denounce its own members who owned slaves, he asserted that it was guilty of slaveholding and withdrew, with many of his followers, to form a Congregational Church. Late in 1833 he initiated a series of debates with Joseph Danforth, the local agent for the American Colonization Society. [27] A Utica crowd jeered his call for immediate emancipation and hanged him in effigy. The Utica Common Council denounced his stand as incendiary. On February 13, 1834, Johnson plunged headlong into the argument.

When Johnson mounted the platform that night he found himself facing some of his oldest and closest friends, many of whom favored, as he knew, the aims of the American Colonization Society. He began by praising the laudable intentions of the Society and its hopes of "benefitting colored men, of Christianizing and civilizing Africa." But, he added quickly, "I believe the Society and its supporters are mistaken as to the moral nature of their institution."

Students of Johnson will find it easy to anticipate the course of certain arguments taken by the man who wrote earlier, in his *Treatise on Language:*

> Who has not experienced that in the dark no discrimination exists between the color of a Negro and a European? The astonishment is produced by the supposition that the "blackness" which is attributed to us in the dark, is not to be interpreted by the event to which it refers; but that the event is to be interpreted by the word, "blackness," according to its meaning when it refers to Negroes. [28]

Johnson's speech, one of the most passionate of his many public utterances, has been reproduced in its entirety, together with additional notes by the Editors, in the Appendix to these *Proceedings* (see pp. 246–259). In it, Johnson was as vociferous in his condemnation of slavery and the plight of the Negro as any dyed-in-the-wool abolitionist. His attack upon the hypocrisies inherent in the Society's plan for sending the blacks to Africa ("Christianity and this Society cannot live together. Choose ye this night which ye shall serve!") must have shocked the pious and well-intentioned sponsors of the movement. However, what Joseph Dorfman calls the "goading objectivity of his mind" could brook no distinction between the "evil" of slavery and the "evil" of forcing the slave states to give up slavery. "To persuade them," he said, "is a duty; to coerce them is a crime!" As a result, Johnson pleased no one. He offended the Society, the abolitionists, and the proponents of white superiority—a predicament not unknown, certainly, to many advocates of so-called gradualism in America a hundred years later.

Beriah Green berated and disputed Johnson,[29] indeed Johnson felt Green distorted his statements.[30] No doubt Johnson had more supporters in Utica than Green, but the abolitionists were making headway. In the summer of 1834, Charles Stuart, former principal of the Utica Academy, returned from England where he had helped secure emancipation in the British Empire. In January 1835, he gave five antislavery addresses in Utica. But when the antislavery forces issued a call for a meeting to organize a state society, Mayor Joseph Kirkland and several prominent men protested. The Common Council, however, agreed to permit a meeting on October 17. The *Oneida Whig* denounced the council as going against the wishes of nine-tenths of the citizens.[31] When the convention met on October 21 in the Presbyterian Church on Bleecker Street, a mob of several hundred drove them out.[32] Some of the delegates adjourned to Peterboro, the home of Gerrit Smith, who became an ardent abolitionist at this time. No doubt Johnson looked on all these activities with keen interest, but he confined himself to the states' rights issue in subsequent publications—largely those dealing with the introduction or banning of slavery in the new territories.

Johnson also found himself embroiled in the controversy over Sabbath observance, which rivaled temperance as a major reform of evangelical Protestants.

Congress in 1810 had ordered post offices to remain open on

Sundays and the mails to be carried every day of the week.[33] New England clergymen in their home states and in Diaspora protested against the desecration of the Sabbath. The noisy and sometimes disorderly behavior of stage drivers, canallers, and hostelers at the inns shocked the Sabbatarians. They tried to persuade individuals not to patronize steamboats or stage coaches operating on Sundays, and earnest folk organized six-day boating and stage lines. In 1828 a convention in New York City met to form the General Union for Promoting the Observance of the Christian Sabbath. In Utica and other canal cities there were mass meetings for the same purpose.

Johnson had to make sure that he had adequate funds in New York City banks on Monday mornings. In 1830 he persuaded Postmaster General William T. Barry to arrange for Sunday mail service on the Hudson River steamboats.[34] His intervention became known in 1834 to the members of the Session of First Presbyterian Church. They sent three men to remonstrate with him.[35] The records of the Session for the next year are full of references to *l'affaire Johnson*.[36] Johnson claimed that his position was a political issue in which the church had no right to chastise its members. On January 16 he withdrew from the church and five days later the Session tried him in absentia. They voted to suspend him from the communion. Johnson took the question to the public, which annoyed the Session. Thirteen prominent Uticans, including Horatio Seymour and Rutger Miller, came to his defense. They charged that freedom of political opinion "is a freedom which the arm of civil authority cannot bind into compliance; nor the thunders of the Church intimidate into servility."

On May 1 Johnson was excluded from the privileges of the church and on May 17 he was expelled. When the Consistory of the Dutch Reformed Church (founded in 1826 in part by the foes of Charles Finney) asked for a copy of the proceedings before they admitted Johnson to membership, the Session refused to comply for a time. They did offer to see a delegation who could confer with the Session.

Meanwhile Dr. Pierre A. Proal of Trinity Episcopal Church invited Johnson to rejoin the congregation in which he and his father had served as vestrymen. Johnson soon became a vestryman in Trinity and in 1842 came to the defense of Dr. Proal whom a faction was trying to oust.

Johnson evinced little interest in theology as such. For him religion was largely a system of morality, a means of social control essential to curb individual selfishness and to insure community discipline. He elaborated on this theme in 1841 in a series of lectures delivered before the Young Men's Association. The five lectures indicate clearly the scope of his subject and the tenor of his remarks:

> Every Department of Nature Obeys Determinate Laws.
> The Conduct which Results Injuriously.
> The Conduct which Results Beneficially.
> The Art of Controlling Others.
> The Art of Self-Control.

It has been claimed that Johnson anticipated Lord Keynes; others state that he foreshadowed Wittgenstein and the twentieth-century semanticists. Let me suggest that he was also a trailblazer for Dale Carnegie and Norman Vincent Peale.

Johnson in the preface to *Religion in Its Relation to the Present Life* observed:

> Churches occupy the same relation to morality as common schools occupy to literature. . . . This accounts for the experimental fact, that men who abstain from churches are, as a class, unsuccessful in business, unhappy in their families, and liable to sudden calamities.

Johnson developed his points logically and persuasively. No doubt his tone and his advice were proper for a generation which had just witnessed the coronation of Queen Victoria. Here are a few of his representative phrases and sentences.

> . . . the temporal happiness of man [is] the object of God's government. . . .

> . . . the results of gambling and ebriety are pecuniary ruin, loss of reputation, remorse, rage, and suicide.

> [Virtue leads to] riches, honours, public esteem, and influence.

> . . . neither physical, moral, nor mental pleasure is procurable, except for the discharge of our moral, mental, and physical duties.[37]

Another passage is a fine example of Johnson's delight in the balanced sentence.

> If I feel ill-will toward men, they will feel ill-will toward me; if I am censorious, they will censure me; if I hate, they will hate me; if I insult, they will insult me; if I am unsocial, they will desert me; if inhospitable, they will neglect me; if contemp-

176

tuous, they will condemn me; if despicable, they will despise me.[38]

Johnson relied heavily on the Golden Rule. He seemed to have a fairly good knowledge of the Bible. Undoubtedly it was superior to that of President Warren G. Harding, who once observed that if the Golden Rule was faithfully obeyed he would "almost be willing to wipe out the remainder of the commandments." [39]

Johnson preached the good life and especially the Protestant ethic in his letters to his sons at Hobart College in Geneva, New York. Later he collected portions of these letters into *An Encyclopedia of Instruction: or Apologues and Breviats on Men and Manners,* published in 1857. The power of positive thinking permeates this volume. He wrote:

> Mark out for yourself, then, such a character as you desire to possess, and by speaking consonantly thereto you will attain the desired character as certainly as you will a coat, after going to your tailor and ordering it.

Not only does Johnson foreshadow the "positive thinking" of Peale and Carnegie—the phrase, "by speaking consonantly thereto," which is further elaborated in his essay, *The Effects of Language on the Speaker and Hearer,* is part and parcel of the brand of psychotherapy made popular during the 1920's by Dr. Émile Coué: "Every day, in every way, I am getting better and better" became the chant of that troubled generation which had recourse to neither tranquilizers nor legal alcohol. Since we are crediting Johnson with all manner of innovations, why not also hold him responsible for having anticipated both the language and the philosophy of Madison Avenue? I was brought up short when I ran across the phrase "religion-wise" in a Johnson essay, but even more so when I stumbled upon this sentence: "The feeling that causes a man to kiss his wife he can excite in himself at any time by kissing her." The consent engineers and creative thinkers of our time missed a good bet by not reading the works of A. B. Johnson.

Johnson, who always tried to write concisely and without embellishment, wrote to his pastor, the Rev. S. H. Coxe, D.D., of Trinity Church, a letter on May 7, 1867, three weeks before his death. This letter is a clear statement of his religious thinking and bears full quotation.

> The intellect conceives religion to be a unit; but the intellect can also analyze the unit into three distinct and inconvertible enti-

ties, namely, into doctrine, ceremony and piety. Man is likewise a unit in the contemplation of the intellect; but the intellect can analyze him into three distinct and inconvertible organisms; namely, into physical, intellectual and emotional. Each of these organisms claims a part of religion; doctrine is the intellectual part; ceremony is the physical part; and piety is the emotional part. Man's emotional organism pertains to him under all doctrines and ceremonies; and I doubt not piety is felt alike by Jews and Turks, infidels and idolaters, Mormons, and occasionally by avowed Atheists. The great elements in which religions differ, are in doctrines and ceremonies. The intellect is the freest part of our nature, and each sect holds its members to the same doctrine by only an enforced agreement; for naturally no two men ever thought alike without an artificial concert; and hence we may see the impossibility of all sects uniting in one doctrine. The ceremonial part of religion is physical, and like all our physical actions, the ceremonial part is much under the dictation of the intellect, and somewhat of the emotions. When a clergyman turns up his eyes to heaven, the physical turning up is dictated by the emotional feelings. Ceremonial religion, and which I call physical, has been almost as effective as doctrine in dividing Christians into conflicting sects. Now I suppose the difference which divides our Church into high and low, relates to what I term physical religion; and deeming it thus relatively unessential, I prefer the kind of ceremonial which is most effective in engaging the congregations of the Church, and exciting most the feeling of piety in the worshippers.[40]

Coxe cited with approval Johnson's statement that ". . . if he were to go through life again, he would not give employment to any young man who did not habitually attend church."

Finally we must note the role played by Johnson in the beginnings of the American Lyceum movement—another manifestation, like the Oneida Institute, of the upward-and-onward-with-everything spirit generated by the Oneida revivalists. Professor Carl Bode, in his *American Lyceum,* [41] informs us that the movement, which amounted almost to a crusade, began with a manifesto published in the *American Journal of Education* for October 1826, by Josiah Holbrook, a Yale graduate and student of Benjamin Silliman, the chemist and mineralogist who devoted much of his life to popularizing the study of science. Holbrook's manifesto, borrowing heavily from the literature of Dr. George Birbeck's London Institute for the Diffusion of Science, Literarture and the Arts, founded in 1809, called for "associations for mutual instruction in the sciences and in useful knowledge generally."

178

Among the myriad benefits to be derived from a national Lyceum movement, argued Holbrook, would be the "Improvement of Conversation," "Benefitting Academies," "Compiling of Town Histories and Town Maps," "Agricultural and Geological Surveys," and "State Collections of Minerals." Bode credits the town of Millbury, Massachusetts, with being the birthplace of the Lyceum movement, for there, in November 1826, Holbrook "started Millbury Branch Number 1 of the American Lyceum."

Without attempting in any way to disparage Holbrook's role in putting the Lyceum movement on its feet as a national institution, one cannot ignore the fact that Johnson and the city of Utica were almost three years ahead of him. Sometime during November 1823 Johnson got together with Jonas Platt and a number of other Uticans and drew up a plan for a Utica Lyceum modeled after the Mechanics Institutes which were being much talked about in the British journals filtering into Utica. In January, Johnson was elected president of the new organization, and on February 5, 1824, he delivered an opening address "in which I designated some of the purposes which the Institution might subserve." Unfortunately, the only copy Johnson preserved was "badly mutilated by an attempt at verbal emendation" but there is ample evidence that the objectives he outlined were very similar to those projected by Josiah Holbrook. According to M. M. Bagg, Johnson saw the Lyceum as an agent for "encouraging the study and dissemination of a knowledge of natural history and other useful sciences." [42] Johnson's friend, S. De Witt Bloodgood, wrote him on receiving a copy of the lecture and praised him for his "disclosure of the manner in which natural history forces itself upon our notice." Another friend, John Grieg, of Canandaigua, wrote: "It does you much credit . . . exhibiting great research and enlarged philosophical views of the objects of the institution. I wish similar ones were established in the principal villages of the state, as I believe they may be made to promote greatly the interests of science and of useful knowledge." Bagg describes the members as being "the educated young men of the time, chiefly lawyers and teachers . . . its discussion was attended by the public, including the lady friends of the speakers." That the Utica Lyceum broadened its objectives to include the arts as well as the sciences is evident in the fact that Johnson's next two lectures dealt with his language theories and the subject of "Eloquence."

Johnson's early initiative in promoting the Lyceum movement in New York state resulted in his election to the presidency of the

State Lyceum in 1829, and he was asked to be the main speaker at the state convention held in Utica in 1831. He was also invited by Theodore Dwight to address the Fourth Annual meeting of the American Lyceum, held in New York City on May 2, 1834, and although he felt "much indisposed to make such an exhibition of myself in New York" [43] he accepted.

His zeal for progress and reform was endless. He spoke out, under the pseudonym, "Matilda," against "The Immorality of Tight Lacing" in *The Mother's Magazine;* he clamored for the annexation of Texas; he even insisted on learning every last detail of his first wife's autopsy—hoping, doubtless, to discover the fatal flaw in the treatment she was given by the Utica medical profession. Throughout his entire life he was interested in good works (provided they didn't cost too much) and consciously played the role of the Christian gentleman at all times. This was not the posturing of a hypocrite, but the methodology of a man who believed in perfectibility—that one can perfect his character by taking thought and systematically cultivating positive attitudes and good conduct. An individualist to the core, Johnson parted company with those reformers who wanted to use government agencies and even church sessions to enforce prohibition and Sabbath observance. Strong as his personal feelings were against the scandal of slavery, even stronger was his belief in states' rights. Like Thoreau and John Stuart Mill, he was consistent in his approach to individual liberty. Even Fanny Wright, the advocate of free love and women's rights, should be permitted to walk the streets of Utica with her French paramour, but Johnson, of course, reserved his own right not to be seen in their company.

NOTES

I am indebted to Professor Charles L. Todd for several references and suggestions.

1 Carl Carmer, "Upstate is a Country," from *My Kind of Country* (New York: McKay, 1966), p. 18.
2 David Maldwyn Ellis, *Landlords and Farmers in the Hudson-Mohawk Region 1790-1850* (Ithaca: Cornell University Press, 1946), pp. 46–54.

3 *Travels in New-England and New-York* (New Haven, 1821–22), Vol. III, p. 179.

4 The best source on Utica and Johnson's career is the autobiography of Alexander Bryan Johnson. Citations refer to the Hamilton College typescript. Moses Bagg, *Pioneers of Utica* (Utica: Curtiss & Childs, 1877) is a useful account which relied in part on Johnson's material.

5 Edmund Bailey O'Callaghan (ed.), *Documentary History of the State of New York* (Albany: Weed, Parsons & Co., 1849–51), Vol. III, pp. 685–687.

6 Autobiography; Chap. 5.

7 David K. McMillan, "To Witness We are Living: A Study of Charles Finney and the Revival of Religion in and About Utica, New York, During the Winter and Spring of 1826." Thesis at Union Theological Seminary, 1961.

8 April 8, 1823, Johnson to Adams; autobiography, Chap. 4.

9 Autobiography, Chap. 4.

10 *Ibid.*, Chap. 5.

11 The two leaders left their memoirs. Charles Grandison Finney, *Memoirs of Charles G. Finney* (New York: A. S. Barnes & Co., 1876), pp. 6–60; *Autobiography (to 1834) of George Washington Gale (1789–1861)* (New York: privately printed, 1964), pp. 262ff.

12 Report to the Synod of Albany, quoted in *Autobiography and Correspondence of Lyman Beecher* (New York: Harper & Brothers, 1864), Vol. II, p. 90.

13 Quoted in Jane Speakes Shade, "Samuel Dana Dakin, Esq. 1802–1853," M. A. Thesis at State University College Graduate Program at Cooperstown, 1966, p. 38.

14 Autobiography, Chap. 5.

15 *Ibid.*

16 *Ibid.*, Chap. 6.

17 *An Address to the Utica Temperance Society, Delivered at the Second Presbyterian Church, July 29, 1829.* John Q. Adams praised the address.

18 Autobiography, Chap. 8.

19 Utica *Evening Telegraph* (no date) in Volume I of the "Scrapbooks of Alexander Bryan Johnson," Seymour Collection, New York State Library, Albany.

20 Autobiography, Chap. 6.

21 Edgar J. McManus, *A History of Negro Slavery in New York* (Syracuse: Syracuse University Press, 1966), pp. 161–179.

22 *Speech before an Auxiliary of the American Colonization Society, Utica, January 13, 1834* (Utica: Press of William Williams, 1834).

23 Gilbert H. Barnes, *The Anti-Slavery Impulse, 1830–1844* (New York: D. Appleton-Century Co., 1933), was the first to stress the role of the Oneida revivals in the antislavery movement.

24 Wendell Phillips Garrison, and Francis Jackson Garrison, *William Lloyd Garrison* (New York: The Century Co., 1885), Vol. II, p. 259.

25 See Gale's *Autobiography* and Hermann R. Muelder, *Fighter for Freedom* (New York: Columbia University Press, 1959), pp. 25–46.

26 John L. Myers, "The Beginnings of Anti-Slavery Agencies in New York State, 1833–1836," *New York History,* Vol. XLIII (April 1962), pp. 161–171.

27 *Utica Sentinel and Gazette,* January 7, 1834; *Elucidator,* January 14, 1834.

28 A. B. Johnson, *A Treatise on Language,* ed. David Rynin (Berkeley, Calif.: University of California Press, 1959), p. 119.

29 Letter to A. B. Johnson, January 7, 1834, in A. B. Johnson, *Correspondence,* a collection of letters. Copies are deposited in the Hamilton College Library.

30 Autobiography, Chap. 8.

31 October 20, 1835.

32 *Oneida Whig,* November 10, 1835. Ralph V. Harlow, *Gerrit Smith* (New York: Henry Holt and Company, 1939), pp. 121–124.

33 A short account is given in John R. Bodo, *The Protestant Clergy and Public Issues 1812–1848* (Princeton: Princeton University Press, 1954), pp. 39–42.

34 William T. Barry to A. B. Johnson.

35 Autobiography, Chap. 7.

36 James Coddington, Clerk of Session of First Presbyterian Church, Utica, kindly searched the records and supplied me with information. See also autobiography, Chap. 7.

37 Selections are to be found on pages 33, 57, 73, and 78 of *Religion in Its Relation to the Present Life* (New York: Harper & Brothers, 1841).

38 *Ibid.,* p. 125.

39 Quoted in George F. Mowry, "The Uses of History by Recent Presidents," *The Journal of American History,* Vol. LIII (June 1966), p. 12.

40 From "Extract from a Discourse Preached in Trinity Church, Utica, September 15, 1867" in *Obituary Notices of Alexander Bryan Johnson* (Utica, 1868).

41 Carl Bode, *The American Lyceum—Town Meeting of the Mind* (New York: Oxford University Press, 1956).

42 Bagg, *op. cit.,* p. 558.

43 Autobiography, Chap. 8.

ALEXANDER BRYAN JOHNSON
AND THE ADAMS FAMILY

♦ ♦ ♦ ♦ ♦ *L. H. BUTTERFIELD*

The relating of facts is like the gathering of blackberries,
but the publication of reflections is like the
creating of blackberries.

Alexander Bryan Johnson to John Quincy Adams, February 7, 1835

To the nobility of intellect, whether in high political station,
or in low, I am a devoted subject; especially when it is
combined, as in your ancestors, with a confirming nobility
of the moral powers and sentiments.

Alexander Bryan Johnson to Charles Francis Adams,
September 8, 1843

I

EARLY IN JUNE 1843 General Peter B. Porter of Niagara Falls, New York, an old acquaintance and political ally of John
Quincy Adams, addressed a letter to Adams introducing a friend from
Buffalo who was coming to Boston for the celebration on June 17
marking the completion of the Bunker Hill Monument. "Shall we never, my dear Sir," Porter asked before closing, "have the honour and
pleasure of seeing you at the Falls of Niagara? Or, I should rather say,
will you never indulge yourself the high gratification which you could
not fail to enjoy in viewing this splendid exhibition of nature?" [1] On

◇ ◇ ◇ ◇ ◇ *Editor in Chief,* The Adams Papers, *sponsored by the Massachu-*
setts Historical Society and in course of publication by the Belknap Press of
Harvard University Press. Former Director, Institute of Early American History
and Culture. Former Associate Editor, The Papers of Thomas Jefferson; *author,*
John Witherspoon Comes to America *and other works.*

June 19, Adams recorded in his diary that Mr. Calvin Stow of Buffalo presented letters from both Porter and Millard Fillmore and orally reinforced their plea that the ex-President pay a public visit to western New York.

> I do not deceive myself [he commented] by mistaking this earnest desire to hear me for any thing more than mere curiosity, but it is friendly and claims my gratitude. I believe there is not a man in the world more unfit for self-exhibition at public meetings and banquet dinners. When I go to them it is with feelings of a culprit to punishment [rather] than of a victor to triumph. I told Mr. Stow that I could not indulge the hope of ever meeting in public the people of Buffalo, but I should ever be grateful for their kindness and would pray for their prosperity.[2]

Adams could hardly have been more mistaken. He was about to take a tour through the Empire State that was to become a royal progress and that he was to describe soon after it was completed as "in many respects the most memorable period of my life." [3] How this came about requires a little explanation that will introduce some of our cast of characters.

Not long before he received the letters from his friends in western New York, Adams had returned to his home in Quincy from his twelfth consecutive year of service in Congress. His whole life had been a battle against dragons of many shapes and sizes, and now, approaching the age of seventy-six, he was embattled as never before. Year after year from the mid-1830's on, he had defied the gag rules passed by majorities made up of Southern members and "Northern men with Southern principles" who were determined not to let any petitions from the people of the United States relating to slavery be heard in the House of Representatives. Repeatedly threatened with censure and even expulsion, Adams never gave up, again and again sent his assailants slinking away to lick their wounds, and after seven years of combat was about to triumph, for in 1844 no gag was adopted and petitions from the North and West flooded the House.

But there were always more dragons to kill. Currently the most formidable of them was John Tyler. This Virginia slaveowner and states-righter had been elected Vice-President on the supposedly Whig ticket of "Tippecanoe and Tyler too" in 1840 and, when old General Harrison had died after only a month in office, had unceremoniously, and in J. Q. Adams' opinion unconstitutionally, set himself up as the actual rather than the acting President of the United States, thereby

184

earning among frustrated Whigs the title of "His Accidency." Tyler pursued a strictly Democratic line by vetoing Whig financial legislation and vigorously working for the annexation of Texas; and now in June 1843, thanks to the presidential aspirations of his recent Secretary of State, Daniel Webster, Tyler was coming to Boston to participate in the rites marking the completion of the Bunker Hill Monument.

To J. Q. Adams this seemed the last indignity. As a boy going on eight he had himself from the top of Penn's Hill in Braintree watched with his mother the battle that the Monument commemorated. Now he would not travel the few miles to Boston to enter Webster's "gull-trap for popularity" by participating in a "pageant" designed "to bedaub with glory John Tyler the Slave-breeder, who is coming with all his Court in gaudy trappings of mock royalty . . . under colour of doing homage to the principles of Bunker hill martyrdom." [4] The excuse Adams gave for public purposes was ill health, but in the privacy of his diary—that repository in which he deliberately placed his most ulcerous judgments on his contemporaries so that he could remain civil to them face-to-face—he wrote on the day of the celebration:

> I passed the day in the solitude of my Study, and dined almost alone. . . . [W]ith the ideal association of the thundering cannon which I heard, and the smoke of burning Charlestown which I saw on that awful day [in 1775], combined with this Pyramid of Quincy granite, and Daniel Webster spouting, and John Tyler's nose with a shadow outstretching that of the monumental column; how could I have witnessed all this at once, without an unbecoming burst of indignation or of laughter? Daniel Webster is a heartless traitor to the cause of human freedom. John Tyler is a Slave-monger. What have these to do with the Quincy-granite pyramid on the brow of Bunker's hill? What have these to do, with a dinner in Faneuil Hall, but to swill like swine and grunt about the rights of man? [5]

Meanwhile, forces were at work to test ex-President Adams' own popularity—a word he had always used pejoratively and a phenomenon, when associated with himself, that had always made him uncomfortable. No American statesman had ever worked harder to earn the suffrage of his countrymen, and none had more profoundly wished to serve them; but the political manners of his day, combined with the high-mindedness and inhibitions that by then had become Adams trademarks, had absolutely forbidden his lifting a finger—at least in view of the public—in support of his own election to *any* office. To court voters and votes was wicked, and from this conviction sprang his bottomless contempt for the Websters, Tylers, Clays, and Van Burens who did. But in the years following his own rejection by the voters for a second term as President, the whole structure of American politics changed radically. During the re-formation of parties in the 1830's, Adams would have accepted any plausible bid to run again for the highest office, but he would not openly lift his hand to promote his chances and so suffered silently while lesser, more pliant and ingratiating men jockeyed for the honor he thought more rightfully his own. To others he insisted, and he tried to convince himself, that his service as tribune of the Twelfth District of Massachusetts in the House of Representatives was a greater honor. No one seriously believed it then, but the judgment of history suggests that he may have been right after all.

In June 1843 J. Q. Adams' family was divided between Quincy and Washington. His only surviving son, Charles Francis, lived in a new house on Presidents Hill above the old family mansion, with his wife, the former Abigail Brooks, and a growing number of small children. Like many women of her time who had few occupations except the bearing and rearing of children, Abby Brooks Adams enjoyed indifferent health. Her family and physician thought that a trip to "the Springs" would benefit her. (At that time, evidently, this term used without qualification meant Saratoga Springs.) She accepted the suggestion, decided to take her oldest son (then ten and named for his Adams grandfather) with her, and invited her fond and affluent father Peter Chardon Brooks to come with her too. But there were complications. Who would take care of "the President" (as J. Q. Adams was ordinarily called by his family), to say nothing of Abby's younger children, if the Washington contingent of the family did not come on? This included the President's wife and his widowed daughter-in-law, Mrs. John Adams 2d. The illness of sundry members of that large household kept delaying their departure, and at the very end of June the President's wife reported that the whole family of one of her innumerable nephews had been poisoned by arsenic placed in their breakfast coffee by disgruntled servants.

In the end the impasse was settled by the President's deciding to join the party to the Springs. It was unusual for him to indulge in any mere excursion of pleasure; but the affair at Bunker Hill had unsettled him; his wife could not leave Washington until later in the summer; and at the back of his mind, apparently, there was the thought that he might just possibly go on and visit Montreal, Quebec, and even Niagara Falls (which he had never seen) and some of his friends in New York State who had long and pressingly urged their hospitality upon him. Among these was a nephew by marriage, Alexander Bryan Johnson, a banker and publicist of Utica, with whom Adams had corresponded for many years but whose home he had never visited. Charles Francis would stay home with his children and await the arrival of his mother and sister-in-law from Washington.

And so, on July 6 the Adams-Brooks party gathered in Boston, "proceeded to the depot of the Western Railroad," and "started in the Cars" for Springfield at 3:30 p.m. "The Season is delightful," the President contentedly recorded in his voluminous diary record of the trip:

> The face of the Country like the garden of Eden. It is the Season of hay-making, and throughout our way, the mower with his scythe, the cocking of the grass, or the spreading it from the cock to dry, followed in alternate succession, and the atmosphere was charged only with varieties of fragrance. Fields of Indian corn, Rye, Potatoes and Oats interchangeably with pastures covered with grazing cattle, neat and comfortable houses and kitchen gardens and Orchards laden with ripening fruit, attested a genial climate, a fruitful Season and a region of Peace, plenty and contentment.[6]

It was a good opening scene for a chapter in John Quincy Adams' life that was to have its full share of trials, surprises, and rewards.

II

THE ADAMS-JOHNSON relationship went back almost thirty years. One day in 1814, walking with his father on Genesee Street in Utica, Alexander Johnson noticed among the girls leaving a school "one whose bright appearance, mature but slight form and auburn hair greatly interested" him. His father knew her and said she was a granddaughter of President John Adams, being the daughter of Charles, a younger brother of John Quincy Adams. The girl's name was Abigail Louisa Smith Adams, and she lived with her widowed mother, the former Sarah Smith of Long Island and New York City, while finishing her schooling in Utica. Abigail Louisa was only sixteen, but Johnson, who was twenty-eight and nothing if not enterprising, began paying meaningful attention to her which resulted in a brief engagement and an early marriage.[7] From a worldly point of view it was a good match for her. Her father had died when just beginning the practice of law and had left his wife and two infant daughters, Susan and Abigail, totally dependent on their Adams and Smith relatives.[8] Since little could be expected from the Smiths, the Adamses, although they had numerous competing claims of the same sort, provided shelter and financial support for their daughter-in-law and granddaughters at intervals over many years. As Alexander Johnson was to discover, this was sometimes a thankless duty. His sister-in-law Susan Adams married twice, both times badly, had high notions of her prerogatives as the granddaughter of one President and the niece of another, and grew more demanding as she became more dependent.

That, however, is another story. Alexander and Abigail Louisa Johnson had a happy marriage. In his autobiography Johnson says that "The marriage on the side of Bride and Groom was purely intellectual," which is puzzling enough in view of her having borne him eleven children. What he seems to have meant but expressed badly concerning her was that she may have accepted him more through "the persuasion of others" than from any attraction she herself felt for him. He adds with the disarming candor found throughout his autobiography:

> Her mother had, I found subsequently, consulted Col. Benjamin Walker as to my character, and he said I possessed only one fault known to him, and that was too much fondness for money; and this Mrs. Adams deemed in my favour, as she had seen in her own family the consequences of an opposite character.[9]

Alexander Johnson was as much an individualist as any of the Adamses into whose family he had married; and on the frontier— for the Utica to which he had come as a boy in 1801 was truly a frontier settlement—he was an anomaly. He had a Midas touch, undertook and brought off large affairs while still a very young man, successfully invested the large profits that he and his father had made from their store, and complacently recorded in his autobiography the substantial growth of his personal fortune from his bank, real estate, and other ventures year by year. But he went into banking, he said, so that he "might have time and opportunity *to write*." "The labors of the counting-room and the study," said a contemporary, were for Johnson "constantly intermingled, and often the sheet of a treatise in hand and a current balance sheet might be seen on his table together." [10] Like many other self-taught men, he was never happier than when instructing others, and his literary output was truly phenomenal. The National Union Catalog at the Library of Congress has entries under Johnson's name for nearly thirty separate titles of books and pamphlets, not counting contemporary and modern reissues or, of course, his ceaseless contributions to newspapers and magazines. His earliest book was *An Inquiry into the Nature of Value and of Capital,* published in New York City the year before his marriage to Abigail Louisa Adams, but contemporary with it was "an allegorical poem in heroic meter entitled 'the Court of Hymen,' " illustrating, he tells us in his autobiography, "the pleasures and obstructions of courtship." [11] So far as I know, this was never published, but it would be an entertaining find if it survives among his papers. He had opinions on everything, from temperance, religion, and politics to "The Immorality of Tight Lacing" (an article concerning which he contributed to *The Mother's Magazine*), and he saw that they all got into circulation. His two most characteristic titles, as titles, were *An Encyclopedia of Instruction; or, Apologues and Breviats on Man and Manners* ("a condensation of letters written by me to my children of both sexes while they were at School and at College" [12]), and *A Guide to the Right Understanding of Our American Union; or, Political, Economical and Literary Miscellanies.* Each of these volumes runs to over four hundred pages, and both were published in 1857.

There were special circumstances of the time that made all this possible. Johnson lived through the first great age of American printing. With the spread of literacy (thanks to the common-school movement), the improvement of roads and stage lines, the laying of the earliest railroads, and the immense expansion of the postal service, printers set up shops in every village. They issued newspapers, schoolbooks, almanacs, and the sermons and political tracts that were spawned in an age of fervid theological controversy and political partisanship. Mrs. Johnson's sister Susan married as her second husband a country printer, one William R. H. Treadway, about whom we know little except that he had a printing shop in Hamilton, N.Y., which produced lawbooks among other things. The availability and cheapness of printing facilities created conditions somewhat like those that G. B. Shaw was later to say prevail in marriage, namely maximum temptation combined with maximum opportunity. The learned and leisured banker of Utica took full advantage of them. Like some of his Adams in-laws, he wrote and published *too much.*

For their wedding trip Alexander and Abigail Louisa Johnson traveled to Quincy. They took with them Abigail's mother and thus demonstrated, as Johnson remarked with a frivolity he seldom indulged in, the truth of the proverb that two persons are company and three are a committee. Like most others who came in contact with the aging John Adams, Johnson was captivated by his grandfather-in-law. He set down scraps of his conversation and began a correspondence with him that lasted a decade. Johnson prided himself on his philosophical detachment from the common concerns of life, but Adams told him this was nothing to be proud of:

> Your Want of a Profession is a serious Misfortune. If I had your Fortune and your head, I would study Law, Physick, or Divinity, or Merchandize or Land Jobbing, I will not say or Stockjobbing; rather than be idle, and without an Object. "Il est plus difficile de s'amuser, que de s'enrichir." You may depend upon it, he is the most unhappy Man in the World, who has nothing to do. . . . As the Mind and Body are made for Action, the most implacable and inexorable Ennemy of human Happiness is Ennui. I wish the English Language had a neat and well sounding Word to express it.[13]

Some years later, when Johnson seriously undertook the study of law, no one was happier about it than John Adams, who suggested books, reminisced about his own legal career, and urged Johnson to curb his "propensity to writing" books so that he could draw more writs. But then he supposed that this advice would be useless: "I never knew a Lawyer who became eminent in his profession without the stimulus of want. You are too happy to be a laborious Lawyer." [14]

In 1815 the Johnsons presented Adams with a great-grandson whom they named John Adams Johnson. Adams had no doubt that he would "be fit for a Merchant, a Farmer, a Statesman, an Admiral [or] a General," provided care was first taken "to make him a Schollar." But, he added, with the rueful jocularity that so often marked his style, "You have given him a name that has sometimes sounded in soft musick, but much more frequently with harsh discord. Whether it will be most beneficial or prejudicial to the Child, is very uncertain." [15]

The most revealing exchanges occurred in 1823, when Adams touched on one of his favorite topics of study and speculation, namely the parallels and differences among the religions of mankind. Good sources for the pursuit of this study, he pointed out, were hard to come by:

> Sir William Jones's works have excited a curiosity for Oriental literature which can never be gratified. I wish our Missionarys would import and translate Sanscrit, and Persian books, we

might possibly learn something useful from them that we do not know which might somewhat abate our Bigotry.[16]

Johnson agreed that "Of the vast Empires of China and Japan, we know little more, than we know of the Moon—a few fanciful stories constituting the whole of our Knowledge." But it seems to be the fate of every individual that he must live physically and intellectually within a narrow "circle in which are located all his hopes and all his fears." [17] In his next letter Adams pursued his idea further and raised a question:

I do sincerely wish that the Mandarins of China, the Bramins of Hindostan, the Priests of Japan, and of Persia, could be influenced with the same zeal de propaganda fide as the Roman Catholicks and Calvinists of this day are for propagating their Creeds, and ceremonies. I wish they would form into societies, open their purses, contribute their diamonds, pearls and precious Stones, as liberally as our people their treasures, for translating their sacred books into English, French, Italian, Spanish, and German—And send Missionaries to propagate them throughout all Europe and all America North and South. We might then know what the religions really are of the great part of the World. We know as little of them now, as we do of the religions of the Inhabitants of Sirius, the dog Star.

But sobrius esto—Stop, pause! Let us consider what would be the consequence; what would our Christian Theologians, from the Pope, to Zinzindorf, Sweedenborgh, Wesley, down to Mr. Moffet say, if these learned priests of all those vast Countries, if they were to appear here with their Brama and Veda and Zoroaster and Confucious, entering among their Parishioners and Congregations and zealously labouring to make converts among them. Do you think these reverend Gentlemen will be tolerant enough to permit them? Would they be contented to preach and write them down, or would they try to inflame the civil power to raise its arm of flesh and strength to drive them out.[18]

Johnson replied sententiously that in a multiplicity of sects lay the safety of each sect. "As a christian, I would be glad to see all mankind christians, nay presbyterians; but so long as they will not, I should rejoice to see every where a toleration in which the mosque and the synagogue, the pagoda and the church, should be harmoniously located along side of each other," and he would be glad to contribute to the building of any one of them. But in the present state of affairs, he considered this a "delicate question" and seldom spoke about it, whatever he might think. Speaking in the similitudes he was so fond of, he gave his own rule of conduct as follows: "I treat a man, in relation to his prejudices, as I treat him in relation to the corns which afflict his feet. They may not be on this toe or that; but so long as I am not apprised on which they are, I fear to press against any." [19] Adams thought this a good maxim, but guyed Johnson a little for preferring Presbyterianism, one of the most authoritarian and "hierarchical" of creeds.[20] Johnson replied with the ardent and highly pragmatic defense of his Presbyterian faith that has been quoted in the preceding study by David Ellis.

On his part, Adams closed this question by accepting the view that men's passions need checks and bridles, but among all the kinds that exist he considered those employed by "the Priests" and particularly by the Presbyterian hierarchy "the most detestable," being little better than those invoked by Osage and Cherokee medicine men. "They have no Authority over me," he concluded, "more than I have over them; I value more your maxims, than all their bulls." [21]

The last surviving letter between Johnson and John Adams is a warm note of congratulations from Utica to Quincy on the election of John Quincy Adams to the Presidency in 1825, and a similar message to the new President begins Johnson's correspondence with the next Adams generation. Though friendly enough, this was to prove a good deal less intimate in tone than the correspondence reviewed above. Uncle and nephew exchanged publications of course, and wrote polite and sometimes thoughtful acknowledgments. On receiving Johnson's *Discourse on Language* at a moment of leisure, J. Q. Adams read it at once and commented at length on its theme of the "insensibility of the People in this our own Country to the merits of our own Literature"—an observation often made before, Adams remarked, "though never to my knowledge with the keenness of severity, and the aptitude of illustration, with which you have presented it to view." He went on to suggest some of the causes of this condition that occurred to him. One of these was:

> We have no private Libraries. Gentlemen in easy Circumstances, and having a taste for Literature, collect a few Books —enough to adorn the upper Shelves of a Mahogany Book case with glass doors, and that is their provision for Life. These Books are often Works of Sterling merit, and sometimes merely of fashionable repute. A Library, even a private Library, deserving of the name, requires a large Space for its location. Our dwelling houses are not built with dimensions capable of holding a considerable collection of Books; and although there are

among us men of opulence, who build large and costly houses,
I know not a single instance, in which room has been found in
such a House, for a capacious Library.

Adams was aware that this explanation really begged the question.
He liked the suggestion Johnson made of establishing "a Library
composed exclusively of native Literature." It would have to be
done under the patronage of "a Society in one or another of our popu-
lous Cities." If the idea were carried out, it

> might among other good effects teach us a lesson of humility.
> Of what would it consist? How long is it since the Aristarchus
> of Edinburgh [Sidney Smith] put the Trumpet to his mouth
> and blundered out—who reads an American Book? Yet there
> was some reason for the question, and you, though in a very
> different Spirit, now ask it again—Who reads an American
> Book? If Americans can produce no books, but such as nobody
> will read, why should they complain that their Literature is ne-
> glected? If the Soil yields nothing but Indian Corn, must we
> interdict the importation of Flour? [22]

However, Adams had high hopes of the Lyceum movement,
which was then just entering its palmy era in America and in which he
and Johnson, like most of their literate countrymen, were active. A
good part of his letter is devoted to the prospects and hazards of this
promising movement in literary endeavor and popular education.

Of Johnson's more elaborate and now celebrated *Treatise
on Language,* Adams—again like most of his countrymen at the time
—could make little and, I am afraid, took a philistine view.

> Without being able to assent to many of its opinions [he
> wrote], and particularly to that which if I understand the work
> forms the foundation of your theory, namely that Sensation is
> the only Source of human knowledge, and that every word not
> expressive of some sensual impression is insignificant, I must
> admit that the view which you have taken of the whole subject
> is new, and sustained with great meditative power—a power
> which I can trace neither to sight, sound, feel, taste or smell.[23]

Probably the most welcome letter that Adams ever received
from his nephew in Utica was one written early in 1839 in which Johnson put forward his views on the proper use of the generous but
politically controversial bequest of James Smithson to the United States
"for the increase and diffusion of knowledge." Adams was to be embattled for a decade in a campaign to see that, in the first place, the
fund was accepted (for powerfully placed states-righters argued that it

was undignified for the United States to receive such a gift from a foreigner and unconstitutional for the Federal government to establish a scientific or educational institution), and that, in the second place, it was used for its true purpose and not squandered on what he once called a rest home for broken-down politicians. Johnson's suggestions were entirely sensible and correct, and fell in with Adams' own. "The capital of the fund," he urged, "should be kept entire for ever, and on interest:—the income only to be used. Buildings, if any are necessary, should be erected only out of the income; though I should hope Congress will erect them at the national expence."

> The cardinal object with me [he continued], is the creation of some benefit which will not exist without the bequest. To feed the hungry is a good object, but the hungry will be fed without this fund. To educate 500 poor young men annually, is a good object; but probably, like the Cadets at West Point, they would nearly all obtain an education by some other means. . . . What good object you select is of less consequence, than the principle that the object shall be a good, created by the fund:—a good that could not exist without the fund.[24]

This was a principle that Adams was determined to see carried out, although for altogether different reasons than Johnson had in mind and did not state. It may have been noticed that the subject of politics is pretty completely skirted in all of Johnson's correspondence with the Adamses. The reason is that he held very different constitutional views than they did, and hence, during the long period of fundamental debate concerning the nature of the American union prior to the Civil War, he was allied—with I believe only a single exception (the national election of 1840)—with their foes rather than with their friends. On the great overarching issue of the relations of the states to the central government, he was one of those whom J. Q. Adams designated "Northern men of Southern principles," or in the political slang of the day, he was a "doughface." In his First Annual Message as President, one of the great prophetic declarations in our history but stillborn then and too little known today, Adams had enunciated the principle that for the Federal government to stand aside, "palsied by the will of its constituents," and fail to promote the happiness and prosperity of the citizens by active measures of internal and intellectual improvement, would be "treachery to the most sacred of trusts." It would leave buried the material, moral, and intellectual resources that Providence had specially furnished to America for her own improvement and that of mankind. In his proposals for developing these, Adams set forth a program for the Great Society almost a century and a half before the phrase was coined.[25]

All this was anathema, or merely funny, to the politicians who had opposed Adams' candidacy and who coalesced immediately after his election to cripple his program and eject him from office at the earliest possible moment. Johnson was not one of these partisans, but throughout his long career as a publicist he lent philosophical respectability to their political tactics. He believed that the maintenance of the Union, or, as he usually chose to call it, the "Confederacy" of American states, depended entirely on restraint of the central power and the initiative and self-reliance of its component parts. In an important paper he published at the beginning of 1850, he quoted the eloquent paragraph I have summarized above from J. Q. Adams' Message of 1825 and then commented:

> All that is thus so well and patriotically stated by Mr. Adams is true, but it is totally inapplicable to our Confederacy, which is a nation for only a limited number of purposes, and can continue a nation by only adhering strictly to the limitations; as we may be assured by the present agitations, as well as by several preceding ones, which brought the Confederacy to the verge of dissolution. The power to which Mr. Adams alludes, exists in our States respectively, who, instead of "slumbering in indolence and folding up their arms," have advanced in their career of public improvements, canals, railroads, plankroads, electric telegraphs, steamboat navigation, steamboat construction, public education, and all other elements of progress, to a degree which no other people ever witnessed; and to a degree which the National Government could not have attained, had it been legally invested with the attributes of unrestricted sovereignty.[26]

Johnson himself was a lifelong entrepreneur and capitalist of such improvements as he enumerates here; and, as an observer of and participant in the prosperity around him, he thought it right to leave local tasks to local enterprise, especially since one great section of the country, based on a different economic system, was so sensitive to the possibility of interference by the national government with its "peculiar institution" of slavery. Johnson was no apologist for slavery per se, but under the Constitution as it was written he held that state and territorial option should be absolute on this question, just as it should be with respect to temperance laws. In innumerable books, tracts, and newspaper articles he argued with logic, plausibility, and consistency for this dogma. If John Quincy Adams' vision of a single and powerful union of states united for benevolent purposes was premature, Alexander Johnson never saw that vision at all. "Liberty is power," J. Q. Adams had said. But, Johnson countered, power consolidated at one center is despotism, and no widespread and expanding federation of political entities will tolerate or can long survive it.

The last letters I find of his among the Adams Papers were directed to Charles Francis Adams in December 1860. Adams was serving as the Massachusetts member of the House Committee of Thirty-Three, which at this late hour was desperately striving to find another compromise formula that could somehow glue together the dissolving union. Johnson's proposal was characteristically consistent with all that he had said so often before:

> If a desire for Union really exists throughout the confederacy (and of which desire I much doubt,) I think it may be consummated by placing slavery in the same category as the constitution already places Religion. The Constitution could be amended as follows: "Neither Congress nor any Territorial Legislature shall make any law or regulation permitting or preventing the existence of Slavery in any part of the United States, but the preventing or permitting shall be left to the exclusive jurisdiction and control of the States respectively."   —I should like to add, "nor shall the merits or demerits of Slavery as existing in any State, be discussed or alluded to in any debate or proceeding of either house of Congress." [27]

The qualifying clause was, of course, a gag which if written into the Constitution would surely have roused J. Q. Adams from his granite tomb under the portico of the First Parish Church of Quincy.

III

A LONG WAY back we left John Quincy Adams, his daughter-in-law, her father Peter C. Brooks, and her little son John Quincy aboard the railroad cars en route from Boston to Springfield, Saratoga Springs, and possibly points farther north and west. Although much supporting material exists, especially in contemporary newspapers, to show how this tour in the summer of 1843 affected others besides the main figure, by far the best record is in Adams' own manuscript diary, only selections from which were included in his son's twelve-volume published edition. [28]

Early in the extremely full entries that the diarist struggled to compose along the way, usually by the dawn's earliest light, it becomes apparent to the reader—even if it did not at the time to the diarist—that the tour was going to become something more than a mere family excursion for health and pleasure. At his hotel in Lebanon, autograph-seekers singled out the ex-President and gave him their usual botheration; and early one morning a perfect stranger who said he was from Albany came up on the piazza and talked to Adams through his chamber window, simply because, he said, he had long wanted "to see me and shake hands with me." [29] Letters of invitation to address this or that society, or the citizenry at large, in towns and cities of New York State were handed to him by individuals and committees who had traveled long distances to pay their respects. The invitations threw Adams into painful quandaries. He was totally unaccustomed to popular homage, and indeed thought there was something contemptible in those who accepted, to say nothing of those who solicited it. But here *he* was, on display himself, and liking it even though he could not admit that he did. At first he put off these importunings on the ground that he was "a mere appendage" to a family party and could not dictate its itinerary.[30] But developments at Saratoga Springs, where the party arrived on July 12, altered the perspective for everyone. Here the ex-President was well known to numerous local and visiting dignitaries. A reception was gotten up for him in the great hall of the Union Hotel and announced in the papers, and he spent a morning shaking the hands of some 500 well-wishers, listening to speeches, and having to reply to them. This threw Mr. Brooks and his daughter Abby into a quandary in their turn. It was clear that the ex-President would like to continue on tour, and Brooks (who had no relish for resort life) at this point also thought he should and was willing to accompany him. Abby would have preferred to stay at the Springs, but knew that this would disappoint her father-in-law, who would probably "not go on without a motive" [31] (meaning his daughter-in-law's health, to which he continued to make pointed public allusions), and so she yielded and went along with the two old gentlemen.

They proceeded by steamer up the lakes to the St. Lawrence, visited Quebec and Montreal, crossed to Ogdensburg in response to a pressing invitation and found the entire village and countryside had turned out to honor the great man, and then continued by lake steamer to Niagara Falls. Their approach was well heralded, for by this time the newspapers—and they were legion throughout the cities and villages of the state—had begun printing and reprinting almost daily stories of the visit the Adams party was paying to the Empire State, spiced with innumerable anecdotes of Old Man Eloquent's prowess as statesman, diplomat, orator, and author; his alert step and fiery eye; his republican simplicity; his erudition; his fearlessness; his capacity for labor; his early rising ("The sun never shines while he is in bed; if he is able to leave it"); his virtues as son, father, and grandfather; and so on *ad infinitum*. In short, he was good copy, for the people of New York State discovered, now that he was too old to run for the Presidency again, that they not only admired but loved him, probably to their surprise and certainly to his. After all, had he not presented petitions against slavery and the slave trade signed by thousands of New York State residents, when no one else in Congress dared to? Had he not crusaded for internal improvements and scientific institutions, for education and public enlightenment generally? And was he not the last physical link actually surviving in public office with the generation that had won independence for America? Such thoughts help to explain the outpouring of public affection that was to engulf him as he traveled eastward through the incredibly rich pathway of American empire, which was also, it should not be forgotten, the "burned-over district" of spiritual aspiration with which J. Q. Adams had many affinities.

It would be impossible to convey the color and quality of this triumphal progress without quoting extensively from both Adams' diary and contemporary newspaper accounts. [32] Both illuminate the management of such affairs in youthful America, before the age of mechanized mass communications had stupefied everyone everywhere with boiler-plate "news," and when the visit of a great man to our town was a novelty to get excited about. Here is a single example of news-writing in that day that will have to stand for many. It is from the *Ontario Repository* of August 2, 1843, reporting in the standard journalistic prose of the day Adams' visit to the village of Canandaigua:

RECEPTION OF JOHN QUINCY ADAMS

This venerable and respected statesman arrived in this village on Friday morning last. Our citizens, anticipating his coming, had convened in public meeting, and sent Messrs. FRANCIS GRANGER and JARED WILSON, as a committee to meet Mr. ADAMS at Rochester, and request him to tarry a few hours in our village. —Mr. Adams has complied with the request, and on his arrival at the crossing of the rail road and the highway, a little distance north of the town, he was met by a large and respectable escort of our citizens in carriages and wagons, and on horseback, all under the direction of Gen. JOHN A. GRANGER, as Marshal. On leaving the cars, Mr. ADAMS took his seat in a barouche ornamented with wreaths of flowers, and drawn by four splendid bay horses, accompanied by the President of the village, and the Hon. Messrs. GREIG and GRANGER. A large number of ladies, pre-eminent for worth, beauty and taste, had come out in carriages, to do themselves honor by thus honoring "the old man eloquent," and followed in the procession immediately next to the ex-President. Our fine village Band, under the direction of Major SPENCER, had generously volunteered its services for the day, and striking up an appropriate air, the procession, nearly a mile in length, amid the roar of the cannon and the ringing of the bells, moved in excellent order through the main street of our village, to the Brick Church, the side pews and galleries of which were filled with lovely women, whose beaming eyes and heaving bosoms, indicated the excitement produced by the venerable man's coming. As Mr. ADAMS walked from his carriage to the Church, the large crowd gathered about its doors, gave three hearty cheers that made the welkin ring, and amid the shouting of the crowd, the thrilling music of the band, and the thundering of the cannon, Mr. ADAMS, escorted by the committee and preceded by the Marshal, entered the church. The ladies all rose to give him welcome.

And this is only the beginning of the *Repository*'s account! Its readers' appetites for the last detail were obviously insatiable.

The other overwhelming impression the documentary evidence conveys is the sheer physical endurance required on the part of all concerned and especially on that of the principal figure, a man seventy-six years old. Handed from committee to committee, endlessly talked at, serenaded by bands, deafened by cannon salutes, kept from his bed by the newly invented firemen's torchlight processions, whirled from factory to prison to young ladies' academy to lunatic asylum and expected to say something appropriate and memorable at each, all in the heat of midsummer and with scarcely two successive meals at the same table or two nights in the same bed, Adams either possessed superhuman strength or ingested it from the torrent of adulation directed at him.

By the time they reached Auburn, the day after their reception in Canandaigua, others in his party had wilted. "I will try to give you a little idea of the doings," Abby Adams wrote her husband in a letter begun at Auburn, and continued at Utica,

> but I am so confused and tired both with your fathers bustle, indecision, and the excessive heat, that I am fit for nothing. I do not mind his parade, for with several ladies, we go to our

room, look on, and wonder and laugh. Old Tyler, or the Elephants [which had recently visited Boston], were nothing to him, but his inability to say no, and his making plans and promising solemnly to abide by them, and just as we are all off giving up to the first person who asks him, without considering us at all, has pretty well worn . . . father out, and I am so cross, I cant speak to him.[33]

Governor Seward, whom Abby described with a distaste perhaps justifiable under the circumstances as "a most ordinary looking, conceited little person," had appeared at Canandaigua and insisted on the party's stopping at his home in Auburn, but no sooner had they arrived than a delegation from Syracuse waited on the ex-President with an invitation to Syracuse. He of course accepted and was "paraded" there too, on the day he was due in Utica. Abby had looked forward to Utica, where she knew her Johnson relatives would take good care of her, but the circumstances of her Saturday-evening arrival were terrifying. Her father-in-law's diary relates that

> such was the confusion in the crowd and darkness . . . that [the welcoming committee] missed of meeting me. I was taken into a Carriage and brought to Mr. Johnson's through a dense mass of population, I know not how or by whom. They brought me by the torchlight procession of the firemen. From the porch of Mr. Johnson's house I thanked them for their kindness and I said I hoped and trusted we should all devote [the next] day to the worship and service of almighty God; and that [on Monday] I should have the happiness of meeting again my fellow citizens face to face, when I should endeavour to find words to thank them for their kindness. —Mr. Brooks was also lost for some time in the crowd; and Mrs. Charles, though in the charge of William C. Johnson, was so much alarmed that she actually screamed.[34]

Mr. Brooks had had more than enough. A. B. Johnson's autobiography records that Brooks had said bluntly that "He was tired of playing second fiddle to Mr. Adams." [35] This is an oversimplification. Now that Abby was in friendly hands, and could rest, Brooks relieved her of caring for little John Quincy, took "the train of cars" for Albany and Boston with the boy and a servant, and left the ex-President to his parades.

Of these there was to be a sufficiency in Utica, for Adams agreed to stay over an extra day "to give the opportunity for persons living in the neighbourhood of the city to come in and see the show" —a remarkable expression to have crept into the diary of John Quincy

Adams! [36] On Monday he clambered over the rough ground of Trenton Falls with the Johnson family, and that evening was entertained in their home "at a large party of our neighbors," A. B. Johnson later wrote, "with a band of music and a supper. The guest danced till a late hour." [37] Next day, among other things, Adams was persuaded to have several "Daguerreotype likenesses of my head . . . taken. All hideous." (But the Adams editors would like to know where they are now.) He also viewed General Tom Thumb; the York Cotton Mills, where he made a speech but in accordance with lifelong principle declined accepting a present of several pieces of cotton cloth; and a girls' school, where the reading of passages from his mother's recently published letters was "so affecting that it made a child of me," and he sobbed out loud.[38] The most interesting event of the day and of Adams' Utica sojourn was reported as follows in a Utica paper as yet unidentified:

JOHN Q. ADAMS AND THE COLORED PEOPLE OF UTICA.

We, with a number of other gentlemen and ladies of the city and elsewhere, happened to be present on Monday evening, when a deputation from the colored people of this city, consisting of Messrs. Woodson, Thompson, Panco, and James Jackson called upon Mr. Adams for the purpose of presenting to him their thanks for the devotion which he had uniformly manifested in the cause of human rights; and particularly for the vigorous and effective stand which he made in Congress in vindication of the Right of Petition as touching the sufferings and rights of their race.

All was done with strict propriety and gentlemanly decorum; and the short and appropriate address to him, which in behalf of the others was delivered by Mr. Woodson, was done in an excellent style, and delivered in a clear, collected and impressive manner, and was listened to with great attention and interest by Mr. Adams and all who were present.

Mr. Adams responded to it immediately: expressing his grateful thanks for the overestimate which they had put upon the value and amount of his services in the case to which they had alluded—saying that he could claim no merit at all for the bare performance of a duty which he had considered as imperatively incumbent upon him, with his views of the subject; and that if he from any cause should have failed to have performed it, he should have considered himself as wholly unworthy of the confidence or suffrages of his fellow citizens of any color. After repeating his thanks for the undeserved favor which they had shown themselves desirous of confering upon him, he took leave of them; wishing them all prosperity and happiness, and a successful issue out of all the afflictions and injustice under which they and their brethren now in bondage of various kinds had so long labored. They then returned in the same gentlemanly and decorous manner which had marked their entrance.

Mr. Adams may surely receive this mark of respect and affection as an abundant offset against the denunciations which he has lately received in the little conventions of abolitionists who occupied the Wesleyan Chapel in this city with their fanfaronades on this and various other corelative topics the last week.

We cannot follow in detail the dancing patriarch's further progress through New York State, but it was more of the same. In Albany, which he had passed through less than a month before without stirring more than a ripple of interest, the demonstrations dwarfed everything that had gone before, with cannons, bells, torchlights, and receptions on the steps of the Capitol and in the Governor's chamber. Adams spoke for half an hour to shouting multitudes in Capitol Park. According to the reported versions, his speech, although billed as nonpolitical, turned out to be a "Give 'em hell" performance: "I entreat you in the name of God *to send your petitions on to me.* (Tremendous cheering and laughter.) I trust this is not trespassing too much on politics. (Renewed cheering and laughter.)" [39] To Adams, however, who was told that the only fault of the speech was that it was not long enough, "it was but the crowning proof how unfit I am for such occasions." [40]

He had ample opportunity for more ruminations of this sort during his return to Pittsfield and Boston on "the morning Cars" from Albany. On this last leg of the journey he traveled quite alone, and no one paid the slightest attention to him. From the Boston "depot" he walked to his son Charles' office in Court Street. Charles was not there, nor could his father get word of him at the livery stable where Charles kept his horse. Back at the station the ex-President had a long search for his trunk, "which had disappeared." He then "returned to the Stable; took there a hack; stop'd at the Railway depot and took my trunk and came out alone to my home at Quincy. . . . I found the family at dinner. My wife, my Son John's widow, Mary Catherine [(Hellen) Adams], and her daughter, Mary Louisa." [41]

About a week later, Abby Adams arrived home, having rested during the interval at the Johnsons'. She had found herself "quite charmed" by the "unaffected kind manner" of her host, who "appears, from what I learn here [in Utica], to stand quite alone as a lovely domestic character." [42] She brought along with her to Quincy two of the Johnson children, William Clarkson and Sarah, for a return visit. William was already well known in Quincy, for he had enrolled at the Harvard Law School in 1842 and had often visited the Adams homes there. His earliest impressions of Abby had been mixed. He found her "a good looking" and "very pleasant young woman," but possessing "an endless tongue and a great number of small children." [43] (There were five in 1842.) But his attachment to the family steadily increased. Charles Francis was particularly grateful and kind after his wife's happy stay in Utica. William gives a pleasant picture of life at Quincy during his summer visit in 1843:

> The girls practice their music every day; and yesterday, the President, Charles, Hull [Charles' cousin] and I went a fishing with several other gentlemen. We went in three boats,—the president, four other gentlemen and I, being in one; and we caught over a hundred Haddock, besides a few Cods and some other fish. I caught about 30 haddock, and had the best luck of the boat. The whole party caught over 200 Haddock, eight or ten codfish, a few tautogs, two bushels of Perch, and 3 of mackerel. I never knew such Sport and the day was delightful. We dined at Cohasset on Chowder made from our own fish, and then went to an evening party at Hingham, thus ending the day. [44]

One of the invitations that J. Q. Adams had received during his progress through New York State and that, as his daughter-in-law reported, he had not had the self-restraint to decline, was to address a public gathering at the laying of the cornerstone of an astronomical observatory in Cincinnati. He now asked William Johnson to accompany him on what was to prove another epic jaunt westward. From William's hand, in letters to his father that survive among Johnson's papers, we have one of the best accounts of this expedition, in the course of which William became devoted to his formidable great-uncle. [45]

Eventually William was to form an even stronger tie with the Adams family. In 1843 Mary Louisa Adams, the granddaughter from Washington whom J. Q. Adams had found among his family at Quincy when he returned from Albany, was not quite fifteen. She was a third cousin of William, who was just twenty. Probably they met for the first time on this occasion. Ten years later they were married, Mary Louisa becoming William's second wife. Their descendants, who were and are numerous, were thus to be doubly descended from two Presidents of the United States. Few occurrences in his long and productive life, one may be sure, could have been more gratifying to William's father, the literary and philosophical banker of Utica.

NOTES

1 June 12, 1843. Adams Papers, Massachusetts Historical Society.

2 All quotations from the diary of John Quincy Adams are from the original in the Adams Papers, Massachusetts Historical Society. This manuscript, in fifty volumes, may be consulted in the microfilm edition of the Adams Papers issued by the Society, 1954–59, Reel Nos. 4–52.

3 Diary, October 2, 1843.

4 Diary, June 13–16, 1843.

5 Diary, June 17, 1843.

6 Diary, July 6, 1843.

7 Alexander Bryan Johnson, autobiography ("rough draft"), Chapter 3. This version of the autobiography is in the possession of Leonard J. Wyeth, Jr. of Dayton, Ohio, a descendant of its author. A note by Johnson, dated at Utica, February 7, 1867, on the front flyleaf of the first of the four bound volumes states that this is a "rough draft" and that a fair copy has been made and bound in five volumes. Two or more typescripts, deriving from either the draft or the fair copy (which the present writer has not seen), are in the possession of other descendants of A. B. Johnson. Since the draft is unpaged, references here are to chapters only.

The present writer wishes to acknowledge the kindness not only of Mr. Wyeth but of other Johnson descendants whose family papers he has been allowed to examine and quote as indicated in the notes below. It is very much to be hoped that all the papers of A. B. Johnson, now widely dispersed, will one day be brought together for permanent preservation and the use of scholars in the remarkably varied fields to which Johnson contributed. Some portions of those papers as they existed at Johnson's death, including correspondence between Johnsons and Adamses, have not to this day been located, although they are probably extant.

8 To indicate the complexity of the Adams-Smith-Johnson relationships, it should be noted that Charles Adams' marriage to Sarah (usually called Sally) Smith in 1795 was the second marital alliance between the Adamses and the Smiths. In London in 1786, Charles' older sister, Abigail, had married Sarah's older brother, William Stephens Smith, a dashing Revolutionary colonel then in the diplomatic service, who was to undertake many ventures in the course of his life but to succeed in few besides his courtship of the younger Abigail Adams. In 1808 the Smiths settled in Chenango County, New York; after a sad and troubled life, Abigail died in 1813, and three years later her husband died, leaving his affairs in great disorder. There is a sketch of Smith in the *Dictionary of American Biography;* see also Katharine Metcalf Roof, *Colonel William Smith and Lady* (Boston, 1929).

9 Autobiography, Chap. 3.

10 *Obituary Notices of Alexander Bryan Johnson* (Utica, 1868), pp. 8, 13.

11 Autobiography, Chap. 3.

12 *Ibid.,* Chap. 17.

13 January 11, 1815. Original owned by Mrs. Waldo C. M. Johnston, Old Lyme, Conn., a descendant of A. B. Johnson of Utica.

14 December 16, 1822. Original owned by Mrs. Johnston.

15 October 13, 1815. Original owned by Mrs. Johnston.

16 February 12, 1823. Original owned by Mrs. Johnston.

17 February 22, 1823. Johnson, autobiography, Chap. 4.

18 March 1, 1823. Original owned by Mrs. Johnston.

19 March 14, 1823. Johnson, autobiography, Chap. 4.

20 March 26, 1823. Original owned by Mrs. Johnston.

21 April 22, 1823. Original owned by Mrs. Johnston.

22 September 26, 1832. Original owned by Alexander B. Johnson, Darien, Conn.

23 December 8, 1836. Original owned by Alexander B. Johnson, Darien, Connecticut. The letter goes on in a very civil way to question the validity of Johnson's discoveries on the grounds both of theory and common sense. Adams' comments in his diary while he was reading the "Treatise" are somewhat sharper and are especially interesting for their analysis of Johnson's use of language and his literary style and method as reflections of his temperament. Thus on November 26 Adams wrote:

"It is a work of an extraordinary character; and deserving of much consideration at least from me. It assumes the merit of a profound discovery, undetected by all the writers upon metaphysics of former ages. There is something of the Jeremy Bentham character about it. A free use of neologies—words of the author's invention, but deficient both in euphony and precision. A style deeply studied; affecting originality—antipathetic, highly figurative, and often stranded upon the commonest rules of Grammar. He quotes Berkley, Locke, Hume, Descartes and Reid, as mere schoolboys utterly ignorant of his great discovery, and consequently committing egregious blunders, which it has been reserved to him to expose. But instead of quoting them in their own words, he gives his own version or paraphrase of particular passages in their writings and then shews the absurdity of his own conceptions which he imputes to them. He has long and perseveringly and painfully meditated his subject into a system which has unity and consistency and some ingenuity of invention. But I find it very difficult to understand him, and am doubtful whether he has really presented some new views of language, or whether his book is a mere bundle of common truisms mystified into an appearance of metaphysical refinement."

See also Adams' further comments on the "Treatise" in his diary entries of November 28 and 29 and December 1, 1843.

24 February 8, 1839. Adams Papers.

25 J. Q. Adams' First Annual Message to Congress, December 6, 1825, is most readily available (though in a text not perfectly reliable) in James D. Richardson (ed.), *A Compilation of the Messages and Papers of the Presidents, 1789–1897* (Washington, D.C., 1896–99), Vol. II, pp. 299–317.

26 *A Guide to the Right Understanding of Our American Union*, p. 40. A footnote by the author states that this section or chapter of the book was first published January 1, 1850, doubtless in a newspaper.

27 December 7, 1860. Adams Papers.

28 Charles Francis Adams (ed.), *Memoirs of John Quincy Adams, Comprising Portions of His Diary from 1795 to 1848* (Philadelphia, 1874–77). For the (published) entries relating to the Adams-Brooks family tour of New York State and Canada in 1843, see Vol. XI, pp. 389–405.

29 Diary, July 10, 1843.

30 Letter to Rufus King, President of the Albany Young Men's Association, July 9, 1843. Adams Papers.

31 Abigail Brooks Adams to her daughter, Louisa Catherine, July 13, 1843; to her husband, Charles Francis Adams, July 16–17, 1843. Both in Adams Papers.

32 A collection of mounted newspaper clippings relating to the tour is in the Adams Papers, M/JQA/62, Microfilms, Reel No. 255. Quotations below from newspaper accounts are drawn from this collection.

33 July 29–30, 1843. Adams Papers.

34 Diary, July 30, 1843.

35 Autobiography, Chap. 12.

36 Entry of July 31, 1843.

37 Autobiography, Chap. 12.

38 Diary, August 1, 1843.

39 *Albany Argus,* August 4, 1843. Preparation of this speech, the final effort of his month-long trip, had been agonizing. In the Adams Papers, Microfilms, Reel No. 527, is a page of rather pathetic notes for it, reading in part:

"I came among you alone [which, as we have seen, was not literally true] —my companions have been the whole people of western New York. . . . What I have seen and heard and enjoyed will serve for pleasing meditation and reflection for the short remainder of my days. I come not as a public man, but I linger in the public service—I remember [i.e., mention] it only to tender my service to one and all."

40 Diary, August 3, 1843.

41 Diary, August 5, 1843.

42 To Charles Francis Adams, August 6, 1843. Adams Papers.

43 To his father, A. B. Johnson, August 26, 1842; A. B. Johnson, autobiography, Chap. 12. To his stepmother, the second Mrs. A. B. Johnson, October 3, 1842; original owned by Alexander B. Johnson, Darien, Conn.

44 To his father, August 18, 1843. A. B. Johnson, autobiography, Chap. 12. Present-day Adamses still sail and fish off the point on the South Shore of Massachusetts Bay then called Cohasset Rocks and now called The Glades.

45 Copies of these letters are in A. B. Johnson's autobiography, Chap. 13.

IV

ESSAYIST AND SATIRIST

That a man thrown so early into the active and
what with most men would necessarily be the
absorbing business of life should accomplish so much in
literature, and accomplish it so well is indeed
extraordinary.

M. M. Bagg in Pioneers of Utica

JOHNSON'S MISCELLANEOUS
ESSAYS AND FICTION

◆ ◆ ◆ ◆ ◆ *THOMAS F. O'DONNELL*

IF WE EXCEPT the early *Inquiry into the Natural Rights of Man* published anonymously as a pamphlet in 1813, Johnson turned to belletristic writing comparatively late. Through the earlier years, to be sure, he had incorporated short essays and moral injunctions into letters to his growing children; many of these are to be found among the so-called "Breviats"—short pieces—in *An Encyclopedia of Instruction* (1857). But not until 1841, apparently, did he publish anything resembling fiction. This was *The Philosophical Emperor: a Political Experiment; or, The Progress of a False Position* (Nine years later, in 1850, Johnson was to publish another piece of fiction entitled *The Philosophical Emperor,* almost entirely different from the first, but subtitled "An Experiment in Morals." I shall refer to the earlier version as *Philosophical Emperor A* and the later as *Philosophical Emperor B*.) David Millar has dealt with the early version in these *Proceedings*.

Johnson was then in his fifty-sixth year when he finally turned to fiction: this fact takes on significance later, when we venture an evaluation, both historical and critical, of that fiction. Why did he wait so long? The question can be answered in terms of Johnson's own

◇ ◇ ◇ ◇ ◇ *Chairman, Division of Languages, Utica College. Coauthor,* Harold Frederic *(1962),* Back Home in Oneida *(1965). Editor,* Harold Frederic's Stories of York State *(1966),* J. K. Paulding's The Dutchman's Fireside *(1966).*

background, temperament, and earlier pronouncements. Although Moses M. Bagg testifies that Johnson "made diligent use of the old Schuyler library" and read "romances and poetry," [1] we have Johnson's own word for it that he did not read widely. "I read almost nothing," he confessed to Simeon De Witt Bloodgood in a letter in 1832, "although I have a reputation of reading much." [2] The literal truth of this statement may be discounted, because Johnson does manifest a familiarity with Shakespeare, Milton, Swift, and certain eighteenth-century poets, including William Cowper. What he actually meant, no doubt, was that he read little contemporary writing of any kind, especially contemporary romance or fiction.

Long before he turned his hand to his own variety of fiction, Johnson had developed, and often expressed, the philosopher's traditional distrust of the mimetic arts. In the letter to Bloodgood already cited, he maintains that "the same innate cruelty of our nature" which in other times "led to the gladiatorial fights of Rome—to the jousts and tourneyments of the Middle Ages and subsequently to the bullfights of Spain and the cock fights of England" finds its outlet in his own time in

> novels and romances, through highly wrought representations of fictitious cruelty. . . . When I accidentally [note the significant adverb] cast my eyes on these modern fictions and see, as in one of Scott's novels, snares preparing trapdoors constructed to immire to destruction some beautiful and faultless woman, I as uniformly and indignantly cast from me the book, as I should an invitation of some South Sea cannibal, to make a dinner with him on a human victim. [3]

Some months later, in a letter to G. A. Worth, Johnson's scorn for romancers was further directed at two of his fellow Americans. "I never read any of Cooper's trash and never shall," he tells Worth in a sentence that reflects more, alas, on Johnson than on Cooper. "But Irving tells very pretty stories," he goes on with only less contempt, "and I mean to add them to my stock of nursery amusements; though they will never be as popular as Jack the Giant Killer and Tom Thumb." [4]

Here, then, is Johnson's explicit attitude toward fiction in 1832: at its worst it is extremely harmful, a verbalized extension of man's least admirable characteristic, his cruelty; at a higher level, it is a kind of verbal toy suited to the children's playroom, but hardly for the philosopher's study or practice. Certainly there is nothing new in this attitude: it has been shared by many intellectuals at least as far back as Plato; it is part of the humanistic tradition of the Renaissance, which insisted that the imagination be rigidly controlled by learning and judgment; we find it expressed again and again in Milton and later by men of the Enlightenment who feared lest the hoyden, Fancy, corrupt her majesty, Reason. As far back as 1668 John Dryden—himself blessed with one of the most imaginative of minds—maintained that "Moral truth is the mistress of the poet as well as of the philosopher. Poesy must resemble natural truth, but it must *be* ethical." Because he found little of either "natural truth" or ethics in *Tom Jones,* Samuel Johnson labeled Fielding's novel "vicious" and "corrupt." Benjamin Franklin —A. B. Johnson's master in so many ways—would have substituted the adjective "useful" for Dryden's "ethical"; but he too held belletristic writing in suspicion. "I approved for my part," Franklin says in the *Autobiography,* "the amusing one's self with poetry now and then, so far as to improve one's language, but no farther," [5] and derogated some of his own best pieces by labeling them "bagatelles." And even in his own time, A. B. Johnson was hardly alone in his antipathy for romantic fiction. In 1814, the year of the publication of Scott's *Waverly,* which ushered in an era of prose romance, James Kirke Paulding was already lamenting "the pernicious examples held up in those mischievous books of chivalry from time to time manufactured by" Sir Walter Scott. And in 1819 the same Paulding (whom Johnson may have known through a common friend, Judge Morris M. Miller of Utica) published a widely read essay entitled "National Literature," in which he called for "rational fictions," rather than fiction requiring "the aid of superstition, the agency of ghosts, fairies, hobgoblins, and all that antiquated machinery which till lately was confined to the nursery."

Not until nine years after the letter to Bloodgood that put him squarely among the losers—the antiromantics—did Johnson revise his attitude toward fiction and try his own hand at it in *The Philosophical Emperor A.* This is a lengthy, satirical, political allegory based chiefly on the Bank issues of the Jackson administrations, but geared also to the Van Buren administration, the election and sudden death of William Henry Harrison, and the first few days of the Tyler administration. For a number of years afterward, he seems to have published no other fiction. And then, suddenly, between November 1849 (he was then sixty-three) and March 1852 fourteen different pieces of his fiction appear in *The Knickerbocker Magazine,* including pieces in twelve successive issues in 1849–50. During this period he also probably wrote a number of other pieces that did not appear until *An Encyclopedia of Instruction* was published in 1857. During this remarkably productive period, between 1841 and 1857, he also published *The Meaning of Words* (1854), *The Physiology of the Senses* (1856), two pamphlets, and many articles on banking and politics.

But it is only the fiction in *The Knickerbocker Magazine* that concerns us here, for it poses a number of questions. Why, for one, did Johnson write the stories in the first place? Why so many in such a short time? How did he happen to place them in *The Knickerbocker Magazine,* which was, after all, the leading literary periodical of the day, numbering among its contributors such contemporary giants as Longfellow, Hawthorne, Whittier, Holmes, and Bryant, as well as lesser-known New Yorkers? Next—and the questions become more interesting as we proceed—why did the stories stop so suddenly in 1852? And finally, why, in view of the frequency of his appearance in the magazine between 1849 and 1852, was Johnson not invited to contribute to *The Knickerbocker Gallery,* an anthology published in 1854 as a tribute to the *Knickerbocker* editor, Lewis Gaylord Clark?

Our present knowledge of Johnson provides us with only speculative answers to these questions. We know, because he tells us often in his autobiography and elsewhere, that he was disappointed with the unenthusiastic reception of his early works on language, which reached a pitifully small audience. And Johnson, despite his occasional statement that he wrote primarily for himself, wanted readers: in 1828 responding to Fanny Wright's encouraging remarks about *The Philosophy of Human Knowledge* (the first book version of *A Treatise on Language*), he frankly admitted, "My object in the publication is, I confess, fame—the fame arising from useful authorship. I am too fond of this bewitching ignus fatuus; and the stimulation of such fame can alone make me continue the lectures." [6] At about the same time in a letter to Timothy Flint he wrote, "I literally starve for lack of excitement—a mouthful of praise is a luxury to me. . . . The expectation of such a reward from the wise, the reflecting, and the liberal, was all I expected from my book; and as yet I have received too little to tempt me further in the painful and laborious occupation of book making." [7]

But the fame Johnson sought refused to come, chiefly because his audience, even for *The Philosophical Emperor A,* remained so small. Then, in a manner not yet clear to me at least, he made a happy contact with *The Knickerbocker Magazine,* one of the most widely read periodicals of the day. Did Johnson know Lewis Gaylord

Clark, the editor? Very probably he did. Johnson's election to honorary membership in the New-York Historical Society in 1826, his activities in the State and National Lyceum movements, his wide acquaintance in the banking circles of New York—all these would make an acquaintance with Clark not only possible but probable. Or he could have known Clark through Willis Gaylord, Clark's uncle, prominent editor of *The Genesee Farmer and Albany Cultivator,* or through Richard B. Kimball, a Wall Street lawyer and banker who, like Johnson, was a writer by avocation and a contributor to *The Knickerbocker;* or through his old friend, Henry R. Schoolcraft, another contributor. Or perhaps Clark, who liked satire, had read *The Philosophical Emperor A,* admired it, and invited Johnson to contribute to his magazine.

The strongest possibility, however, is that Johnson connected with Clark and *The Knickerbocker* through his old friend Samuel Dakin. Early in the 1840's Dakin, then living in New York City, quietly "bought into" *The Knickerbocker,* which was in financial difficulty. Although no literary historian that I know of mentions Dakin's connection with the magazine, Johnson tells us about it in the autobiography. In Dakin he had, in a sense, a powerful friend at court.

All this is, of course, calculated speculation. The probability of a special, personal contact with Clark is, however, of some importance, because, quite frankly, the appearance of Johnson's fiction in *The Knickerbocker* is rather difficult to explain otherwise. It seems to me to be anomalous, out of place in a periodical that was publishing mainly the very kind of fiction and poetry for which Johnson had previously expressed so much contempt. But there it is, and at last Johnson had the large audience that his earlier writings had never achieved. The opportunity to spread some of his basic ideas by the mere expedient of sugarcoating them in fiction was an appealing one, and required only a minor compromise of method and not of substance. And so during the next thirty months the stories appear: twelve of them in successive issues, and, after a hiatus of almost a year, three more.

Now let us consider them, first as a group. Again quite frankly, they read like the work of an elderly man with more wisdom and experience than concern for the dramatic or artistic. They betray a conviction, natural in a philosopher like Johnson, that fiction at its very best can only be a means, never an end in itself. They reflect no awareness whatever of new concepts of literary art, or of what Poe and Hawthorne had long since done to the short story form. They are full of what Poe, at the very time Johnson was writing, was belaboring in his widely heard lecture ("The Poetic Principle," 1848–49) as "the heresy of the Didactic." In both form and content, they are stories—moral allegories and fables—out of the eighteenth century. Men of the Enlightenment from John Dryden to Benjamin Franklin would have approved of them; but they are a full generation behind the general taste of a reading public whose appetite was being shaped by romantic writers, both great and not so great, in 1849–50. By now the emotional and sentimental had all but routed the intellectual from American fiction, and we were entering a decade which Fred Lewis Pattee has aptly labeled "The Feminine Fifties" because of the predominance of the literary ladies that Hawthorne complained about as a "damned mob of scribbling females."

Remembering that it is fiction we are discussing, consider the very titles of some of these pieces: "How to Live Where You Like, A Legend of Utica"; "How to Prosper, or the Fatal Mistake"; "How to be Happy"; "Story of the Man Whom Nobody Can Benefit, and the Man Whom Nobody Can Injure"; "The Obstacles to Success." They have the ring of coin long before minted by, for instance, Benjamin Franklin himself. In form they are undramatic, consisting almost entirely of straight narration, with practically no characterization through dialogue, no attempt at suspense, no nuances in viewpoint. There are no characters in the common sense of the word; only abstractions in shadowy human form. And always at the end, sometimes clearly explicit, sometimes implicit, is the moral, the lesson, the admonition.

But neither are the stories as artless as I have perhaps just made them sound. Although there are few carefully developed climaxes of the kind that we now expect in fiction, there *are* reversals, undramatic though they may be. These reversals are the result of the inexorable operation of cause and effect that is the concern of Johnson's fiction as it is of much of his other writing. So also is there a real concern with motivation, especially with motivation based on responses to "verbal" (hence questionably valid) concepts. In *The Philosophical Emperor B,* which appeared in two installments of *The Knickerbocker* in May and June 1850, the title character sets out on a journey (somewhat like Samuel Johnson's Rasselas) to test his theory that "no class feels happy or unhappy by reason of its position, but only by reason of falling below its accustomed position or rising above it." [8] In the course of the story, three groups of characters representing roughly the lower, middle, and upper classes are each reduced, by *fiat* of the Emperor,

214

one step on the socioeconomic ladder: a group of contented agricultural slaves are relegated to the mines; their previously happy owners are turned into slaves; and *their* socioeconomic superiors are reduced to a kind of middle-class penury. All three groups lament their fall from various kinds of fortune. But it is not the actual, the *real* change in condition that bothers them most: it is the "social," or what might be called the "artificial" change. The physical discomforts that come with the change are tolerable: it is the loss of *status* that they cannot bear.

This story—except for *The Philosophical Emperor A,* the longest piece of fiction that Johnson wrote—also has allegorical political overtones. They are not so obvious, however, as in *Philosophical Emperor A,* and the modern reader needs no key to the work in order to appreciate its satire. Is the title character, this second "philosophical emperor" who wanders incognito through his realm to test his theories, Martin Van Buren? Perhaps, but if so, it is not important to know that he is, as it *was* important to know the real identity of the characters in *Philosophical Emperor A.* In the second version Johnson is using his own ideas and convictions, rather than political history, as a basis for his fiction, and it is his structural sense that shapes the story, rather than events in contemporary politics, as was the case with *Philosophical Emperor A.* Consequently the piece is much more satisfactory as fiction. In it Johnson also allows himself plenty of ironical play, some of it reminiscent of Swift. Toward the end of the story, for example, the Emperor rewards a faithful corporal who had helped him to escape from captivity by making him head of a regiment. The ex-corporal is a capable soldier but cannot stand the social pressures of his new position. "He possessed no pedigree . . . while all his new associates were continually boasting of their ancestors." In the end the unfortunate man, who wanted nothing more than his corporal's rank, hangs himself in shame and "ignobility," a grim example of a man defeated by empty concepts like "ancestry," "position," "status."

Most of the stories are simple moral fables dealing with the consequences of human frailty. In "How to Live Where You Like; a Legend of Utica" (November 1849), Lucinda Tompkins is unhappy in her native frontier home in old Fort Schuyler. At the death of her father she inherits three boxes: one is labeled "open this; I shall not be offended"; the second, "touch not till the other is expended"; and the third, "nor this until the other two are ended." In a scene reminiscent not only of the casket scenes in *The Merchant of Venice* but of a host of other casket scenes in world folklore, Lucinda opens box one and finds a written legend saying "live where you like," together with a large sum of money. She is able now to leave dull and desolate old Fort Schuyler and move, first to Schenectady, then to Albany, and finally to New York City. Here she acquires a spendthrift husband, aptly named Mr. Lusher, whose extravagances force her to open the second box. In it she finds another legend reading, "live where you can" and a smaller sum of money. When Mr. Lusher dies, Lucinda opens box three, in which she finds a third legend reading "he only can live where he likes who likes where he lives" and enough money to start her on the return trip to Albany, to Schenectady, and finally back to old Fort Schuyler, which now doesn't seem so dull and desolate as it once did.

Another piece, "The Hermit of Utica" (March 1850), tells the story of old Pardee, who lives in gloomy solitude "in a little hovel, which was situated somewhere near where Hopper-Street now intersects Genesee . . ."—in other words, only about three blocks away from Johnson's home in one direction and from today's Munson-Williams-Proctor Institute in the other. We learn that old Pardee was once a highly respected citizen of Philadelphia, but has become a hermit because of what happened to his son. The younger Pardee had made a Faustian contract with Satan—in Philadelphia! — who agreed to supply him with unlimited wealth as long as he (young Pardee) avoided the cardinal vices of the drunkard, the gambler, and the libertine. When he turns to these sins, the young man is snatched away in the night by Satan. The distracted father moved to Utica to brood about his son's fate until his own dead body is found in his "hovel" one cold winter morning.

These two stories are representative of most of Johnson's fiction in purpose and execution; they are explicitly didactic and unexciting in development, consisting almost entirely of straight, undramatic narration. They are latter-day "exempla," designed to warn the reader against moral error; and Johnson continues this line in such stories as "Feminine Perfections; or the Unreasonable Bachelor," "How to Prosper; or the Fatal Mistake," and "Obstacles to Success."

Into at least three other stories, however, Johnson laces his ideas about the nature of man and his language. These pieces, more subtle and substantial than the simple moral fables, can, like *Philosophical Emperor B,* engage the reader who knows anything at all about Johnson's semantics and philosophy. Take, for instance, "The Argumentative Husband and the Husband Who Denied His Wife Nothing; or, A Secret Worth Knowing." This is a light-hearted application of Johnson's convictions about the differences between words and things. Jackson and Jenkins, friends in young manhood, marry and establish their own households, Jenkins in Philadelphia, Jackson in New York. Over the years, both are fairly successful, but Jenkins becomes famous for his indulgence: he is known as the husband who never denies his wife anything. When Mrs. Jackson hears of this she nags at her own husband to emulate his old friend—to buy, for one thing, a new house. Jackson demurs for as long as he has strength enough, but finally gives in and, against his better judgment, buys the new house. Now he is almost wiped out in a financial panic, although his old friend Jenkins sails through it unscathed. Finally Jenkins goes to Jackson to learn his secret: how can he be so indulgent to his wife's demands and still remain solvent? Jackson gives him the answer: while it is true that he doesn't deny his wife anything, he doesn't *give* her anything either—anything, that is, except words and promises. Like most wives, Jackson maintains, she is content with these. She doesn't really need or want *things*: she wants *words*. Jackson's stock of inexpensive words keeps his wife happy, and himself in solid financial condition.

"How To Be Happy"—despite its uninspired title, one of Johnson's best pieces—is a kind of extension of the fourth part of *Gulliver's Travels*. A Nantucket whaler lands in the country of the Houyhnhnms, where its crew kills an arrogant horse who tries to carry them off into slavery. The captain of the whaler takes the dead horse's two colts back to Nantucket and sells them to a farmer. Eventually they are hitched blindfolded to a grinding-mill and trudge in endless circles in the dark. One of the horses, named Grey, imagines all kinds of pleasant things as he goes about his work; he delights in the sounds and smells that surround him. The other horse, named Black, reacts oppositely: he deduces all kinds of unpleasant things from exactly the same sounds and smells that Grey loves so much. This goes on for a long time, until the farmer removes the blindfolds and the two horses see that they have been treading the same path. Grey, the happy Houyhnhnm, points out the inescapable moral—essentially the same as that of *Philosophical Emperor B*—"happiness depends not on the road we travel, nor on the incidents we encounter, but on our own reflections thereon."

But for the most explicit application of his ideas in fiction, Johnson turned to an Indian story entitled "The Three-Fold Nature of Man: a Legend of The Oneida Indians." The introductory part of this story is about the Indian village at Oneida Castle, some twenty miles west of Utica, and its chief, "Schonondoa," who is fond of repeating the legend proper that now follows—a legend which "seems to evince," as Johnson points out, "a knowledge, not too extensively known by white men, of the three-fold nature of man, making him a kind of triune being." Whoever has read Johnson's presumably final work, *Deep Sea Soundings* (1861), knows what is to follow in the Indian "legend."

Catena, an Indian woman, is the sole survivor when her hunting party is massacred by a hostile tribe. Instead of returning to her village of "Agoneseah" Indians, Catena stays alone in the wilderness for several years. As time passes, she wishes she had a daughter to care for her in her old age. She prays for such a daughter at a nearby spring, and a voice tells her she will have a daughter. When Catena repeats her prayer, the voice tells her again, a bit sharply this time, to return to her shelter: she will have a daughter. Catena repeats the request a third time, and the voice replies, angrily now, that she "shall have a daughter with a vengeance." When Catena returns to her wigwam she finds not one, but *three* baby girls identified in Indian heiroglyphics as Appetita, Limbina, and Intellecta. Appetita develops into the only one of the three who can eat; Limbina, the only one who can move her limbs; and Intellecta, the only one who can utter words. One night three strange little women appear to Catena and admit it was they who separated Catena's daughter into "the three constituent parts of a human being—the intellectual, physical, and moral parts." Now they remedy the situation: Appetita and Intellecta melt into Limbina's body, and the three become one whole person, a considerate, affectionate, and helpful daughter. Still later, a young Agoneseah chief wanders by, woos and wins the new Limbina. From them descend in a direct line Schonondoa and the whole tribe of Oneida Indians, who still live near the spring that runs through Oneida Castle.

This Indian "legend," which was published in August 1851, is one of the last pieces of Johnson's fiction to appear in *The Knickerbocker*. There were two more: "The Philosophical Sparrow," and "The Lunatic Asylum of Boresko," neither of them distinguished or even memorable. And suddenly there were no more.

In 1854, only two years after the appearance of Johnson's last story in *The Knickerbocker,* a group of Lewis Gaylord Clark's friends, all of them contributors to the magazine, edited and published an anthology called *The Knickerbocker Gallery*. The purpose of the book was to raise money to buy a home for Clark, who apparently was once more in financial difficulty. The Foreword of *The Knickerbocker Gallery* says that all "remaining" contributors to the magazine had been asked to write for the anthology. Curiously, however, Johnson, who had been one of the magazine's most regular contributors from 1849 until 1852, is not represented in the book. This pointed omission would seem to indicate that Johnson's line to *The Knickerbocker Magazine* had been cut off. Why? Once more I can only conjecture that his fiction was considered by other influential writers to be too antiquated, too out of date for the magazine's and the anthology's audience.

And yet his fiction was not without its admirers, especially among his fellow bankers. In 1850 and 1851, during the hiatus between the two groups of his stories in the *Knickerbocker,* Johnson's efforts in this field received a curious accolade that originated in America, was picked up in England, and finally appeared again in America. In February 1851 *Hunt's Merchants' Magazine* published an article entitled "Character of an American Banker: A. B. Johnson, Esq., The President of the Ontario Branch Bank," with a prefatory explanation: "The following sketch of the character of A. B. Johnson . . . although originally published in an American journal, the *Utica Teetotaller,* first met our eye in the *London Bankers' Magazine* for December, 1850." After praising Johnson's character and acumen as a banker, the anonymous author of the far-traveling tribute—presumably, since he was writing for the *Utica Teetotaller,* one of Johnson's fellow townsmen (or, as Stillman Drake suggests, possibly Johnson himself)—turned to Johnson's fiction. "Mr. Johnson is the author of several books, evincing much thought and study, in all of which chaste literature and utility are combined. His stories have the same merit. They have been written for a practical purpose, and not merely for amusement or literary fame." Johnson wrote his stories, the critic goes on to say, "to correct a fault" in one of his children, or "to impart wholesome instruction." In his stories, Johnson tries "to combine amusement and instruction, and for this purpose they are valuable contributions to the literature of the times. . . . Mr. Johnson writes because he has something to write about, and is always guided by the law of his life, *utility*. . . . We have perused his stories with pleasure and instruction, and regret that his series have come to a close."

Even this encouragement from *The Teetotaller,* endorsed by London bankers and American merchants, was not enough to prolong Johnson's career as an imaginative writer. After 1852 he wrote a few more pieces of fiction that were published, along with all the *Knicker-*

bocker stories, in *An Encyclopedia of Instruction* (1857). But after that there were no more. His excursion into fiction was over, and the large audience that he had enjoyed for a brief time was gone. From 1857 on he apparently abandoned all attempts at belletristic writing and went back to straight exposition in books, pamphlets, and articles.

As I have indicated from the very outset, it has never occurred to me to make great claims for Johnson's fiction. It can be read with appreciation and sympathy, as I have already said, only by those who have at least a nodding acquaintance with his work. But this, after all, is something. No biography of Johnson could be complete without a careful scrutiny and analysis of this fiction and Johnson's own attitude toward it. Eventually such an examination may shed some revealing light on this amazingly many-sided man. The fiction will never have a life of its own, but it is certainly a significant part of Johnson's.

NOTES

1 M. M. Bagg, *Pioneers of Utica* (Utica: Curtiss & Childs, 1877), p. 322.
2 Autobiography, Chap. 6.
3 *Ibid.*
4 *Ibid.*
5 Benjamin Franklin, *Autobiography* (Boston: Houghton Mifflin Company, Riverside ed.), p. 34.
6 Autobiography, Chap. 6.
7 *Ibid.*
8 *Encyclopedia of Instruction,* p. 98.

A NOTE ON
ALEXANDER BRYAN JOHNSON'S
PHILOSOPHICAL EMPEROR

◆ ◆ ◆ ◆ ◆ *DAVID MILLAR*

Johnson's one sustained attempt at humor, The Philosophical Emperor *(referred to in the previous essay by Thomas O'Donnell as* Philosophical Emperor A*), attracted even less attention than the author's language works. Among the few who know of its existence today, however, there are those who feel that it may be one of the most incisive and polished political satires produced in America during the first half of the nineteenth century.*

As usual, Johnson subsidized its publication, and one thousand copies were printed in New York by Harper & Brothers. Johnson tells us, however, that "as no pains were taken to bring the book into notice, and I never avowed it, the book failed to attain any popularity." With his customary nonchalance he added, "I think it was an experiment in political discussions that merited attention." Johnson sent a copy of the Harper edition to Park Benjamin, editor of the New York literary weekly The New World, *and offered him all the proceeds on a new edition of 3,000 copies "if it could be made popular and sold." Benjamin, one of the more influential literary arbiters of the Knickerbocker period, flattened the eager author with the following appraisal: "I shall be happy to . . . promote the sale of your work, but I am convinced that the task would be futile. No book sells to the extent of 3000 copies unless it is of a popular character. People will not give themselves the trouble to think enough, fully to appreciate a political allegory, no matter how much pervaded by evidences of superior talent."*

Professor Millar gives us some of the flavor of Johnson's ill-fated attempt to get away from what he called "the old mode of literal discussion."

THE EDITORS

◇ ◇ ◇ ◇ ◇ *Assistant Professor of History, Hamilton College.*

221

IN THE presidential elections of 1840 William Henry Harrison, the Old Hero of "Tippecanoe and Tyler too," defeated the incumbent President Martin Van Buren of New York. One year later Alexander Bryan Johnson wrote and "caused to be published anonymously" *The Philosophical Emperor,* a political allegory in which he sought to explain the origin and cause of Van Buren's defeat.[1] Johnson believed that Van Buren's defeat "was mainly owing to his persistence in the subtreasury scheme; by which the money of the country . . . was kept secluded from public use, producing by its abstraction, a scarcity of money, and a consequent derangement of business, which was felt injuriously by everybody." [2] Johnson also believed that the subtreasury scheme resulted directly from the Panic of 1837, which resulted from the Specie Circular of 1836, which in turn resulted from President Andrew Jackson's conflict with Nicholas Biddle and the second Bank of the United States; hence the opportunity for an allegory upon the progress and effect of a false position in politics.

The allegory begins therefore with President Andrew Jackson as the Philosophical Emperor of Boresko, and with Nicholas Biddle as his majesty's sturdy confectioner.

> Boresko, as every person knows, is no inconsiderable part of a large continent. The customs of the government and the manners of the people possess as little resemblance to our customs and manners as the quadrupeds of Australasia, whose heads are usually where their tails should be, resemble our quadrupeds. But the peculiarity most interesting to Americans of the present day consists in the unacquaintance of the people with gold and silver. The whole commerce of the country is transacted by a currency which is based on sugar. . . .
>
> But sugar being a heavy commodity, its use became gradually superseded by a species of sugarplum, pretty to behold when new, very light and portable. To manufacture these employed many confectionaries, situated in different parts of the empire, and who conducted the business with more or less magnitude, and manufactured plums of more or less relative goodness. . . .
>
> The government, however, whose revenue and disbursements amounted daily to a hundred thousand plums, had long patronised a confectionary of which it was the part owner, and of the purity of whose plums it was satisfied. . . .
>
> The system was nearly coeval with the empire, and resulted in the mutual benefit of the nation and the confectionaries.[3]

In the course of time, the philosophical emperor, so called because of his fondness for experimenting in the science of government, and his confectioner fell out. It was rumored that a shopkeeper of the confectionary had imbibed a sympathy for Old Lady Felderal *(Hamiltonian federalism)*. No proof existed of this malign interference in the politics of the confectionary, except that the shopkeeper was accused of giving sugarplums to her friends when he refused them to friends of the emperor. His majesty's plumkeeper *(the Secretary of the Treasury)* requested the confectioner to discharge the obnoxious shopkeeper, and appoint in his place a nominee of the plumkeeper. But the sturdy confectioner bluntly refused. He mounted a very high horse, which is often employed in Boresko by short men on great occasions, and, riding directly to the department of the plumkeeper, delivered a lecture on independence, and concluded by declaring that he would retain the shopkeeper, emperor or no emperor.[4]

The emperor's first impulse was to have both the confectioner and the shopkeeper shot under the second section of the articles of war *(an obvious reference to Jackson's execution of two Englishmen, Alexander Arbuthnot and Robert Ambrister, in Spanish Florida in 1818);* but shooting, being attended with several inconveniences, was eventually abandoned. Besides, the emperor imagined that he could so manage the controversy as to try an experiment in the science of government. The emperor wanted to originate no measure that was not popular, whatever might be its merits, and to repeal all that were unpopular, whatever might be their utility; in short, he desired popularity. The emperor believed that men and measures are unpopular in exact proportion to their merit, and popular in exact proportion to their demerit. The emperor resolved, therefore, to destroy the confectionary. The confectionary was useful enough to make its destruction eminently foolish; and fools were numerous enough to make its destruction eminently popular. Thus reasoned the emperor. But while his majesty was intent upon making a great experiment in politics, he was unconsciously commencing a great experiment in morals. He was trying the effect of a false position.[5]

The doctrine of false position, according to Johnson, has been but little studied in the United States. Johnson, therefore, explains the doctrine by means of an allegory within the allegory.

> A young lady, being on a visit at a noble friend's mansion, was betrayed by complaisance into an admission that she was very fond of potted sprats *(herring)*, though she abhorred the sight, taste, and smell of them. This little falsehood brought her into a false position as respects her noble friend, who, to oblige her young guest, provided for her nothing but potted sprats.

She had said she liked them, and she now must eat. . . . Down, therefore, went the sprat. . . . The whole inner woman suffered a state of rebellion; when a new actor appeared upon the stage (duly called, however, by regular succession), in the shape of fever, first mild and gentle, then importunate and bold, then raging and then outrageous. The fever introduced, in turn, a new agent in the shape of a physician, grave and knowing; who introduced two others more knowing still, who introduced various cathartics, diaphoretics, lancets, leeches, blisters, and glysters, which together introduced debility, epilepsy, and catalepsy; which, to the astonishment of no one but the doctors, introduced death, who ended the false position.[6]

Similarly, Johnson summarizes the larger allegory.

The interference of his late majesty (*Jackson*) in the appointment of a shopkeeper to the government confectionary gave birth to a repulse on the part of the confectioner (*Biddle*). This begat his majesty's doubts in relation to the constitutionality of said confectionary, which doubts begat the struggles of the confectioner, which struggles begat the veto, which begat the pressure, which begat the removal of the deposits, which begat the panic, which begat an entire prostration of business, which produced the expansion, which begat the land speculations, which begat excessive deposits, which begat alarm for their safety, which begat the requirement of mint-drops, the prohibition of small sugarplums, and the recommendation of prodigal expenditures; which latter begat the distribution law, which begat the collapse, which begat the vaults and safes, which begat the rejection of sugarplums in payment of duties, which begat the denial of any obligation to provide a currency for the nation, which begat the doctrine that people expected too much of their rulers, and that government must take care of itself, and the people take care of themselves. These results all made themselves, and were as unexpected to the emperor as to any of his subjects. Such is forever the trouble of a false position. Every step is made compulsorily, with reference to the one that precedes; while, in a true position, every step is made voluntarily in contemplation of the one which is to follow.[7]

Johnson hoped that *The Philosophical Emperor* would serve a useful purpose.[8] Aphorisms, for example, abound.

Men, though prone to trust Providence in matters that they can control by their own right hand, are equally prone to trust their right hand in matters that Providence alone can control.[9]

Falstaff claimed that he could tell a true prince by instinct: so emperors tell by instinct what is constitutional.[10]

Wise men know the difference between words and things, but weak bretheren confound the two.[11]

Providence has so infused into men "the rule of contrary," that they delight in exalting the humble; hence humility is young ambition's ladder.[12]

In conclusion, I would like, as I have done throughout my remarks, to use Johnson's own words. Johnson would object to my use above of the summary of his allegory. In his Preface he says that

The whole has been laboriously collected by me from numerous folios, and so condensed, that, if the reader shall indulge the bad practice of skipping instead of reading, he will miss the deep learning that my pages contain, and which has been seasoned so as to possess just pepper enough, salt, and other mild condiments to make it palatable as well as wholesome.[13]

If by "skipping instead of reading" I have missed the "deep learning" of Johnson's satire, I hope, nevertheless, to have conveyed the flavor.

NOTES

1 *The Philosophical Emperor: A Political Experiment; or the Progress of a False Position; dedicated to the Whigs, Conservatives, Democrats and Loco Focos individually and collectively, of the United States* (New York: Harper & Brothers, 1841).
2 Autobiography, Chap. 11.
3 *The Philosophical Emperor*, pp. 7–9.
4 *Ibid.*, pp. 5, 20–21.
5 *Ibid.*, pp. 6–7, 21–23.
6 *Ibid.*, pp. 23–26.
7 *Ibid.*, pp. 101–102.
8 Autobiography, Chap. 11.
9 *The Philosophical Emperor*, p. 35.
10 *Ibid.*, p. 39.
11 *Ibid.*, p. 71.
12 *Ibid.*, p. 89.
13 *Ibid.*, p. iv.

APPENDIX

Aware of the impossibility of providing full textual material to illustrate the studies included in these Proceedings, the contributors have included many brief citations from Alexander Bryan Johnson's various works. Fortunately, because of the interest in Alexander Bryan Johnson generated by the centennial conference, most of his major books will soon be available to the twentieth-century reader through modern reprints published by Greenwood Press.

In addition to his ten published books, Johnson produced many essays and speeches in pamphlet form, only a few of which were reprinted in such collection as A Guide to the Right Understanding of Our American Union *and* An Encyclopedia of Instruction. *Among these lost and forgotten pieces by Johnson, the two that follow here are rare and representative examples of Johnson's passionate concern with some of the more pressing issues of his time. By including them in an Appendix to these Proceedings the Editors hope, among other things, that they may tempt future scholars to probe further into the mystery of this remarkably prolific and questing American.*

The first selection is one of Alexander Bryan Johnson's earliest known published literary compositions. The second, which is discussed briefly in the paper by David Ellis, is a sample of Johnson's oratory at its best.

AN INQUIRY INTO THE NATURAL RIGHTS OF MAN, AS REGARDS THE EXERCISE OF EXPATRIATION. DEDICATED TO ALL THE ADOPTED CITIZENS OF THE UNITED STATES.

◆ ◆ ◆ ◆ ◆ ◆ ◆ ◆ ◆ ◆

JOHNSON'S twenty-page essay, *An Inquiry into the Natural Rights of Man, as Regards the Exercise of Expatriation,* published as a pamphlet in 1813 by Pelsue and Gould in New York, remained totally unknown to modern Johnson scholars until the Utica Conference in 1967. Writing in his autobiography some fifty years after the work was published, Johnson said, "I retained no copy of the above work and probably no copy is extant." Fortunately, one hundred and fifty-four years later Johnson's great grandson, Bryan Johnson Lynch, ran across a copy in his library and made it available to the Conference. Johnson's name does not appear on the title page. It was ascribed to a "Gentleman of the City of New York."

The essay is one of three known literary efforts composed by Johnson during his stay in New York City from 1811 to 1814. The other two were the *Inquiry into the Nature of Value and Capital,* published a few months earlier, and an unpublished allegorical poem called "The Court of Hymen." The twenty-six-year-old author's sudden burst of literary activity was probably occasioned by his precipitous withdrawal from the New York investment market after the American declaration of war against Great Britain in 1812. Ten years were to elapse before he did any further serious writing.

Johnson, in a brief introduction to the *Inquiry,* gives us this statement of intent:

The United States being engaged in a war with that foreign nation which is the birthplace of many of its citizens, had induced the author of the following sheets to submit to the public some thoughts he has long entertained of the rights individuals have of leaving the country of their birth, and of assimilating with another nation. His object is to rescue the character of such persons from the obloquy which he thinks an unjust prejudice casts upon them when they espouse the cause of their adopted country. . . .

Years later, in the autobiography, he added: "I was induced to this performance by the claims of Great Britain to impress from American vessels all persons of British birth;[1] and also by an awkwardness I felt in favouring the American war against England where I was born."

The essay takes the form of an imaginary dialogue between King and Subject, and scholars will find no difficulty in recognizing Johnson's hallmark on each page. Practical matters, quite naturally, are given first priority. The King is concerned by what we might now call "the brain drain," and laments the steady flow of artists and laborers from their native shores. The Subject's advice to the King is just what one would expect from Johnson—namely, "Raise the price of such skill and labour to their worth in other countries," or take the consequences. Later, when the King asks, "Does not every good man love his country?" the Subject launches into an analysis of such purely emotional attachments, clearly foreshadowing the author's hardheaded approach to courtship, marriage, and similar institutions. The King's reference to love of country, says the Subject, is "an appealing to prejudice and not to reason . . . let us consider the nature and the rise of that principle we call love of country." The dissection which follows is as neat and workmanlike a job of cutting through abstractions as any Johnson performed later in his works on language. Finally, the King raises the question of the Subject's right to take up arms against the country of his birth. The reply is simple and to the point: "All control assumed by a government, foreign to his residence, is an assumption of power operating against his natural rights . . . he may justly resist such power with all the means of which he is capable."

Although there is no indication that the pamphlet received wide circulation, it must have provided some comfort to those emigrés who, like Johnson, were haunted by their own consciences and by the hostility of visitors from the homeland. Of greater relevance, however, is the light shed by this early composition upon those driving forces behind Johnson's quest for recognition and success in his adopted land.

He had arrived in New York in 1811 with a large sum of money, acquired through his own and his father's efforts in Utica over the short space of ten years. He was admitted into the higher echelons of New York society, attended parties in company with high-ranking captured British officers who promptly snubbed him, hobnobbed in Washington with President Madison and his family, proffered advice to a Secretary of the Treasury, and probed the marriage market among the best families of New York and Washington without finding a single candidate who measured up to the standards he had set for the future Mrs. Johnson. All of this is implicit in the reply of the Subject to his King when the latter inquires into the real reasons for his new allegiance:

> He may have a further reason for such a preference: if he should find himself from a humble unaspiring individual, who readily acknowledged many grades of superiors to a hopeless height beyond his possibility of attainment, suddenly transformed, by this change of residence, to a situation where he need acknowledge no superiors, and where the first society of the nation stand and welcome his admission amongst them; and where hope and ambition may reasonably flatter him with the possibility that he or his descendants may, at some future day, be honoured with the first offices of the nation.

Johnson, as he confessed in the first pages of his autobiography, was "tinctured with republicanism at an early age"!

THE EDITORS

NOTE

1   The British view of expatriation and the right of impessment to which Johnson objected was based on Blackstone's edict that "it is a principle of universal law that the natural born subject of one Power cannot . . . put off or discharge his natural allegiance to the former; for this natural allegiance was intrinsic, and cannot be diverted without the concurrent act of that Prince to whom it was first due." This doctrine, rejected by the Americans during the Revolution, was not officially set aside by the British until the Naturalization Act of 1870 whereby British subjects, whether natural born or naturalized, were permitted to renounce their allegiance apart from an act of Parliament.

THE INQUIRY

INTRODUCTION The United States being engaged in a war with that foreign nation which is the birth-place of many of its citizens, has induced the author of the following sheets, to submit to the public some thoughts he has long entertained of the rights individuals have of leaving the country of their birth, and of assimilating with another nation. His object is to rescue the character of such persons from the obloquy, which he thinks an unjust prejudice casts on them, when they espouse the cause of their adopted country; in opposition to that of their nativity. He has conveyed his ideas in the form of two dialogues, between a king and his subject; and though the present publication is called forth by the present war, he would wish it to be understood, that his remarks are intended not to apply to any particular foreign country and its subjects; but to any foreign country and the natives of it, who may find themselves under the circumstances mentioned in the dialogues. If no such circumstances do really exist; then the persons he supposes operated on by them, can also not exist; and his design in writing is of course useless: but if persons do exist, under the circumstances he has endeavored to describe, then he hopes his design will not be useless; and their taking an active part at present, or hereafter, in the concerns of the country they have adopted, may not subject them to the charge of incorrectness of conduct, which he thinks is now, often, secretly cast on them.

Dialogue I

KING: You were born within the limits of my kingdom, and therefore are subject to its laws; and these laws forbid your emigration.

SUBJECT: If a number of persons were to associate and bind themselves to form a new community, (which might be the case with a body of people who should, by voluntary and mutual agreement, emigrate to establish a settlement) then there would be a palpable obligation on each individual to remain in this community; and he might well be taxed with treachery and bad

◇ ◇ ◇ ◇ ◇ *Originally published by Pelsue and Gould, New York, 1813.*

LANGUAGE AND VALUE

conduct, who should desert the settlement. But in the course of time were either of these first settlers, at their death, to leave children, the same obligation could not be supposed to bind them to the settlement, that bound their fathers; and, I think, were they to determine to leave the country, they could not justly be accused of treachery, or breach of faith, or any other crime; and if they were detained by force, it would be an act of tyranny. From this I would infer, that men, in nations, are situated as these offspring would be in this supposed new settlement; therefore, that it is no breach of any obligation, and no crime, for a man to leave that country, where, by chance, he commenced his existence; and, at his pleasure, assume a residence in any other that may please him better. And because such removal is no crime, and no breach of any natural obligation, all laws to prevent it are unjust, and the government that inflicts them is, in this particular, highly tyrannical.

KING: But the prosperity of my kingdom depends upon its manufactures and its commerce; and were we to permit mechanics and sailors to depart, our manufactories would be deserted, and our ships unnavigated; because, as some other nation might offer greater prices for their skill and labour, they would resort to that nation; and the consequence would, to us, be fatal.

SUBJECT: This may be an argument for you to keep them, but can be none for them to stay. By the prosperity of your kingdom, you mean that state of things, which enables you to live in the enjoyment of all your accustomed ease, splendor and authority. When your nobility use the same expression, they have reference to the magnificence and authority they possess. When your naval and military commanders, and your wealthy commoners, use it; they also have reference, each individually, to his own peculiar comforts, which, they believe, the giving of this natural liberty of departure would interfere with or abridge. For most, if not all, of the old governments of the world have, more or less, so familiarized their subjects to the commission of abuses against their inferiors, (and of which this right, in question, may be an instance) and have so accustomed them to all the regulations which give authority to these abuses, that the idea seldom intrudes on their minds, that this state of society, is unjust and encroaching at every step on some of the natural rights of man; and that the government, under which these regulations are perpetuated, differs widely, in its spirit, from what was contemplated in the original formation of every government, namely, to preserve to each individual his natural rights, by guarding him from the unjust pretensions of his neighbours. Nor do they reflect, that their government has attained to its present power by gradual or violent assumption of authority; and that, from being a mere *instrument,* created by the people for their convenience, it has become the *principal;* and not only considers the people as its instrument, but as its property.

KING: But will you not allow, that the departure of our mechanics and marines would transform the nation from a powerful to a contemptible state? Would it be desirable, by any reasoning man, that a change should take place, which would tend to destroy that immense fabric of human skill and grandeur, which our nation now presents; and which makes it stand conspicuous as the inventor and encourager of all the arts and sciences, which tend either to adorn our nature, or to administer to its pleasures or its comforts?

SUBJECT: You have taken it for granted, that giving permission of removal to your artists and marines, would be the same thing as an act of expulsion; and that it would have the effect of leaving you destitute. I think, a different result might be calculated on. No man will leave the country of his birth and education, the country where are centred all his relations and acquaintances, if he cannot materially better his situation, in life, by the removal. Now, were this removal permitted, and its operation found injurious to the prosperity of the state, the remedy would be apparent, and in the natural course of events, would be applied; either, by foresight, in raising the price of such skill and labor to their worth in other countries; or, by its own correction in the natural rise which always follows a diminution in the number of artists and laborers.

KING: But if the price of their labor were enhanced, we could not manufacture to that advantage which now enables us to undersell other nations; and therefore our commerce would cease, since there would be an impossibility of vending when manufactured. Thus would be produced all the evils I before suggested. And, moreover, the emigrant artists would teach foreign nations to manufacture for themselves, and thus also vitally affect us.

SUBJECT: The West Indian planter may give the same reason for keeping his negroes in slavery; and perhaps a still better reason, in saying, that the nature of the climate renders it impossible to cultivate the soil by people of European extraction; therefore, however much he infringes on the natural rights of these poor victims (and I believe few of them will contend but they do infringe) yet they must submit.

The question I wish to decide, is not whether your nation would carry on the same degree of commerce, and with the same profit; but whether this forced detention is not an actual infringement on the natural rights of any portion of the community on whom it is practiced.

KING: In the present state of the world, nations are governed by policy, and though in a mere abstract question of right it may be said, that they ought to be permitted to depart; yet it cannot be supposed that such a consideration would induce a government to permit the exercise of that right when it would interfere with its general policy.

SUBJECT: I grant you, no person who is acquainted with human nature will suppose, that those who have had the disposition to obtain power over others, will voluntarily yield to any measure which would affect that power. As such, I do not expect of your wealthy manufacturers, that they should be willing to permit the departure of their poor artizans; nor of any other branch of your population, that they should subscribe to any alterations of customs (however tyrannical) which they suppose would affect their individual interests. But this I do say, that your artizans, mariners and others, have also an interest to pursue, and those who may wish to remove have a natural right so to do; and they do no more than justly assert this right, when they refuse to permit the interested motives of other persons to detain them in a state which they dislike; and that it is no crime, or breach of any natural obligation, for them to break through, or evade this restraint, by any means in their power, and to remove to any other country, or government, they may think proper.

Dialogue II

SUBJECT: I think it has been shewn, that man has the natural right of removing from the country of his birth, to any other country. I will now endeavor to make it appear, that the government from which he removes can, thereafter, have no just right of control over him; and that the separation, so long as it continues, entirely suspends the natural connexion which subsists between governors and the people they govern. For if we examine into the natural object of all governments, we shall find that the only reasonable cause that can be assigned for their institution, is that they were erected to be an equitable tribunal to which the societies that created them might refer all questions of individual rights, arising between any of the members. That for the purpose of making such reference effectual, the members may have agreed to enforce its decisions. They may also have given it some power of direction, in cases of offensive war, and of invasion by persons of other communities. These could have been the only legitimate objects, and all the additional powers governments assume are encroachments on the natural rights man had reserved to individuals. No government, therefore, has any natural right over any person who is not living in the community which it governs; and when an individual leaves a community and removes to another, all the ties that subsisted between them have an end. For the object of government being to regulate the differences that arise between men of the same society; a man removing from that society, is without its jurisdiction and power of legislation, and it can render him no service, his new abode having a government of its own. The connexion is dissolved by a removal in like manner, as it is at present between a county sheriff and the members of his county, whenever they step beyond the limits of his shire.

KING: Such may have been the foundation of governments, and perhaps the first form they assumed; but as the state of society changes, the government is also required to change: and now, a nation is understood as forming a large political body, composed of governors and governed, to which nation every human being, who may be born within its precincts, is considered as forming a new member. Owing such allegiance to the existing government as to be bound to defend it against either foreign or domestic foes. That this allegiance is unalienable. And that if the members depart from the government to that of some other nation, the departure must be considered not as the exercise of a natural right, but as a permission, subject to be recalled whenever their services shall be considered necessary, either to make conquests, or to preserve those already won: and that to refuse obedience to this recall, is a breach of obligation; and to appear in arms against the forces of the government, (even though they come to invade your own property, in your new dwelling) is the heighth of enormity, and deserving death.

SUBJECT: I can readily conceive that persons who have power, would, for the purpose of preserving it, make such regulations (and enforce them too) as you have enumerated; and as many other regulations as they may think conducive to the same end, or any other end they might wish to attain. For such I conceive is the nature of man, that his own good is the chief object of all his actions; and it is not that I expect to see this order of our nature reversed, and that governors should act differently from what they now do, that I speak. It is for the purpose of having these subjects better understood; that those who are aggrieved may know that they also have the same principle of action, and that it is no greater crime or disgrace for them to follow its dictates, than it is for their governors. I therefore say, that a man has a natural right of removing from the country of his birth; and should do so openly, or by stratagem, as the case may require, (whenever he has not voluntarily bound himself to remain) and wishes to remove. And that after his removal he becomes a member of the country to which he removed; and the very circumstance of his being without the jurisdiction of the government from which he came, is a dissolution of all the natural ties that can subsist between governors and governed; and therefore it is no breach of any duty for him to refuse returning at their call; and no greater crime to appear in arms against them, than it is against any other nation.

KING: But is it no crime for a man to desert the country of his birth? and more especially to appear in arms against it? Does not every good man love his country?

SUBJECT: This is appealing to prejudice, and not to reason; and this principle, like many others, we take on trust and seldom examine. But now for the better answering your questions, I will consider the nature and rise of that principle which we call love of country.

And first, I believe it will be commonly found that we like the particular district in which we are born, better than any other district in the nation; and that we generally like the particular village or place of our birth, better than any other part of that district. This arises from its being, most generally, the residence of those friends and relations, who from our frequent intercourse in infancy and youth, are the most endeared to us in after life. Also from its being the theatre of our youthful actions and enjoyments; themes which most persons reflect on with pleasure; and frequently with a pleasure increasing with the distance of the period. Therefore, (for such is the nature of man) whenever this town or village is named, it immediately brings to his recollection all the before mentioned circumstances of pleasure; and as the reflecting on them in a manner renews the pleasure, and that this pleasure is always produced by the mention of the place, he views them as one object, and the place is endeared to him from its combination with these pleasant reflections. I believe if we pursue this principle, we shall find that in every instance of our love for any particular place, it arises from certain circumstances of pleasure, which that place was the theatre of. And as this theory is so beautifully illustrated (though on other subjects) by Mr. Alison, I shall forbear to press it farther, as it must be evident to every person who has read that gentleman's celebrated production on taste.

Secondly, wherever a man is educated, he is accustomed to see performed, and also to perform all the offices of life in some peculiar manner; and because he is so accustomed, any deviation from this manner, immediately appears to him ridiculous and improper: and as every community differs, more or less, in its customs, in its opinions, and generally in its language; he naturally entertains a prejudice against foreign communities, for acting contrary to his settled opinions of correctness. This prejudice is seldom removed until he becomes so familiar with foreign manners as to see them frequently tested by experiment. It is then, perhaps, he first perceives how nearly equal all customs are for promoting their various objects, and that a change in any country would seldom be an improvement. I believe this prejudice forms the principle reason why people of uncivilized and remote nations, who have few opportunities of visiting other countries, are generally found to possess a greater love of country than people differently circumstanced, and more refined: and I doubt not, but an inhabitant of the frozen regions of Lapland, does, in consequence, feel a greater love of country, than a refined man of civilized society, who has encompassed the world for his instruction and amusement.

It is this prejudice that is most efficient, in giving a bias to the people of a country, when any question is agitated involving the interest of their own nation, in opposition to that of a foreign one. For no man can be so insignificant in society, but, if he thinks at all on any contest, he must find his feelings incline to one party in preference to the other. I believe it is a principle of our nature, of which each individual must readily recollect instances in himself, that it is scarcely possible for him to keep his mind neutral in the most contemptible affray he may witness. The bias created by the foregoing prejudice, against those whose manners differ from our own, is, therefore, generally sufficient to awaken our solicitude for the success of our own nation in any war in which it be engaged; and even to awaken the solicitude of those whom the contest can affect, neither in person, relations nor property.

Another cause for this solicitude may be found in the self-important opinion each man entertains of himself, and which produces in him a feeling as if he was degraded by every defeat suffered by his country; and exalted by every victory. This way of thinking, is most common to those who have visited foreign countries; for each individual finds himself identified, as it were, with the country of his birth; and treated in a manner proportioned to its importance or insignificance. We, therefore, find that men, in a foreign country, always acknowledge the place of their birth, if they come from a great nation; and sometimes conceal, or deny it, if they come from one that is insignificant or degraded.

I have now shewn several of the causes which, I believe, naturally produce that feeling which we call love of our native country. I will now endeavour to show several other causes, which are equally efficient in producing that love, which many persons feel, for the country of their adoption, and which make them prefer it to the country of their birth.

First. It has been said, that we naturally feel a love for the country of our birth, arising from a recollection of the many enjoyments it has been the theatre of in the gay times of our infancy and youth. This can operate only on those who have had such enjoyments. But should a man have been unfortunate in the country from which he removed, should the recollection of it bring to his mind scenes of unhappiness and trouble, he would as naturally, and with as much propriety, couple the idea of dislike to that country, as a person, under other circumstances, would that of liking. Again—if a man, after his having removed, enjoy greater prosperity, more health, or any other pleasing transition; he would very naturally, in expressing his opinions, say, that he preferred his present country for such and such reasons, of superior enjoyment. For this also is, I believe, the nature of man, that his likings and dislikes always proceed from the degree of pleasure and satisfaction, or pain and dissatisfaction, the subject produces in him; and if so, for him to prefer that to all others which does not most contribute to his pleasure and satisfaction, would be against the order of nature, and, of course, impossible. If the country a man has resorted to, does, by its climate, by its institutions, by the cheapness of the means of life, by the facility it presents of acquiring property, or by the greater political liberty it allows, or by any or all of these, contribute more to his pleasures and comforts, than his native country, he cannot help giving it a preference. A man, born in England, France, or elsewhere, who finds America, or any other country, contribute most to his comforts, is no more to blame for liking America, or this other country, the best, than an Englishman or Frenchman, differently circumstanced, (and who received most comforts in his native country) would be, for liking that native country the best.

KING: But if a man is not able to find as many comforts in his native country as he does in another, is it not most generally his own fault? And if he complains of misfortunes and sufferings, have they not generally been produced by vices and infringement on the law? Now, if these be facts, (as I believe they are) then the point I contend for is proved; namely, that none but bad men have such causes of complaint; and therefore none but bad men prefer another country to their own.

SUBJECT: I will grant you that some men may prefer a foreign country; and on account of sufferings, produced by misconduct in their own. Yet it does not follow that every person who prefers a foreign country, does it from that cause. A man born of poor parents, in a country where it is extremely difficult to obtain by the price of labor, the mere necessaries of life, will very naturally prefer another country, when, on his removal to it, he finds that the same labor will not only procure him the necessaries, but also the comforts, and some of the luxuries of life. He will be still more inclined to prefer it, if he came from a country where he had been considered as a mere blank in society,; and on his removal finds, that in his new residence, he is considered as a person of some importance; and that the rulers of the nation are indebted for their places, to the suffrages of persons like himself; and that the favor of such persons is accordingly sought by every one who has the ambition of ruling. Another man, however honest, who finds himself the native of a country, where by the superior wealth of others, he is an unimportant and insignificant individual, will very naturally prefer another country if he should find, that his capital, before considered as small, is there (owing to the different state of society) considered as a competence, or perhaps an affluence; bringing with it all the numerous real and imaginary comforts either of those states are capable of producing. He may also have further reason for such a preference: if he should find himself from an humble unaspiring individual, who readily acknowledged many grades of superiors, to a hopeless height above his possibility of attainment, suddenly transformed, by this change of residence, to a situation where he need acknowledge no superiors, and where the first society of the nation stand and welcome his admission amongst them; and where hope and ambition may reasonably flatter him with the possibility, that he or his descendents may, at some future day, be honored with the first offices in the nation.

To men thus situated (and in many other situations that could be mentioned) it would be a want of proper sensibility if they did not feel the superior advantages of their new situation, over their former one; and they cannot help prefering the situation which presents more, to that which presents fewer, inducements. It is quite natural and correct, that persons, so situated, should feel a solicitude on all questions that they may think have a tendency to increase the prosperity of their new residence, or to abridge it; that they should consider any question involving these points, as involving their own interest. It has been said, that we can seldom remain neutral in any contest that comes within our knowledge. It is, therefore, not to be wondered at, if the consciousness of advantages persons enjoy, superior to what they enjoyed in a former country, should give them a bias in favour of the preferable residence, though it were engaged in a contest with the nation of their birth. That this effect does not always take place, arises from the several causes of love of country which have been mentioned; but, perhaps, from no one so frequently as from that pride the person has assumed in identifying himself with the nation of his birth; and consequently considering its defeats as subjecting him to less respect; and its victories as adding to his personal consequence. When these circumstances are sufficient to counterbalance great advantages, experienced in a new residence, it is a triumph of pride and prejudice over reason and philosophy; and the person justly subjects himself to the charge of ingratitude; since his persevering in his new residence is, as it were, an open acknowledgment of the superior comforts it affords him.

KING: But does not the general voice of the world unite in condemning the man, who does not love the country of his birth?

SUBJECT: A man may prefer the country of his residence to the country of his birth, and yet bear it no hatred. This is a mistake to which people, in argument, are frequently liable. They do not reflect, that of any two things a man may prefer one of them, and still bear no dislike to the other. It is quite frequent and reasonable, that a man should prefer the country of his residence to that of his birth, since the very circumstance of his choosing it for his residence is the effect of that preference. Self-interest has so great an influence over our opinions, that it is not at all unnatural for it, in time, to overcome the impressions of former prejudices, and to give us a fair and honest bias in favour of the country of our residence, even in its wars with the country of our birth. It is true, that there is a general prejudice against those who express a dislike to their native country. This frequently arises from the persons, who censure, feeling, at the time, those emotions of pleasure which have been described, namely, a recollection of the scenes of their youth; the places where they have spent many joyous and happy days; the residence of their friends and relations, and the numberless other reflections which occur to all men, though, perhaps, to few men alike. Now the love of country, though springing from the recollection of such various combinations of past or anticipated enjoyments, yet each man takes it for granted, that every other person ought to have the same feelings he himself has; and if they have not, he immediately feels the same disgust at their conduct which he thinks he should merit if he were to express himself as they do. He thinks his love of country proceeds from having correct principles, and not from the certain accidental causes which made his country agreeable to him.

He also thinks that the want of the same feeling in another person, proceeds from a want of principle; and not from certain accidental causes which made his country disagreeable to him.

He does not reflect that had he the same causes for disgust that the other person has, he would in all probability have the same disgust. Neither does he reflect that had the other person the same causes for love that he has, he, in all probability, would have the same love.

I can readily conceive that a man may have just cause for real dislike to the country where he chanced to be born, even though the instances already adduced only go to show that the man who likes the country of his birth, may still, very honestly, and without any discredit to his principles, like an adopted country so much better, as to advocate and aid, in a cause even against the country of his birth, when he shall think the interest of that adopted country demands it. Yet I also believe that a man may have sufficient cause to aid the adopted country, out of real dislike to the country of his birth; and without that dislike being any cause for discredit to his principles, I suspect there are few dispassionate men who cannot conceive such situations. And to give an instance, few see the representation of Coriolanus, as drawn by Shakespeare without sincerely sympathizing with his feelings, and entering fully into his schemes of vengeance against his ungrateful country.

I am, however, far from supposing that all men who have a dislike for their country, have such grounds for their dislike as would be approved of by the world. Their grievances may be theoretical and imaginary. They may spring from their own want of assiduity, and from many other causes, which to an impartial judge, might be thought unsound. Yet if we reflect that a great part of those ties which give a love of country, spring in the best of men, from a recollection of the pleasures that country has afforded them; and perhaps from a reflection of the further pleasures they consider it doomed to be the theatre of; I think we then cannot blame others, for a dislike, when they have no such past or future pleasures to reflect on; even though their not having any has been produced by a want of sufficient industry on their part, or by any other suggested causes. There is, however, another portion of men who, for the commission of crimes, have been justly punished and disrespected; and who, on removing to a new country bring a dislike to that of their birth, on account of the punishment there inflicted on them. Of these men, though it may be truly said that they deserved their punishment, yet as they have not the same motives for the love of country, which if better men, perhaps they would have had, they also cannot be expected to have the love. Neither ought they to be blamed for not having it, without that blame alludes to those evil practices which prevented them having the same causes of attachment, that if good men they might have had. I think this must sometimes be what men mean by saying that no good man can dislike his country. They do not blame a man for not loving his country, when he has no cause of love; but they consider his having no cause must proceed from a persecution or punishment for illegal and vicious practices. I think, however, that though this may sometimes be the case, yet it is not always so; and that a man may be very virtuous, and for sufficient and just reasons dislike the country of his birth. Also, that a man may very naturally prefer another country to the place of his birth, and still like them both; and that for such a preference numerous causes frequently exist, and that they do not subject the person, on whom they operate, to any just censure or reproach. I shall now conclude with this observation, that if these dialogues prove what they are intended to prove, it will then appear—

First—That a man has the natural right of removing from the country of his birth, to any other country he may choose; and that he is only asserting this right, and justifiably too, when he evades or breaks through any laws made to prevent his removal.

Secondly—That all just connexion, between government and governed, is entirely interrupted by a separation: that a man is subject to the government under which he lives, and no other: that all control assumed by a government, foreign to his residence, is an assumption of power operating against his natural rights; and that he may justly resist such power with all the means of which he is capable.

Thirdly—That circumstances may exist to make a man prefer the country of his residence to that of his birth: that when they do exist, it does not argue any want of correct principles, for

244

the person to be biased towards the country of his residence, in every contest it may be engaged in, including a contest with the country of his birth; and that a different conduct, would rather argue the want of a proper sense of gratitude for benefits received.

Lastly—That a man may even feel a dislike to the country of his birth and education, and have good and sufficient reasons for his dislike; and, therefore, neither be depraved in taste nor incorrect in principle.

SPEECH BEFORE AN AUXILIARY OF THE AMERICAN COLONIZATION SOCIETY

♦ ♦ ♦ ♦ ♦ ♦ ♦ ♦ ♦ ♦

JOSEPH DORFMAN, in notes prepared for the Johnson Centennial Conference but not included in the paper which appears in the *Proceedings,* refers to Johnson's *Speech Before an Auxiliary of the American Colonization Society* in these terms:

> The consistency which Johnson displayed on such matters as monetary doctrine and policy is completely missing in his writing on the slavery issue. Indeed, within this single essay we find him expressing almost directly contradictory views. As a strong advocate of personal liberty he vigorously condemned the institution of slavery on moral and ethical grounds. Yet another facet of his Jefferson-Jackson liberalism forbade the interference of federal authority into the affairs of the states which included, of course, the states in which slave holding was lawful. Possibly contributing to his dilemma in dealing with this vexing question was the goading objectivity of his mind. . . . Perhaps also, being cognizant of political and economic reality, he realized what a tremendous shattering upheaval would occur if there were a sudden elimination of slavery. Caught in this ambivalence, he fell back on the quixotic solution of appealing to the conscience of the slaveholders.

One cannot help but agree that these inconsistencies exist in Johnson's views on the slavery question. On the other hand, one might suggest that these very contradictions parallel other seeming contradictions which crop up in Johnson's work and, to some extent at least, mark him as highly consistent in his inconsistencies. For example,

246

Johnson was a strong temperance man and condemned the use of alcohol in any form, but he staunchly opposed the Maine Liquor Laws and all other proposed legislation limiting the consumption of alcohol. His "logical positivist" approach to experience, including mystical and religious experience, in no way kept him from becoming a pillar of his church in Utica, or caused him to decry the more extreme forms of revivalism which swept through Oneida County. It is highly doubtful that Johnson himself would have regarded his attitude toward the slave question as "quixotic," although others on both sides of the argument certainly did.

The circumstances leading up to Johnson's speech have been related in detail by David Ellis. A few notes might be added, however, concerning the nature of the organization which Johnson so roundly denounced at the meeting held in Utica on January 13, 1834.

In a *Statement of Facts* published by the Colonization Society of Massachusetts in 1831, the objectives of the National organization were described thus: "To promote and execute a plan of colonizing (with their own consent) the free people of color residing in our country, in Africa, or such other place as Congress shall deem expedient." By 1831 auxiliary Societies existed in all the New England States, New York, New Jersey, Pennsylvania, Maryland, Virginia, North Carolina, Alabama, Tennessee, Kentucky, Ohio, and Indiana. Two hundred county and town auxiliaries were also reported. These groups were supported by private donation, and the organization's objectives had been officially endorsed by the legislatures of fifteen states. General Lafayette, whom Johnson had entertained in his home in 1825, was listed as one of the vice-presidents. According to the *Statement* "nearly all of the ecclesiastical bodies of the United States earnestly recommend the Society to the patronage of the entire Christian community."

During the last years of the eighteenth century, numerous African ports were suggested for the repatriation of former slaves from America; but in 1821 the Colonization Society purchased land on Cape Mesurado (the present site of Monrovia, capital of Liberia), and the first settlers were transported to the colony in 1822, led by Jehudi Ashman, a white American. By 1831 the settlement numbered about 2,000, and boasted six public schools, a newspaper, three churches, "twenty pieces of canon and enough small arms to equip a thousand men." Despite the optimistic hopes of the promoters, however, by the time the Society opened its campaign in Utica there were many discouraging rumors about the mortality rate in the colony where sunstroke and disease were taking a heavy toll of blacks and whites alike. The Society argued vigorously that, after a brief period of adjustment, the former slaves at least would recover their "inherited" immunities to heat and tropical disease—a point that Johnson refuted with the disdainful remark that "climate regards not where the emigrant's ancestors were born."

The subsequent history of the American Colonization Society and the turbulent fortunes of the settlement in Liberia may be found elsewhere. It seems clear, however, that when Johnson stood up to denounce the Society on that winter evening in Utica, he viewed it as an extremely distasteful task, and was fully aware that the position he was to take would be highly unpopular. Writing many years later in his autobiography, he attempted to be casual about the affair, saying that he was impelled to join the debate "by the dearth of better intellectual topics in Utica." Judging from the heat of his rhetoric, however, and from his recording of Beriah Green's threat that "painful correction" might be applied to the author of the address, it seems clear that Johnson for once threw caution to the winds, particularly in his remarks to the clergymen present. The inconsistencies in the speech, as Dorfman has pointed out, are clear enough. No one who reads this speech, however, and who has followed the "goading objectivity" of Johnson's mind through his other writings will question the speaker's integrity when he says:

> Had I the power to make slave holding appear to (Southerners) so sinful as to cause them to liberate their slaves, I should feel by its exercise more exalted than Napoleon; but had I the physical power to compel them to relinquish their slaves, I would rather die than exert it!

THE EDITORS

THE SPEECH

TO THE READER Contrary to his original expectation and present wishes, the author of the following remarks is impelled to publish them, both by the request of many persons, and the greater urgency of avoiding misconception. Having never been a member of any society for either abolition or colonization, and intending never to be of either, he simply means to enjoy, on these subjects, the independence of thought and action which the laws and his circumstances in life enable him to maintain. Anxious, however, to respect the feelings of every human being, he would have presented his views with less pungency of illustration, had not the terms of debate precluded amplification, by limiting every speech to thirty minutes. Yet no offence he trusts can be justly excited by any of his remarks, if the reader will remember that guilt exists in intention alone. Any act, even the death of an individual, is either virtuous or criminal, according as the intention of the actor is virtuous or vicious. The most skilful physician that exists has doubtless caused the death of many persons, when he deemed himself engaged in the most benign acts of mercy. If, however, you can show a physician that his prescriptions are deleterious, you may fairly denounce the medicine, without criminating the physician. Having, then, in the following remarks, both at their commencement and conclusion, disclaimed all imputation against the motives of the Colonization Society and its supporters, (and to act differently would be insanity,) the author trusts that the reader will constantly discriminate that the remarks are intended to illustrate the speaker's views of the moral tendency and character of the acts of the Colonization Society, and hence cannot detract from the highly meritorious intentions with which those acts are performed.

RESOLUTION "Resolved, That this meeting deeply deplore the unfortunate condition of the colored population of this country; and commend to the zealous support of the philanthropist and the Christian, the American Colonization Society, as the instrument, under Providence, which is best calculated to ameliorate the condition of the free negro, and secure the ultimate emancipation of the slave."

MR. CHAIRMAN, As I intend to vote on the resolution which is before this meeting, and as I shall vote differently from many of

◇ ◇ ◇ ◇ ◇ *Originally published by the Press of William Williams, Utica, N.Y.*

my friends who are present, I perhaps owe to them, and I owe to myself, to state some of the reasons that will influence me in the vote which I shall give.

I avow the highest respect and esteem for the motives of the Colonization Society and its supporters. I doubt not they deem themselves engaged in the most effectual methods of benefiting colored men, of Christianizing and civilizing Africa, and of strengthening the interests and institutions of our country. Nay, the intelligence and patriotism which are united under the banners of the Society, constitute the most formidable difficulties in the cause which I am to advocate. Even on this floor we find among its friends those to whom we look for the exemplification of every virtue; especially am I constrained to notice one, whose honest zeal in this cause is but an emanation of the zeal which often delights me, as I occasionally hear him, vehement in the cause of righteousness, in the sacred desk. Still, I am bound either to forego all the dictates of my judgment, or to declare the moral nature of their institution.

The Society proceeds on the assumption that it will colonize free people of color with their own assent. This alone reconciles community to the proceedings of the Society. Still, in this fundamental feature, the proceedings of the Society are based on a fallacy.

In some countries of Europe no criminal can be executed unless by his own consent; that is, he must confess himself guilty. Without this confession, the most positive testimony is insufficient to convict him. This provision, so theoretically strong in favor of prisoners, is practically the means in many cases of condemning the innocent. The process consists in applying tortures to a suspected person until he shall confess himself guilty.

To my apprehension, the confession of guilt, thus extorted, is analogous to the assent of colored men to be transported to Liberia. We apply to their minds a torture which is as effective in compelling a consent to be transported to Africa, as physical tortures are effective in compelling a consent to be executed.

The degradations which beset the colored man are ever present. He cannot enter a church, a canal-boat, a tavern, a steam-boat, without being consigned, regardless of all his merits, be they perchance ever so great, to the most degraded position.

He is practically excluded from every post of honor and profit which usually stimulate other men to virtue and industry. Who ever heard of a black juryman, a black lawyer, a black judge, a black physician? What merchant will take a black shopman? what mechanic a black apprentice? In the absence of all stimulants which excite white men to honor, I am surprised at the decency, (be it ever so little,) that colored people exhibit, of even this state. Were they as open in their sensuality as the beasts of our fields, I could not accuse them with their excesses; for the principle, "Eat, drink, and be merry; for to-morrow we die," is unmitigatingly applicable to their condition. Were they more idle than they confessedly are, more reckless of consequences, more regardless of reputation, and every way worthless, I could not upbraid them with these miserable attributes. I can see in my own bosom a sufficient reason for their depravity, in the treatment which they receive at our hands.

Far be from me any accusation against my white fellow citizens. I am stating facts of which I may be as guilty as any other man. I merely show that men thus situated are as effectually coerced to yield their assent to transportation, as the poor wretch on the wheel of torture yields his assent to be executed. Believing this, I say we act fallaciously when we soothe our consciences towards African colonization, by saying that we colonize none but those who assent to be transported.

This is not the only fallacy which is connected with the colonization cause. We further soothe our consciences in sending the blacks to Africa, by saying that though the whites, whom we have sent as missionaries and officers, die with terrific rapidity, yet the blacks, being indigenous to the climate, enjoy a greater immunity from disease than the whites. This position I deny. Exemption from the diseases of climate is not inheritable. It is a personal privilege, which attaches to those alone who are born in the climate, and which is forfeited by a removal from the climate.

Are we not told that emigrants from the south suffer less from the climate than emigrants from the north? Is not this alone sufficient proof that the climate regards not where the emigrant's ancestors were born, but simply where the emigrant himself was nurtured?

I entertain another objection to the Colonization Society. No principle is clearer to my mind than that God's commandments include equally white men and black. "Thou shalt love thy neighbor as thyself" is as obligatory on us in relation to colored men, as the command, "Thou shalt do no murder." If the last forbids us to kill a black man, the former commands us to love a black man as we love a white. If either is applicable to a black man, both are.

Like the reverend gentleman who addressed us on Thursday evening, on behalf of colonization, I am fond of reverting to these elements of duty. Some persons may think they possess no connexion with the question, but I deem them important. Christianity has so moulded our views of right and wrong, of virtue and vice, that we can in no way so effectually settle the morality of any question, as by ascertaining its religious character. Many men think that their conduct is uninfluenced by the Bible, and independent of it; but they are mistaken. A man may doubt whether he shall be judged by the Bible in the world to come; but he is a superficial observer, if he discover not that in this life at least he is judged by the Bible. His acts must be regulated by it, to a degree at least, if he would not be an outcast from society.

Females are told, and correctly, of the peculiar obligations of their sex to the Christian religion. I believe the blacks may be told with equal propriety of their obligations to Christianity. Of all men they should the most revere religion. We heard, on Thursday night, that in Rome four hundred slaves were massacred, because their master had been murdered, and the murderer, who was supposed to be one of the slaves, could not be discovered. This butchery was said to be the regular law of that civilized empire. Whether this was before Christianity, or subsequently, we are not informed; but it could but have been in the infancy of the Christian era. What, think you, prevents similar outrages now? Is it our humanity? Possibly; but it is our humanity as formed and modified by our religion. The blacks are indebted to Christianity for even the trouble and expense that are taken to remove them to Africa. Were we like the Romans, or rather like the Spartans, to whom we were also referred, we should probably like them find a far less expensive and more expeditious way of removing our blacks, than the slow process of colonization.

Religion, then, effects much for the blacks; and it may effect more, till they shall enjoy all the benefits which result from an entire conformity of our conduct with Christian principles. "Thou shalt love thy neighbor as thyself." If this command be applicable to our conduct towards colored men as fully as to our conduct towards white men, and if Christianity be an authoritative reality, this single command involves the whole merits of our controversy. Now I call on the clergy who are present, to tell me if this command is not intended to embrace our conduct towards the blacks? I call on them to answer this question distinctly.

"Thou shalt love thy neighbor as thyself." Is this a command which expediency can annul? If expediency can annul this command, expediency can annul the Sabbath, expediency can annul the decalogue, expediency can annul the Bible itself, and Christianity with it. I call on clergymen to maintain such a doctrine if they dare, either openly or covertly, either by precept or practice, either by inference or by consequence. They may as well preach deism, as that our conduct towards the blacks is not sinful.

If, then, "Thou shalt love thy neighbor as thyself" is authoritative over our conduct towards the blacks, I object to the Colonization Society that it is an instrument and means by which our violation of the above command is gratified. The Society removes the blacks to Africa, because we insist on violating this command. The Society thus, like a brothel, makes itself subservient to the sin of the community.

Is a society with such an object to be fostered by our churches? Is it to be taken under the special care of our clergy? Is it to be the theme of their eulogy on the Sabbath, and the object of their prayers at any time? No. If such a society must exist, let the clergy keep aloof from it. Let them enforce on the consciences of men the law of God, which, when obeyed, will render the Society useless, rather than enforce on the feeble and debased blacks that God's law cannot be obeyed, and that their only refuge is this Society.

In all ordinary cases of hatred between man and man, that is, when the parties are white men, our ministers will not lend themselves to gratify the prejudices of one party, by transporting from his home and country the injured individual; our ministers will fearlessly go to the persecutor, or send to him their session, or other ecclesiastical coadjutors, and tell the offender that he must repent, or expect no fellowship in this world, and no forgiveness in the next. These opposite courses of conduct to the black man and the white cannot both be right; and I call on our clergy to beware lest they give infidelity occasion to infer from their practice that they disbelieve their own precepts.

I admit that, at present, as we have been exultingly told, all the ecclesiastical authorities of our country are with this Society, and nearly all the Christian ministry. They are but men; and the missionary aspect of the Society has blinded them to its real character. They are in this particular like Ambrosio, the saint of Madrid, who was seduced by a demon, under the semblance of the Virgin Mother. Nothing but the missionary character of the Colonization Society has enabled it for a moment to sustain itself with Christians; and in this particular they have yet to learn, and they are fast learning, that they are violating the injunction which prohibits them from effecting good by means that are evil.

By the sufferance of this meeting, the resolution before us is discussed as though it presented for our decision the relative merits of colonization to Africa, and immediate, universal emancipation. The question limits us to no such alternative. It presents no such issue. Nefarious, however, and incendiary, as many persons deem the theory of immediate emancipation, yet so indefensible on any principles is the Colonization Society, that I am willing it shall be tried on that issue, prejudged as it probably is by passion, and misapprehended as I suppose it to be by prejudice. Leaving then for the present the Colonization Society, I will say a few words on the theory of immediate emancipation.

All that is meant by immediate emancipation, is simply the assertion of a duty: Duty requires that all men shall emancipate their slaves immediately. Emancipation is a duty which they owe to the slave, to Christianity, to the character of their country. I mean to assert no right of compelling the slave holder to emancipate his slave; but merely to assert the right of canvassing wherein duty lies, and the right of creating a public opinion, which shall make slave holding appear in all the sinfulness with which Christianity has invested it. We need not therefore fear that our efforts will produce disunion; for we rely on nothing for the emancipation of slaves, but the voluntary acts of slave holders themselves. We rely on nothing but what will be as operative, should the Union be severed, as it is at present. Truth and opinion circulate and ramify without being indebted to any constitutional license, nor can they be arrested by any constitutional disruption.

I yield to no man in devotion to the Union. I yield to no man in love to our southern fellow citizens. I admire the chivalrous south. Slavery itself has produced an exaltation in the character of southern men, by the conscious dignity which freedom must ever feel in the presence of slaves. Had I the power to make slave holding appear to them so sinful as to cause them to liberate their slaves, I should feel by its exercise more exalted than Napoleon; but had I the physical power to compel them to relinquish their slaves, I would rather die than exert it. To persuade them is a duty; to coerce them is a crime. Such, at least, are my understanding of the principles of abolitionists; and in these principles I see no cause for alarm at the north, no cause for offence at the south. I will not even adopt the suggestion made the other night by the agent [1] of the American Colonization Society, and petition Congress to suppress slavery in the district of Columbia. I want not the sword of the law, but the peaceful and more potent sword of the Spirit, operating on the hearts of slave holders themselves. Could we force emancipation on the south, we should but remove slavery from the southern blacks, to place it on the southern whites; for what I pray you is slavery, but to be compelled to act contrary to our own volitions? Could we force emancipation on the south, we should ourselves be slave holders, and our white brethren at the south would be our slaves. I never have invoked the laws of man to enforce the laws of God, and I never will. The laws of God are never so potent as when they stand uncontaminated and unsupported by the passions that forever mix with our legislative support of them. We are most unjust to Christianity, if we deem it unable to conquer slavery. It has vanquished, even at the south, an enemy, in comparison with which, slavery is but a pigmy to a giant. If Christianity is able to maintain in total celibacy a large body of men and women in the most voluptuous parts of Europe; if it has been able to abolish throughout Christendom polygamy and concubinage, we need not fear the result, in its encounter with slavery.

But we are told that our views can never influence the south; that slave holders cannot hear us; and if they could hear, they would disregard our opinion. I believe experience will not justify these assertions. Within a few years the slave system has been greatly meliorated. Formerly, in some slave holding states, the murder of a slave was a slight offence, subjecting the offender to only a pecuniary penalty; while now it is statutably punishable with death. The slaves are also better fed and better clothed than formerly. These improvements were concessions to the public opinion of the north. Indeed, we must wholly mistake human nature, if we believe that southern men are insensible to the opinion which we form of their conduct; and most especially we must mistake the southern character. Of all the inhabitants of our continent, I should select southern men as the most sensitive to the breath of either approbation or censure, blow from what nook of the globe it may. Their sensitiveness is all that can make northern discussion of slavery injudicious. Fretted, as they probably are, between the embarrassments that practically attend any disruption of the ties of slavery, and the desire to free themselves from the consequences that attend the retention of slavery, (and among these consequences the public odium of the north is not the least pressing,) they probably deem our discussions as unkind and unnecessary, as we deem them beneficial, ultimately, to even the south itself.

A gentleman the other night told us of a Carolinian, I believe, who became possessed of ten slaves. His conscience would not permit him to retain them in slavery, and he gave them their liberty. I could not see why this instance was adduced by an opponent of immediate emancipation. To me it is a powerful proof that the duty of immediate emancipation is already responded to by the consciences of slave holders, and that we possess great encouragement to persevere in preaching the doctrine loud and long.

But this benevolent slave holder was not content with manumitting his slaves; he sent them to Liberia. Here the history of this transaction ended. I wish it had been extended a little farther. I want another chapter. The *finale* would be more pertinent than all the rest to the real object of our discussion—the merits of the Colonization Society. I wish to discover what influence the Colonization Society exerted in this transaction. Did it enable this conscience stricken individual to relieve himself by something short of unconditional manumission; by commuting the pains of slavery to transportation for life to Liberia? I should also like to see the full measure of gratitude which these slaves owe to this Society, for enabling their master to satisfy his conscience by exiling them to Africa. How were the bodies of these ten human beings, men, women, and infants, prepared for the fearful disease which they were all to encounter in what is termed the seasoning?

How many of these perished a miserable death amid strangers and pestilence? And how many that escaped the slaughter were found missing in the flight? for missing seems to be a term of some significance in the fearful records of colonization. Possibly this benevolent slave holder, (how thankful soever he may now feel to this Society,) may, at the day of final account, discover, that in this act of vaunted mercy and benevolence, and in this act of disburthening his conscience, he became a murderer.

I am constrained to say here, that I differ essentially from some respected individuals who the other night expressed a belief that the Colonization Society and the emancipationists are both right. I admit that the emancipationists may fail in effecting their object; but I deny that the Colonization Society is worthy of patronage, whether it fail in its objects, or effect them. It is based on a violation of Christian duty, as I have endeavored to show; and hence, whatever may be the results which it can accomplish, I cordially and unconditionally decline its fellowship and affinity. Sooner would I cast a thousand dollars into the ocean, than cast a dollar into the treasury of that Society. What the ocean ingulfed would effect no evil, though it effected no good; but what the Colonization Society ingulfed might cause the death of a fellow being. These sentiments are not the result of heat and debate, but the cool and deliberate dictates of my judgment, and as long cherished by me as the existence of the Colonization Society. Till lately, I knew not but I stood alone in these views; but I perceive they are becoming common.

Some gentlemen argue this question as if its merits depended on the ability or inability of the Colonization Society to remove all the blacks to Africa. I differ from these gentlemen. The inability of the Society to perform its objects is all that will redeem it from the execration of posterity; precisely as the inability of Nero to effect his object, (when he wished that all Rome had but one neck, that he might behead the whole race at a blow,) is all that redeems his character. Heaven, in its kindest mercy, has not made our powers of executing evil equal to the enormity of our conceptions. Are we men, are we husbands, are we fathers, and shall we possess no better motive for opposing this Society, than that it cannot yield up to the devouring pestilence of Africa—that it cannot crowd into the black hole of Calcutta, one sixth part of the whole human race that inhabits these states?

We argue the question as though nothing were to be consulted but the prejudices, and feelings, and interests of the whites. I will never consent to argue it on such a basis. I deny that we possess any right thus to argue it, but the right of power; and hence, whether the Colonization Society can accomplish its objects, has no bearing on the question at issue, till we have established that the objects of the Society are conscientious and right. I have endeavored to show that they are unconscientious and wrong; that they trample on that fundamental command, "Thou shalt love thy neighbor as thyself," which our Savior deemed of equal dignity with our love to God, and which, together, he declared comprehend all religion. Christianity and this Society cannot live together. Choose ye this night which ye will serve.

For myself, I deny being a partizan on this question. The views which I have uttered are my own; I have never read a paragraph written professedly against the Colonization Society, or in favor of emancipation. I have never before spoken on this question, and have never canvassed its merits, except in the privacy of my own thoughts. Invited by public handbill, as we have all been, to discuss the question, I have availed myself of the opportunity to speak with the candor that is the privilege of freedom. I have already disclaimed all imputation against the motives of any man; and so far from possessing the slightest hostility to the dignified, able, and I have no doubt amiable gentleman, who addressed us on Thursday evening as the agent of the Colonization Society, I feel no little pain, nay, I feel great pain in saying any thing that shall by the remotest possibility interfere with his feelings, his views and interests. His deportment, his talents, and I may say his appearance, excite in me the most kindly prepossessions toward him; still, let him not complain, (as I thought he did on Thursday,) of the sentiments which are uttered against his Society, even by a brother in the ministry; [2] for, if I am not misinformed, this discussion is the offspring of his own invitation; [3] and, if I correctly understood him that evening, he deemed opposition propitious to his interests. It added, I think he said, many thousands to the funds of his Society. In one respect I am happy to hear the declaration. I hope none of us shall ever find our interests promoted by suppressing discussion. Let discussion be ever held dear and sacred. Providence has constituted us to differ, and Providence will not permit this feature of our nature to be injurious, though we sometimes, in the tyranny of selfishness, would suppress its exhibition.

Look at our national legislature; and to what but conflicting opinion are we indebted for the exaltation that we discover. Men, who by the mere favor of their neighbors leave home not distinguished from the common mass of man, coursing along the surface of society like a ripple on the unruffled bosom of the ocean, are presently, in their new situation, fretted into a wave; and, surging upwards and onwards, by the mighty energy of conflicting opinion, bear aloft on their bosom the whole fabric of society, and seem to us, who gaze on them from the unmoved surface of the world, like beings whom we can scarcely recognize as our fellows.

Let us then not complain of a principle thus productive of good, but rather let us tolerate each other's views; and while I solicit this most humbly for the vote which conscience compels me to give on this occasion, I am anxious to declare that I shall respect no man the less for finding him diametrically and ardently opposed to me in his conclusions.

Utica, January 13, 1834

NOTE A gentleman who was present at the delivery of the preceding remarks, has called on the speaker to review the declarations which treat disparagingly the virtue and attainments of colored men. The speaker never asserted that they are naturally inferior to other men, nor is he possessed of any reasons or feelings for such an assertion. The picture which he drew of colored men conforms to the limited acquaintance with them that his secluded habits have afforded. That even this country (with its discouraging prejudices,) possesses colored men of virtue, wealth, and literature, he is happy to possess this gentleman's assertion for believing; and the more of such instances are substantiated, the greater will be his gratification.

N O T E S

1 Rev. J. N. Danforth, General Agent of the Society.
2 The Rev. Beriah Green, President of the Oneida Institute, a gentleman whose controversial powers seem of a very high order, and who, during several whole evenings, spoke for the negative of the question with an animation and pathos that absorbed the attention of the whole audience.
3 This assertion was contradicted by the friends of the agent. They said the invitation came from some friends of the Colonization cause, and was merely acquiesced in by the agent.

Language and Value *was composed in Linotype Times Roman, with Times Roman display type, by McGregor and Werner, Inc., Washington, D.C. The entire book was printed in offset lithography. Typography and binding design by Joan Stoliar.*